HUGH POULTON

Who are the Macedonians?

HURST & COMPANY, LONDON

First published in the United Kingdom by
C. Hurst & Co. (Publishers) Ltd.,
38 King Street, London WC2E 8JT

Printed in Hong Kong

ISBNs
1-85065-200-7 (cased)
1-85065-238-4 (paper)

ACKNOWLEDGMENTS

It would have been impossible to write this book without the help of a number of people. I especially thank Nicolas Balamaci, Steve Bowman, Richard Clogg, Abdi Faik, Stoyan Georgiev, Sami Ibrahimi, Anastasia Karakasidou, Donald Kenrick, Evangelis Kofos, Mahi Nesimi, Sasho Ordonoski, Vladika Mihail, Mihail Petkovski, Emilija Simoska, Feroz Yasamee and Shaip Yusuf for their help in various ways. Of course I accept full responsibility for the opinions expressed, and for any errors. I also wish to thank Christopher Hurst and Michael Dwyer for their role in the production of the book, and Sebastian Ballard for making the maps.

London, August 1994   HUGH POULTON

CONTENTS

NOTE ON TRANSLITERATION AND NAMES

The complexity of 'the Macedonian Question' is reflected in the problems of transliteration of names from Bulgarian, modern Macedonian, Albanian, Greek, Serbian and Ottoman Turkish with their different orthographies. Place-names are given in the form of the appropriate modern state to which they now belong and, where it appears relevant in the text, with alternate forms in brackets—for example Bitola (Manastir) and Florina (Lerin). However, Constantinople is used instead of Istanbul for the period before the Ottoman conquest of 1453, and Salonika is used for Thessalonika before 1913. As regards people: Ottoman names have been transliterated to the forms used in modern Turkish—e.g. 'Hüsyin Kazım Bey' and 'Şemsi Paşa'. Albanian names are given in their Albanian forms. Greek, despite its different alphabet, does not pose a problem of consistency: the various Slavic languages, however, do.

Bulgarian names have been transliterated using a modified Library of Congress base with the 'er golyam' transliterated as 'â'—e.g. Dimitâr—and the pre-1946 'er malâk' word-ending ignored. Serbian names, due to the long association with the Latin-script Croatian, are given in their usual Latin alphabet (Croatian) form with the appropriate diacritical marks—e.g. Novaković, not Novakovich. Similarly for place-names connected with the portion which was within former Yugoslavia and is now independent—e.g. Kruševo and Kičevo. This has not been done to prejudice the various nationalist arguments which are discussed in the text, but purely because the existence of Yugoslavia for most of the twentieth century has made such usage standard.

However, with many of the names of people this has proved impossible. One problem concerns the fact that the modern Slav Macedonian language only appeared in written form after the Second World War, and both Bulgaria and the new Macedonian state claim some of the same historical figures as their own. Another problem is that, especially in the initial period after the Second World War, there were a number of people who fled from Tito's Yugoslavia to Bulgaria, and some of these became major figures in the Bulgarian state/party apparatus. Others, as detailed in Chapter 6, were tried and in certain cases executed for pro-Bulgarian leanings. In view of this, to try and use separate orthographies for the names of people depending on whether they identified as 'Bulgarian' or 'Macedonian' would be profoundly problematic. To overcome this, all Bulgarian and Slav Macedonian names of people have in the main been transliterated the same. Thus 'Gotse Delchev' not 'Goce Delčev', 'Chento' not 'Čento', 'Kolishevski' not 'Koliševski' and so on. However, even to apply this consistently raises problems, especially when deciding to use 'j' (the usual Serbian/Yugoslav Macedonian transliteration method) or 'y' (the Bulgarian one) for the same letter in contemporary names/titles. As a general rule, the 'j' has been kept when referring to names which are clearly associated with what was Yugoslav Macedonia —thus *Nova Makedonija* not *Nova Makedoniya* for the newspaper published in Skopje. Similar problems occur over the use of 'c' or 'ts'. Obviously Yugoslav Macedonian names like 'Crvenkowski' (the current Prime Minister of FYROM) have been transliterated using 'c'. Again it must be stressed that such transliteration does not in itself carry any nationalist/political overtones. The author apologises for any confusions or apparent inconsistencies.

ABBREVIATIONS

ASNOM	Anti-Fascist Assembly of National Liberation of Macedonia
ATA	Albanian Telegraph Association
AVNOJ	Anti-Fascist Council for the National Liberation of Yugoslavia
BBC SWB	British Broadcasting Corporation Summary of World Broadcasts
BCP	Bulgarian Communist Party
BMORK	Bulgarian Macedonian Adrianopolitan Committee
BTA	Bulgarian Telegraph Association
BWP(C)	Bulgarian Workers' Party (Communist)
BZNS	Bulgarian National Agrarian Union
COMECON	Council of Mutual Economic Assistance (the Communist economic association)
CSCE	Conference on Security and Co-operation in Europe
CUP	Committee of Union and Progress (the Young Turk party)
DPS	Movement for Rights and Freedom (the ethnic Turkish party in Bulgaria)
DPTM	Democratic Party of Turks in Macedonia
DSK	Democratic League (the main Albanian party in Kosovo)
EAM	National Liberation Front (of Greece)
ELAS	The military wing of EAM
EO	Supreme Macedonian Committee, also called the External Organisation—as opposed to the Internal Organisation (IO) of VMRO on the ground in Macedonia
FRY	Federal Republic of Yugoslavia (rump consisting of Serbia and Montenegro)
FYROM	Former Yugoslav Republic of Macedonia
IO	*See under* EO

JNA	Yugoslav army (of the Socialist Federal Republic of Yugoslavia)
KEV	Commissariat for Jewish Affairs (in Bulgaria)
KKE	Communist Party of Greece
KPJ	Communist Party of Yugoslavia
LC	League of Communists
LCY	League of Communists of Yugoslavia
MAAK	Movement for All-Macedonian Action
MAKIVE	Macedonian Movement for Balkan Prosperity
NATO	North Atlantic Treaty Organisation
PASOK	Penhellenic Socialist Movement
PDP	Party for Democratic Prosperity (the main Albanian party in Macedonia)
PSER	Party for the Complete Emancipation of Romanies in Macedonia
PSR (Albania)	People's Socialist Republic of Albania
RFE/RL	Radio Free Europe/Radio Liberty (Munich)
SDS	Union of Democratic Forces (in Bulgaria)
SDU	Social Democratic Union (formerly SKM-PDP)
SFRJ	Socialist Federal Republic of Yugoslavia
SKM-PDP	League of Communists of Macedonia/Party for Democratic Renewal
SNOF	Slav National Liberation Front (of Greece)
SR (Macedonia)	Socialist Republic (of Macedonia)
TMORO	Secret Macedonian Adrianopolitan Revolutionary Organisation
TMPO	Secret Macedonian-Revolutionary Party
UMO Ilinden	United Macedonian Organisation/Ilinden (in Bulgaria)
UN	United Nations
UNHCR	United Nations High Commissioner for Refugees
VMRO	Internal Macedonia Revolutionary Organisation
VMRO-DP	VMRO-Democratic Party
VMRO-DPMNE	VMRO-Democratic Party of Macedonian National Unity
VMRO-ob	VMRO United (the Comintern's attempt to take over VMRO)
VMRO-SMD	VMRO-Union of Macedonian Societies
YVE	Protectors of Northern Greece

MAPS

Macedonia in South-eastern Europe

Geographic Macedonia

1

INTRODUCTION

Terminology

The concept of who the Macedonians are is, at the time of writing, a highly controversial one and is often somewhat confusing for the casual observer. From the outset, mention should be made of the three ways of identifying 'the Macedonians', which are often interrelated and overlapping. The first two relate to the citizens of geographic areas. One of these is the geographic area bounded to the north by the Skopska Crna Gora and the Shar Planina mountains; to the east by the Rila and Rhodope mountains; to the south by the Aegean coast around Thessalonika, Mount Olympus and the Pindus mountains; and to the west by the lakes of Ohrid and Prespa.[1] This area forms a geographic unit based around the Vardar/Axios, the Struma/Strimon and the Mesta/Nestos river valleys, and is generally referred to as geographic Macedonia. It comprises approximately 67,000 square kilometres and is currently divided between the Former Yugoslav Republic of Macedonia (FYROM), Greece and Bulgaria. This geographic area is often subdivided either into two units—lower Macedonia comprising the large coastal area and equating more with modern-day Greek Macedonia, and upper Macedonia relating to the higher valleys in the north—or into three units equating to the political division of geographic Macedonia in the Balkan wars. These three units have been named either after the respective country—i.e.

1 This is the usually accepted definition. There were and are, however, different definitions: see H.R.Wilkinson, *Maps and Politics: A Review of the Ethnographic Cartography of Macedonia*, Liverpool, 1951.

1

Yugoslav Macedonia or Greek Macedonia—or after the main geographic features of each—Vardar Macedonia for the portion which went to what became Yugoslavia and is now temporarily named FYROM; Aegean Macedonia for the Greek portion; and Pirin Macedonia for the Bulgarian part. In this latter terminology there is no expression for the small slice of geographic Macedonia which went to Albania.

The second way of identifying 'Macedonians' relates to all the citizens of the independent political entity which at the time of writing is called by the temporary name of the Former Yugoslav Republic of Macedonia. The third use of the term 'Macedonian' is an ethnic one and currently refers only to the Slav populations either in geographic Macedonia or, more narrowly, in the FYROM.

This book attempts to cover all three forms of 'Macedonian'. However in the modern era, which will make up the bulk of the text, it will concentrate on the citizens of the current Former Republic of Macedonia, and those outside this entity but in geographic Macedonia who consider themselves to be ethnic Slav Macedonians. This is because, despite the impasse over the name of the newly-independent state with its capital in Skopje, the term 'Macedonia' is used outside Greek circles to describe it. Similarly, the term 'Macedonian' is widely used in the same ethnic sense as 'Serb', 'Croat' or 'Greek' are used. The contradictions between the ethnic and civic use of all these terms in the Balkans and the ensuing confusion over citizenship and ethnic identity will be looked at in greater detail.

As is by now readily apparent, there is the continuing problem of names which is at the heart of many of the current political controversies and is discussed in greater detail in the subsequent chapters. At this stage it is merely noted that the majority of Bulgarians continue to view the Slav inhabitants of Macedonia as Bulgarians and believe that the current Macedonian language is a dialect of Bulgarian. Similarly, to the majority of Greeks the terms 'Macedonia' and 'Macedonian' are wholly Greek proper-ty, and they view the use of these terms by their northern neighbour to describe the state, its people and its language as a combination of national theft, historical insult and irredentism against their northern province (which is also called Macedonia). As well as these rigid majority attitudes among Bulgarians and Greeks, there also exist a small number of extreme nationalist Serbs who deny the existence of a separate Slav nation of Macedonians, rather claiming them to be Serbs—although in recent times the number of such people holding this view has dropped.

In such a controversial area it seems impossible to avoid offending some or even many, although needless to say this is not our aim. Given the above, the use of the term 'the Macedonians' is always problematic and usually needs some form of explanation, and it is hoped that the explanation we have given is sufficient to avoid misunderstandings. In Chapter 1, dealing with antiquity, the term generally refers to the inhabitants of the area, and thus the language 'Macedonian' refers to their spoken language which has since disappeared. In the later chapters the term refers to the Slav inhabitants of the area.

The peoples of Macedonia

This book deals with the topic of group identity: ethnic groups, minorities and nations, as well as the modern political phenomenon of nationalism. Some of the peoples who inhabit the geographic area have both a long-claimed history and a definite sense of themselves as a people separate from their neighbours, whose existence as such has lasted over the centuries. Although, as indicated below, this can be seen at times to be artificially propagated by modern nationalists rewriting history and backdating their own modern concepts on to history, it appears reasonable to hold that some nations have predated the onset of modern nationalism. Other groups have also seen themselves—and been regarded by others— as different or distinct but without the same definite historical cohesion, often brought about by historical circumstances like identification with a particular line of rulers, which the first group enjoys. Still other groups appear to have made little impact on the course of history, yet in the present problematic climate of nationalism which so pervades the entire area, they have emerged as important players. Furthermore it can be argued, as indicated in Chapter 7, that in the modern world nations can in certain circumstances and under certain conditions be seen to be created—a process of ethnogenesis.[2]

2 The most frequent use of such ethnogenesis has been in Third World developing countries where the post-colonial governments have tried to create modern
   nations within the often highly arbitrary colonial borders. In many of these

Moreover, while some nations can be created, conversely some can disappear entirely.[3]

In the geographic area of Macedonia all these variants are readily visible. Throughout its long history, the area has seen successive waves of incoming peoples and population movements as well as a shifting geo-political situation. The Balkan peninsula, with Macedonia at its centre, is one of the most ethnically, linguistically and religiously complex areas of the world. Its geographic position has historically resulted in it being disrupted by invaders from Asia Minor to Europe and *vice versa*. Many of the invaders became incorporated into other groups, both new and old, affecting those groups at times profoundly and at other times insignificantly. The three peoples in Macedonia with the longest claim to continuity are the Greeks, the Vlachs (possibly descendants of Romanized elements of the original Thracians), and the Albanians who claim descent from the ancient Illyrians. The Slavs, an Indo-European people originating in east-central Europe, had begun to cross the Danube into the Balkans by the sixth century AD. In the seventh century combined assaults of Slavs and Proto-Bulgarians, a Turkic people from the area between the Urals and the Volga who had come via the steppes north of the Caspian Sea, led to the founding of the first Bulgarian state in 681. In 864, under the direction of their leader Boris, the Proto-Bulgarians converted *en masse* to Christianity and this greatly helped them coalesce with the Slavs, who had already been converted. Thus by the

countries nationalism has used anti-colonialism and anti-imperialism as major factors in the attempt to establish cultural unity. While this had relative short-term success in the initial post-independence period, the basic problems of founding a more permanent cultural unity have emerged in many of these new states causing severe tensions and even break-up of some states. Other modern examples of not always successful ethnogenesis include: the Moldovans of what was Bessarabia—who with justification can be seen to be really Romanians and who have reverted to this; the Uzbeks, Turkmen and Kazakhs of what was Soviet Central Asia—this a fairly successful attempt by Stalin to divide and thus reduce the power of the Turkic-speaking peoples of that area; and in former Yogoslavia (apart from the case of the Macedonians under discussion) the Montenegrins and the Muslims (for these last two see Hugh Poulton, *The Balkans: Minorities and States in Conflict*, MRG, London, 1991 and 1992). Other failed attempts at creating nations have been the Yugoslavs—a non-starter, as will be shown—and the new Soviet Man, which in practice tended to be a façade for Great Russian assimilation.

3 E.g. the Kashubs, Slav-speakers who used to be located around the Gdansk area and have become totally assimilated by the Poles.

end of the ninth century they were as one people speaking a Slav-based language (although modern Slav Macedonian historians in Skopje claim that the Macedonian Slavs have always been a separate people from those in Bulgaria).

From the tenth century onwards Roma (Gypsies), originating from northern India, began to move into the region and progressively spread throughout the whole of the Balkans including Macedonia. By the end of the thirteenth century the Serbs, another Slavic people, were establishing hegemony over much of the Balkans, and in 1282 King Milutin took Skopje from the Byzantine empire and opened the way for Serbian penetration into Macedonia. Disunity in the Balkans allowed the Ottoman Turks, an Asiatic people who had gradually eroded away the ailing Byzantine empire, to invade the peninsula from Asia Minor in the fourteenth century through Macedonia and the Maritsa valley. The gradual Ottoman conquest culminated in the defeat of the Serbs at Kosovo Polje in 1389 and opened the way for a complete occupation of the Balkans. The fall of Constantinople in 1453 saw the end of the Byzantine empire. Ottoman rule over Macedonia was to last until the twentieth century. During this period Turks and other Muslim Turkic-speaking peoples from the Ottoman empire settled along with large numbers of Sephardic Ladino-speaking Jews who had fled from intolerance and persecution in Western Europe or been expelled from there.

Natural and unnatural demographic change

The foregoing overview, which is enlarged in later chapters, both introduces the different peoples who in modern times have lived in Macedonia, and illustrates the profound demographic changes which Macedonia has undergone. These factors of instability and change have assisted the process of shifting allegiances and group identities. Such changes can take many forms. The most drastic is extermination or expulsion of a particular group, as demonstrated by the barbarities of the so-called ethnic cleansing measures taking place in Bosnia-Hercegovina in 1992-3. Another method of change is assimilation, which can take many forms. At one end of the spectrum is peaceful assimilation which is largely a natural process whereby an ethnic group, usually a small minority, gradually coalesces from choice over a period of time with another group, usually a dominant majority. While such apparent peaceful assimilation may often be due to the dominant economic power or control of the education system by one group, and thus it may be ingenuous to describe such a process as peaceful, nevertheless the element of outright compulsion is not pronounced.

At the other extreme is forcible assimilation whereby it is usually denied that a particular ethnic group exists and its members are forced on pain of death, imprisonment or expulsion to declare themselves to be part of another group and to abandon their customs and culture and adopt new ones. Between these two poles are a variety of others usually involving, as already noted, assimilation not so much by force as by control of the education system and the corresponding denial or restriction of education rights to the minority in question. In Macedonia all these modes of change have been pursued including in this century the extremes of outright genocide and 'ethnic cleansing' and mass expulsion.

Nationalism

The impact of modern nationalism on Macedonia and its peoples has been momentous. It is one of the prime reasons for the area becoming the 'apple of discord' in the Balkans and the centre of such intense controversy, which has continued unabated to the present and in the past has been responsible for much bloodshed. Although it is beyond our scope to attempt an analysis of nationalism as a phenomenon, it is necessary to note that for the purposes of this book it is seen as an activist ideological movement which aims to unite all members of a given people on the basis of a putative shared culture. As such it claims to represent the whole collective, however defined, and is antagonistic to competing cultural claims on the totality or parts of this collective, which is deemed by the adherents to constitute an actual or potential nation.[4] Nationalism and nationalists come in many shapes and forms: from 'modernisers' to religious 'reactionaries', from

4   There are many books on and theories about nationalism. Particularly useful for the English-reader are Anthony Smith, *Theories of Nationalism*, Duckworth, London, 1971; Ernest Gellner, *Nations and Nationalism*, Oxford University Press, 1983; Elie Kedourie, *Nationalism*, London 1961, and *Nationalism in Asia and Africa*, Meridian, 1970; Benedict Anderson, *Imagined Communities: Reflections on the Origin and Spread of Nationalism*, Verso, London, 1983; Hugh Seton-Watson, *Nations and States: An Enquiry into the Origins of Nations and the Politics of*

'organic', 'blood and soil' nationalisms to 'rational' ones. At times, although each particular group claims to represent the whole 'nation', there may be rival groups competing for the same body of people—'modernisers' versus 'reactionaries' or whatever. Although, as noted above, there have demonstrably been groups of people who can be seen as forming distinct 'nations' from antiquity onwards,[5] most observers see nationalism as a modern phenomenon which originated in Europe at the end of the eighteenth century or the beginning of the nineteenth century. Its advent on the political stage is closely linked to that of the modern state and the ensuing mass participation (in theory) of all its adult members, as well as to the needs of a modern economy. This latter needs a literate educated workforce able to communicate freely with all inside the polity. The events of the French Revolution and the ensuing Napoleonic wars, perhaps for the first time in modern history, showed fully the enormous latent power of 'the nation' and nationalism as a means of mobilising the masses, as well as spreading the ideas of popular sovereignty as the foundation of political legitimacy.

Whether one sees nationalism itself as a defensive reaction to the power of Revolutionary France—this first occurred in Eastern Europe, primarily among German-speaking peoples divided among a patchwork of states—or whether one sees its origins in Revolutionary France itself with such crucial events as the Declaration of the Rights of Man and the Citizen, and the *levée en masse* of 1791 serving to release the potential power of the new doctrine, is perhaps a matter of choice. The latter alternative stresses the modernising aspects of the new creed, while the first view stresses its suitability as a cultural defence mechanism against a perceived threat. These two views are often used as the basis of a division between 'civic' nationalisms, based primarily on an existing state territory (the French model), and 'ethnic' nationalisms based primarily on the ethnic unit, however defined, which is often not co-terminous with existing state boundaries (the German model). In the latter case factors like language, history, culture and religion become crucial in defining the ethnic group.

Nationalism, London, 1977; Eric Hobsbawn, *Nations and Nationalism since 1780*, Cambridge University Press, 1990; and Tom Nairn, *The Break-up of Britain*, Verso, London, 1981.

5 See John Armstrong, *Nations Before Nationalism*, Chapel Hill, NC, 1982, for a comprehensive review.

Hence history often assumes enormous significance for nationalists. Additionally, the boundary between nationalism and chauvinism—i.e. between claiming an equal place for one particular group in the 'family of nations' and either denigrating others or claiming a superior position—is sometimes a fine one. Nationalists naturally tend to emphasise the perceived positive aspects of their particular nation, and especially in instances where one or more group claims the same territory it is a relatively small step from this to furthering one's claim by claiming superiority, often ransacking history for examples, real or imagined, to back up the claim. This is exemplified in the struggles in central Europe in 1848 when the so-called (and self-claimed) 'historic' nations like the Germans and the Magyars claimed that their particular nationalisms were more justified than Romanian, Czech, Serb or Croat ones.

A powerful weapon for nationalists is the use of history to show the past control of a territory by a state to which the modern nation can claim affinity. In the Balkans this sometimes contentious issue of different nations claiming the same historical ancestors as their own is further complicated by population migrations whereby a particular people has inhabited different areas at different times, and the political changes whereby different states associated with different modern nations have at different times controlled the same piece of land. Macedonia is a prime example of this.

The new creed of nationalism emerged when Macedonia along with most of the Balkan peninsula was under Ottoman control, as it had already been for some centuries. In spite of having at one time advanced almost to Vienna and appeared to threaten Western Europe, the Ottoman empire declined and by the early nineteenth century was in a state of decay with its economy stagnant, the once efficient bureaucracy corrupt, and the army demoralised. At the same time, and partly because of this degeneration,[6] the awakening of the Balkan peoples began, aided by the intervention and interest of the Great Powers, especially Russia and Austria-Hungary.

Geographically the Balkan peninsula is mountainous with dif-

6 The first 'national' revolts by the Serbs in the early nineteenth century were in many ways protests against the collapse of the old system and the ensuing loss of law and order and growth of powerful and rapacious local officials. The formulation of these revolts into essentially nationalist aims came later.

ficult communications, the result of which is that communities tend to be compartmentalised rather than unified. The Ottoman empire, up till the last quarter of the nineteenth century, was run ostensibly according to religious (Muslim) precepts. The *Shariat* (*Şeriat*), or Holy Law, was in theory the law of the empire—although in practice much of the state law became progressively independent of Islamic precepts and there was a gradual secularisation of public law. The empire's population was, in line with traditional Islamic thinking, divided not according to language, ethnicity or nationality but by religion—the *millet* system—and religion has traditionally been one of the main factors in differentiating between various groups. The concept of nationality as expounded in the ideology of nationalism was a late arrival to the Balkans (and even later to Turkey proper). The whole nature of the *millet* system and group identity in the Ottoman empire is looked at in greater detail in Chapter 3.

Although there were inevitably some people who accepted the religion of the new rulers—the majority of the Albanians, numbers of Slavs (the Pomaks of the Rhodope mountains, the Torbeshi of Macedonia and many Bosnians) and Greeks—the Ottomans were non-assimilative and multi-national without the technological and institutional facilities for integrating and unifying the subject peoples. This contrasts with Western Europe where the new 'nation-states' were mostly able to transcend regional loyalties—this process often aided by a long preceding period of strong centralising and unifying rule as in France. In the Balkans, however, the various peoples managed to retain their separate identities and cultures, and many of them retained a sense of a former glorious history when they controlled a particular area which, with the national awakenings in the nineteenth century, they once again claimed. As noted above, such claims tended to be at the expense of their neighbours who likewise made historical claims to the territory in question.

Thus the penetration of nationalism into the Ottoman empire and the ensuing national awakenings, which caused Ottoman power in the Balkans to begin crumbling in the mid-nineteenth century with the establishment of the Serbian state in the north around Belgrade and of the Greek state in the south around Athens, often gave rise to hostility between the previous Ottoman subject peoples. This hostility was to reach its zenith in the struggle for Macedonia at the beginning of the twentieth century. This whole issue of the rise of nationalism in the Balkans and the Ottoman response and the fight for Macedonia is the subject of Chapter 4.

2

THE SOIL FOR NATIONALISTS

The beginnings

The earliest human remains in Macedonia date from Mousterian times, and along with similar remains found in Thessaly and Epirus are the first signs of human life in the lands which correspond to modern Greece. The first signs of continuous occupation date from the early Neolithic period, carbon-dated to 6200 BC in the Macedonian coastal plain. This civilization, which lasted about 1,000 years, originated in and maintained contacts with western Anatolia. Towards the end of this period an intrusive culture characterised by the use of 'barbotine' pottery (clay marked with the finger-nail) appeared in northern Thessaly and western Greece, probably originating from Macedonia and the area which was till recently Yugoslavia. This marked the first of many interactions between Greece, the central Balkans and Anatolia.[1]

Throughout the long Neolithic period lasting 3-4,000 years, Macedonia and Thrace were occupied by people of a different culture to those in the south of the Balkan peninsula. The population of all these areas was hybrid with a noticeable cultural difference between these settlements within the Mediterranean climatic zone and those like Upper Macedonia and northern Epirus which were outside it. The latter exhibited a less refined culture which, on the evidence of stereotypical mother-goddess figures found in excavations, may have been matriarchal societies. In the first two phases of the early Bronze Age from 2800 to 2200 BC, migrants

---

1 N.G.L. Hammond, *A History of Greece to 322 BC*, 2nd edn, Oxford University Press, 1967

from Anatolia arrived in the peninsula. While the Neolithic dwellers and these arrivals spoke non-Indo-European languages, in the middle and late Bronze Age (2500-2000 and again in 400-350 BC) Greek-speakers flowed in from the Pontic regions.[2]

These new arrivals were strongly patriarchal and organised into kindred clans, each with its own king, council and meetings of freemen—features common to other groups like the Hittites and Romans. They were pastoral and not seafarers. Their earliest signs are in central Macedonia, beginning around 2200 BC, and their culture began to spread at this time to inland Epirus, then densely forested and inhabited by nomads. Trade with Troy greatly helped progress on the coast, especially Halkidiki, but while advances were being made in central and southern Greece, the Macedonian hinterland and Thessaly lagged behind. The Mycenaean civilization of 1400-1200 BC led to a homogenous Mycenaean culture throughout the Greek mainland, but it did not penetrate Epirus and upper Macedonia. According to Herodotus, the Dorians moved before the Trojan war to southern Thessaly and south-west Macedonia where they were called '*Makedoni*'. After the Trojan war these Greek-speaking people moved south to the Peloponnese.[3] This was probably due to the invasion of the Greek peninsula after the fall of Troy down the Vardar-Axios valley (evidence is provided by the arrival of pottery of the 'Lausitz' culture of the Danube valley *circa* 1150 BC).

Already a clear pattern emerges of Macedonia as a transit route for movement into the southern Balkan peninsula and Greece proper. The geographic and climatic differences, especially between Greece proper and upper Macedonia with its continental climate, were also a factor which helped to keep Macedonia on the fringes of the Greek culture by then burgeoning in the area to the south. Macedonia remained peripheral to the ensuing great changes to the south until the fourth century BC. The people of Greece proper, unaccustomed to the different climate, were attracted more by Halkidiki and, somewhat less, by the coastal plain. The peoples of Macedonia remained a mixture. The everyday language of the people was distinct from that of its southen neighbours but today it has almost vanished. The inhabitants of Macedonia at

2   Hammond, *op. cit.*, pp. 37-8 and footnote.
3   Herodotus 1. 56; 9. 26, in Hammond, *op. cit.*, p. 59.

this time were of sturdier build than the southern Greeks and apparently more phlegmatic.

Within the variety of peoples at this time living in Macedonia there was a residue of Greek-speaking tribes who remained in southern Macedonia at the end of the Bronze Age. In about the seventh century one of these *Macedones* expanded its sphere of influence into the coastal planes of lower Macedonia, which became the kingdom of 'Macedonia' and whose descendants were the 'Macedonians' proper of the Classical period. Their rulers claimed a traditional suzerainty over the cantons of upper Macedonia and worshipped Greek gods, especially Zeus and Heracles. The other Greek tribes of upper Macedonia became intermingled with other peoples—Illyrians, Paeonians and Thracians. The southern Greeks planted city-states, which so characterised their political organisation, on the Halkidiki peninsula and a few elsewhere on the Macedonian coast. In the early fifth century the royal house of Macedon was recognised as Greek by the presidents of the Olympic games. Their kings considered themselves to be of Greek descent, their ancestor being Heracles, son of Zeus. The royal house of Lyncus in Upper Macedonia claimed descent from the Bacchidae who fled from Corinth *circa* 657.

As Hammond, basing his conclusions on Herodotus, Thucydides, Isocrates and other Classical sources, summarises:

> The men of the royal house certainly spoke Greek. They also spoke the language of their people, 'Macedonian', which contained words of early Greek origin but was not intelligible to contemporary Greeks. The Macedonians in general did not consider themselves Greeks, nor were they considered Greeks by their neighbours.[4]

Moreover, the political institutions of Macedonia in the fourth century were more akin to those of Molossia in Epirus and of Illyria, Paeonia and Thrace than to those of the Classical Greek city-states, and while the Macedonian dynasty both encouraged economic trading with the Greek states and attracted Greek cultural

4 Hammond, *op. cit.*, p. 534, quoting in his footnotes the following sources: Hdt. 1.56.3; Th. 2.99; Hdt. 5.22; 8. 137–9; Isoc. 5.105 (Heracles); Str. 326 (Lyncestae); Plu. 'Alex' 51.6; Th. 4. 124. ifin.; 'Vorsokr'. 85 B 2 (Thrasymachus). See Kalléris, *Les Anciens Macédoniens,* for a glossary of ancient Macedonian words.

influences to their courts, their political systems remained impervious to Greek influences. The Macedonian people themselves appeared to hold little affinity for the Greeks who had settled in city-states on the coasts of Halkidiki. Situated between the Greek states in the south and the more backward north, they had, under pressure from both, become solidified into a compact people.[5] It was at this moment that Philip of Macedon entered the stage.

Philip of Macedon and Alexander the Great

When King Perdiccas died and his infant son Amyntas was elected king with Perdiccas's brother Philip as regent, Macedonia was in danger of dismemberment. However, Philip's genius totally transformed the situation and he bequeathed to his son Alexander a situation where Macedonia had changed from being on the periphery of Greek affairs to dominating them, as well as being poised to expand into a vast empire.

Philip incorporated the territory between Lake Lychnidus (today Lake Ohrid) and the river Nestos into Macedonia, but left Illyrian and Thracian tribes under vassal kings in a colonial relationship. In Epirus he extended and strengthened the kingdom of Molossia. With Thessaly, which unlike Macedonia was a member of the Greek League, he made an association ostensibly on even terms. He did not actively try to destroy so much as pacify the other Greek states and incorporate them into a federal union. In other words he extended the kingdom of Macedon to its 'natural' geographic area and despite his conquests did not extend it to other parts of Greece, with which his relationship was different; for Philip, Macedon and Greece were separate entities. He had a variety of distinct positions depending on which unit is considered. These variations are reflected in his titles: king of Macedon; king over vassal kings in the Balkans; '*Archon*' of the Thessalian League; '*Hieromnemon*' on the Amphictyonic Council; and '*Hegemon*' of the Greek League in time of war.[6]

Demosthenes viewed the peoples of Macedonia as barbarous riffraff led by a king (Philip II) who not only did not belong and was unrelated to the Greeks, but could not even boast a

5 Hammond, *op. cit.*, pp. 535-6.
6 *Ibid.*, p. 575.

respectable foreign heritage.[7] Such bile from the sworn enemy of Philip and Alexander should not be give undue weight. The royal family of Macedon perceived itself as Greek in culture at least. Other Greeks at the time judged Philip primarily to be one of them. His court at Pella was Greek in manners, and he can be seen as having brought Hellenic culture to the rest of the Balkans. His plan of expansion for surplus populations—a classic version of '*Lebensraum*'—was to benefit Greece as well as Macedon. He admired Greek thought and even employed Aristotle to teach Alexander. However the constitution of Macedon described it as 'the kingdom of Philip and his descendants' in contrast to the position of the Greek republics as defined in the Charter of the Greek League.[8]

Philip's notably delicate handling of the Greek states was not carried on by Alexander. The rough treatment of his ruthless lieutenant Antipater as governor of Athens effectively ended the freedom from overt outside control that Greeks had enjoyed for more than 1,000 years. Thus some form of backlash, like the vitriolic outburst of Demosthenes, was perhaps inevitable. However while the distinction between Macedon and Greece proper has been stressed, it must be noted that the two were akin in many ways. As Hammond points out, if they had combined under Philip as *hegemon* of the Greek League and king of Macedon, the Greco-Macedonian era 'might have been a reality rather than a catchword for the historian'. Similarly if Alexander had lived longer he might have forged a stronger cooperation between Greece and Macedon that could even have withstood Rome. Both were close to success before their deaths.[9]

The Romans

After Alexander's death, his huge empire split into three parts — Macedon (including Greece), Syria and Egypt—and their mutual hostilities allowed Carthage to rise as an empire in the western Mediterranean. Also following Alexander's death, the rapid spread of *koine* based on Attic Greek made any distinction between Greek

7 Quoted in John Crossland and Diana Constance, *Macedonian Greece*, London, 1982, pp. 9 and 15.
8 Hammond, *op. cit.*, pp. 575.
9 Ibid., p. 651.

and the language of 'the Macedonians' an academic one which opposing camps continue to fight over.[10] That Greek so easily subsumed the local Macedonian dialect would indicate that the dialect in Philip's time was not far removed from Greek after all. However, before Latin arrived with the Roman legions, there were two main rivals to Greek as the common language in the Balkans: Thracian in the north-west and Illyrian in the north-east. Again Macedonia was a mixed area between all three.

The crucial factor soon became the growth of Rome, which resulted in a fundamental shift in power arrangements culminating in the loss of Macedonian independence in 167 BC after a period of steady expansion of Roman influence into the eastern Mediterranean. The country was initially divided into four nominally independent territories but was eventually incorporated as a Roman province in 146 after repeated uprisings. The expansion and consolidation of Roman power saw the Balkans and Macedonia once more revert to their old role as a border region, this time marking the zone between Latin- and Greek-speaking cultures, and between the western and eastern halves of the empire. Latin was spoken from the Danube down to a line marked by Durrës in Albania, Ohrid, Skopje, Stobi and Sofia and thence due east to the Black Sea. South of this line Greek predominated.[11] However when the empire was divided at the end of the fourth century AD, the border was further north along the river Drina—which was

10 For the Greek view that the Macedonians of Philip's time were Greeks who spoke Greek (and thus by extension modern Macedonia and any reference to it by name is the sole property of modern Greece), see A. Daskalis, *The Hellenism of the Ancient Macedonians,* Salonika, 1966, or N. Andriotis, *The Language and the Greek Origin of the Ancient Macedonians,* Salonika, 1979. For an extreme Slav Macedonian view that the modern Macedonians are a separate people with a 2,500-year history and thus the ancient Macedonians of Philip's time (as well as Aristotle, who is also considered a 'Macedonian') are the ancestors of modern 'Macedonians' see *Glas na Makedoncite,* edited by Kiril Anarhistov, vol. 6, nos 28–9, August–November 1982, Kogarah, NSW (Australia). Emigrés tend to be more nationalistic than those who remain in the 'home' country.

11 Ivo Banac, *The National Question in Yugoslavia: Origins, History, Politics,* Cornell University Press, Ithaca, NY, 1984, 1992, p. 46 puts the line to Skopje and then to Sofia while Hammond, following Jiriček, puts the line slightly further south closer to Stobi—see N.G.L. Hammond, *Migrations and Invasions in Greece and Adjacent Areas,* Noyes Press, Park Ridge, NJ, 1976, and 'Migrations and Assimilation in Greece', in Tom Winnifrith and Penelope Murray (eds), *Greece Old and New,* Macmillan, London, 1983, map 11, p. 64.

the border in the twentieth century between Serbia and Bosnia. Thus the whole of Macedonia remained in the eastern half.

The Vlachs

However, in the eastern half of this new division there were large numbers of people who continued to speak Latin. The largest such group were the Daco-Romanians living north of the Danube from whom the modern Romanians are descended. There were also many south of the Danube, especially in Greece and Macedonia, who also continued to speak Latin. These are the ancestors of the Vlachs and are referred to by a variety of different names. They usually call themselves Aromani or Aromanians while Romanians often call them Macedo-Romanians. This is because many emigrated to Romania from Macedonia during the bloody conflicts in Macedonia at the end of the nineteenth century and the beginning of the twentieth century. The Greeks referred to them as Koutzovlachs—'*vlach*' means 'shepherd' in Greek and in recent times the Vlachs have often been transhumant shepherds in inland Greece, especially in the Pindus mountains. '*Koutzos*' in Greek means 'lame'—possibly a reference to the way they spoke Greek. Winnifrith notes some of the more bizarre explanations both for their names and for their origins, including the supposed derivation of their name from the Roman general Valerius Flaccus, or from the noise of bleating sheep, or the idea that they are descendants of the Roman Fifth Legion—hence the Yugoslav name for them of '*cincari*' as '*cinci*' in Vlach (pronounced *tsintsi*) means five—and sensibly opts for the basic use of the term Vlach which he considers to be derived from a Germanic word for stranger.[12]

Whether they were really descended from 'lost' Roman legions or, more likely, from local inhabitants who adopted a form of Latin instead of Greek as their everyday language is perhaps irrelevant. Such questions fall into the modern nationalist trap of attempting to prove the 'purity' of certain peoples in an area where patently such exercises are both senseless and unproductive. What is indisputable is that the Vlachs managed to continue their

12 Tom Winnifrith, 'Greeks and Romans', in Winnifrith and Murray(eds), *Greece Old and New*, Macmillan, 1983. See also Winnifrith, *The Vlachs*, Duckworth, 1987.

Latin-speaking culture in an area where Greek had become the norm, and it is not so surprising that they became associated with transhumant shepherds—people who, living in the uplands, were less likely to be sucked into the general Hellenic culture. Of course not all Vlachs were transhumant shepherds and not all shepherds Vlachs, and they were to play a leading role in the second Bulgarian empire. Winnifrith points out that the Roman transit route, the Via Egnatia, also probably helped the continuation of a Latin presence, and to this day there are Vlach settlements that have survived in the vicinity of the route.[13]

The Albanians

Illyrian and Thracian are languages which have left little mark on history compared to Latin and ancient Greek since they were not spoken by the educated townspeople. Thracian survived till the end of the Roman empire, while Illyrian is seen by most modern scholars as the forerunner of modern Albanian, although some noted philologists such as the German, G. Weigand, at the end of the nineteenth century saw Thracian rather than Illyrian as the base of Albanian, which also has a large Latin element.[14] Despite these Latin accoutrements, the original Albanians, who called themselves Arbëni and lived in the high mountains from Krujë to the Šar range, represented the Illyrian elements who resisted latinisation from their mountain fastnesses.[15] They remained on the western periphery of Macedonia ready to expand into it.

The Slavs

Macedonia remained subject to repeated attacks and threats from the north, and with the decline of Roman power Huns and Goths swept in and down the Balkan peninsula. Once more Macedonia was on a transit route for invaders, but these invaders have not left as significant a mark on the ethnic/cultural make-up as other invaders, notably the Slavs. This Indo-European people

13 Winnifrith, *op. cit.*
14 Ibid., fn.7.
15 Zef Mirdita, 'Problem etnogeneze Albanaca', *Encyclopaedia Moderna*, vol. 5, 1970, no. 13, p. 39, in Banac, *op. cit.*

originated in east-central Europe and began to cross the Danube and into the Balkans by the sixth century. In the seventh century combined assaults by Slavs and proto-Bulgarians, a Turkic people from the area between the Urals and the Volga who had come to the Balkans via the steppes north of the Caspian Sea, led to the founding of the first Bulgarian state in 681. The conversion of the Slavs to Christianity was greatly helped by the pioneering work of two Greek[16] brothers from Salonika, the Saints Constantine (who took the name Cyril on becoming a monk) and Methodius. They codified the Slav dialects of the Slavs living in the vicinity in order to aid the evangelisation of these people. This was the so-called Church Slavonic or 'Old Bulgarian', originally written in the Glogolithic script. The brothers moved on to evangelise among the Slavs of central Europe but fell foul of Rome whose popes viewed their work in the Slav idioms with distrust. Their disciples were expelled from central Europe but carried on their work in the Balkans where papal influence was less strong. In particular, the great educators Saints Clement and Naum of Ohrid founded a monastery and teaching institute on Lake Ohrid which was to become a centre of Slav learning.

By the middle of the ninth century, Bulgaria had extended its control over Macedonia, and in 864, under the direction of their leader Boris, the proto-Bulgarians converted *en masse* to Christianity, which greatly helped them to coalesce with the already Christianised Slavs; by the end of the ninth century they were as one people speaking a Slav-based language. Some Bulgarian historians claim the ancient Thracians as a third element of the Bulgarians. In the legacy of Cyril and Methodius—carried on by Clement and Naum—the development of Slav literacy was crucial in preventing assimilation of the Slavs either by cultures to the north or by the Greek culture to the south. Thus as Crampton notes,[17] the legacy helped the Bulgarians develop a national consciousness which, though far from that associated with modern nationalism, 'was strong enough to preserve the concept of Bulgaria and the Bulgarians as a distinct religious, cultural and, perhaps,

16 Inevitably there is not a consensus on whether the brothers were actually 'Greek' (however defined), because of the enormous influence of their work on the literary Slav languages—an influence which spread all the way to Russia. Both the Bulgarians and modern Slav Macedonians claim them for themselves.

17 Richard Crampton, *A Short History of Modern Bulgaria*, Cambridge University Press, 1987. p. 5.

political entity'. This sense was cemented by the conquests of Simeon the Great, who had been educated in Byzantium and was chosen as prince in 896. He extended Bulgaria's boundaries in the west to the Adriatic, in the south to the Aegean and in the east to Constantinople. During his reign the head of the Bulgarian church was given the title of patriarch while he himself was given the title Tsar and thus became an equal of the emperor in Constantinople.[18]

Inevitably there was great military rivalry with Byzantium and after varying fortunes Bulgaria's power declined. However, under Samuil, who was based in Macedonia around the Ohrid and Prespa lakes, its fortunes once more revived in the early tenth century. The geographic location of Samuil's empire has given ammunition to modern nationalist historians from Skopje who assert that in this period the Slavs of Macedonia were distinct from those in Bulgaria proper and that Samuil was a Macedonian rather than a Bulgarian ruler. However this appears to be a typical case of backdated nationalism. Others claim him as Armenian, and Winnifrith points to the possibility that he was a Vlach.[19] Whatever his true ethnic descent may have been, Samuil's army was soundly defeated in 1014 by Basil II, emperor of Byzantium—revealingly known as 'Basil the Bulgar-killer'—and Macedonia once again fell firmly under Byzantine control till 1230. A factor in the decline of this first Bulgarian empire was the rise, from its centre in upper Macedonia in the tenth century, and rapid spread of Bogomilism, a Manichean doctrine resembling that of the Albigensians. This creed, which became deeply entrenched among the lower clergy, tended to encourage popular discontent with its view of the state as the manifestation of evil.[20]

Despite their catastrophic defeat by Basil II,[21] the Bulgarians

18 Ibid., p. 4
19 Winnifrith, *op. cit.*
20 Crampton, *op. cit.*, p. 5. Since Bogomilism started in Macedonia, and by aiding the articulation of popular discontent could thus possibly be seen as having rudimentary socialist overtones of 'class war' etc., it has unsurprisingly been used by the post-war Communist regime in the ethnogenesis of the Macedonian nation. For example: 'Bogomilism came into existence under the influence of the old teaching [i.e. that of Clement and Naum who, of course, are portrayed as true Macedonian patriots] as revolt against feudal exploitation and so against the official church which was the lackey of the feudal lords and the state.' Doné Ilievski, *The Macedonian Orthodox Church*, Skopje, 1973, p. 20.
21 15,000 were captured on the slopes of Belasitsa mountain and blinded by Basil's

were able to revive under the Asenids (who are also claimed, with more evidence, to have been Vlachs[22]) and retake Macedonia briefly in 1210, only to lose it again. The area was then divided between the Greeks of Epirus in the west, the Greeks of Nicea in the east, and the Serbs—another Slavic people who were rapidly expanding their influence from the north and north-west (from Kosovo), and who were for a brief period Latin Catholics, due to the attack on Byzantium by Western Christian powers in the course of the fourth Crusade of 1202. Norman attacks from Italy through Albania and into Macedonia and beyond had already started in the late eleventh century and continued through the twelth. The result of this penetration by the west was a temporary introduction of Catholicism on territory controlled by Norman and other western invaders. This included southern Macedonia. However, this Latin empire only lasted from 1204 till 1261. One aspect of this ill fated incursion by western Europe was to weaken Byzantium and even discredit it in the eyes of many Orthodox believers, some of whom later even viewed the Ottomans as protection from Rome and thus a blessing.

In 1282 Milutin, the Serbian king, took Skopje from Byzantium and by the end of the century had established hegemony over much of the Balkans and penetrated deeply into Macedonia. The apogee of the Serbian empire came under Stefan Dušan, in whose capital, Skopje, he took his coronation in 1346. His empire stretched from the Danube to central Greece and from the Drina to western Thrace. After Dušan's death in 1355, the Serbian empire disintegrated. The chronic disunity in the Balkans allowed the Ottoman Turks, an Asiatic people who had gradually eroded away the ailing Byzantine empire, to invade the peninsula through Macedonia and the Maritsa valley. The gradual Ottoman conquest culminated in the defeat of the Serbs at Kosovo Polje in 1389, which allowed the Ottomans complete control of Macedonia and the Balkans. Constantinople held out for some time behind its redoubtable defences, but eventually it fell in 1453 and the Byzantine empire was no more. Stability had finally been brought to

troops who left only one man in every 100 with one eye to lead the others back to Samuil. Samuil was so stricken that he died shortly after, but legend has it that he sent his remaining troops out to collect the eyes and put them into Lake Ohrid in a gold casket— hence the lake's shimmering surface.

22 R.L. Wolff, 'The Second Bulgarian Empire: Its Origins and History to 1204', *Speculum*, vol. xxiv, 1949, pp. 167-206.

Macedonia in the shape of the Ottoman conquerors who brought
with them Islam and their own form of social divisions.

The Jews

Although the Jewish population of Macedonia, which was to
be such an important element in Salonika, came during the Ottoman
period after their expulsion from Spain at the end of the fifteenth
century, Jews had been living in Macedonia before then. Some
date their arrival to the sixth century BC when they were brought
in by Phoenician merchants as slaves, while others assert that
they arrived about the same time in the wake of Darius's conquests.[23]
Paul of Tarsus in the first century AD mentions Jewish communities
in Salonika, while the 1931 excavation of the large and obviously
wealthy synagogue in Stobi indicates that wealthy Jews were
prominent in Macedonia slightly later. After the Council of Nicea,
a long series of laws and edicts were promulgated by Roman
and later Byzantine emperors which worked to the disadvantage
of Jews. The first such law was the 'Cunctos populus' decree of
Theodosius which called for the forcible conversion of Jews, and
other similar edicts from Heraclius and Leo III of Byzantium
followed. Although these were not consistently applied even in
Constantinople, they did result in a movement of Jews from
the major centres, especially Constantinople and Salonika, into
the Slav lands to escape persecution.

The Serbian empire established by Stefan Nemanja in the twelfth
century had a number of Jewish centres in Macedonia, for example
in Kastoria, Ohrid and Skopje. Dušan's codex of laws, published
in 1349, which lays down that Orthodoxy is the only recognised
religion, did not mention the Jews, but as Pomeranz states, it
seems that at least in the newly-captured lands the Jews had to
pay a poll-tax—a Byzantine institution continued by Dušan—and
thus their status was more or less the same in both the Serbian
and Byzantine empires. However, the medieval Serbian state was
more tolerant towards the Jews—and towards the Ragusa (Dubrov-
nik) Catholics—than the Byzantine empire. This was in contrast

23 This section is based upon Frank Pomeranz's 'Judaica Illyrica' in the *South Slav
   Journal*, Winter 1982/3, vol. 5, no. 4 (18), which reviews a number of works on
   Jews in the Balkans, especially Mirko Mirč's essay 'Jews in the Balkan Peninsula
   and in the ancient Serbian State before the advent of the Turks'.

to western Europe where continuing racial and religious persecution resulted in Jews fleeing to the Balkans even before the Ottoman occupation. As early as 1360 Jews expelled from Hungary by Louis the Great were taken in and protected in Bulgaria by John Shishman. Those fleeing western persecution went to Turkey and to Salonika. In the latter these new Yiddish-speaking Ashkenazi arrivals overwhelmed the ancient Romaniot (i.e. Greek-speaking) element. These in turn were overwhelmed after 1492 by Ladino-speaking Jews from Spain, making Salonika the spiritual and economic metropolis of the Jews of south-eastern Europe.

The Roma (Gypsies)

The Roma originated from India. From the fifth century onwards Roma filtered into the Persian and later Arab empires of the Middle East, early groups of them reaching Byzantium in the tenth century. In the Balkans, where Ottoman rule lasted longest in Europe, the majority of them are Muslim. Traditionally independent and the product of migration and adaption, the Roma have in all countries remained predominantly outside the various socio-economic systems in operation, be they feudal, capitalist or even socialist, by becoming horse-dealers, smiths, musicians and more recently scavengers. The Roma have historically been persecuted and/or discriminated against in all countries of Eastern Europe and have suffered from racism due to their colour.

Seeds of controversy

Thus the period before the Ottoman conquest saw the position of Macedonia change successively from being on the periphery of the vibrant Greek world to becoming the centre of the huge empires of Philip and Alexander, a border area between the Latin and Greek cultural zones, a transit route for invading hordes from the north, an integral part of both the Bulgarian and Serbian empires, and a fluctuating border region of Byzantium. While some of the newcomers caused little ethnic change of a profound or permanent nature, others did. In this the Slavs had an especially strong impact; others, like the Jews and (less definitely where formal trade and written records are concerned) the Roma, had less. These newcomers blended, coexisted or fought with the 'originals'—Greeks, Thracians and Illyrians and the later Romans. Thus the pre-Ottoman history gives ample scope for nationalists of a variety of persuasions to claim rights for their 'nation' by referring to their putative ancestors and the relationship which they at times had with Macedonia.

The Greeks claim a consistent heritage from Philip and Alexander through Byzantium to the present day. Critics point out that while Macedon's ruling dynasty in antiquity was Greek, the people were perceived, and saw themselves, as different from the core Greek culture—though just how different remains contentious.[24] They also point out that to classify Byzantium as Greek was— certainly by the end—also highly contentious, especially after the Crusaders had imposed their own states and rulers. Indeed, when Constantinople finally fell to the Ottomans in 1453 many Greeks fought alongside the Ottoman armies, preferring the 'turbans of the infidels to the tiaras of the Latin bishops'.[25]

The argument that Byzantium was not really an extension of Greek culture can be summed up by three points: first, that in spite of the Greek language the Byzantine state was a continuation of the Roman empire; secondly, that Byzantium was subjected to so much foreign penetration that while superficially it was Greek, in reality it was not so—like the Germanic kingdoms of western Europe whose Latin culture concealed an undeniably German society; and thirdly that the rapid Christianisation, especially in the fourth century, marked a fundamental break in cultural continuity—an argument in line with Arnold Toynbee's view of an Orthodox Christian civilization distinct from an ancient Greco-Roman one.[26] One of the most ardent advocates of the second of these arguments, was Johann Philipp Fallmerayer, who in 1830 stated that due to Slavic and other invasions there was no continuity between ancient and modern Greeks.[27] Although this extreme

24 This difference (or not as the case may be) is similar to that between Bulgarians and Slav Macedonians in this century.
25 Douglas Dakin, *The Greek Struggle for Independence, 1821-1833*, London, 1973, p. 15.
26 A.J. Toynbee, *A Study of History*, vol. 1, London, 1934, pp. 63-7. The succinct three formulations are taken from Robert Browning, 'The Continuity of Hellenism in the Byzantine world: Appearance or Reality?' in Winnifrith and Murray, *op. cit.*
27 J.P. Fallmerayer, *Geschichte der halbinsel Morea während des Mittelalters*, vol. 1,

view has been rejected, it is perhaps irrelevant anyway. What people feel should be the crucial factor, and, as noted in the introduction, nations can be created or destroyed on the basis of historical inaccuracies, which are also often the foundation of modern nationalisms. This can also be put to the third argument. Additionally, as Browning points out, there was a reconciliation of Christianity with Classical Hellenistic philosophical thought.

The second point is perhaps the most pertinent since it deals with how people actually see themselves. While many Byzantine subjects, especially in border areas like Macedonia at various times, retained a different core identity beneath the Byzantine exterior, this also worked in reverse in core Greek areas to the south of Macedonia. Bryer points out that the Ottoman occupation can actually be seen as having greatly aided the Greeks to continue as a separate people with a separate consciousness by decapitating the Byzantine 'high' culture, a part-Roman and part-Greek symbiosis, leaving only an undeniably Greek popular 'low' culture as the harbinger of Greek national consciousness.[28] Thus the Ottomans played a vital role in defining and thus partly creating a Greek identity.

For the Bulgarians, despite the catastrophic defeats by both Byzantium and then the Ottomans, the Slavic literary culture based on the works of Cyril and Methodius and their disciples was strong enough to withstand this. That Macedonia was a key area where this was propagated makes it, for them, indisputably Bulgarian. While Dušan for the Serbs made Skopje his capital, and nationalists in the nineteenth and twentieth century claimed Macedonia as 'south Serbia', it never occupied the key role of Kosovo in Serbian national consciousness. Nevertheless, the claims were there and were to resurface with a vengeance and be used by Serbian nationalists. Recent historians in Skopje, making use of the fact that Clement and Naum's great educational work and Samuil's empire were based around Ohrid, claim all these as ethnic Macedonians, and Samuil's state as Macedonian as opposed to Bulgarian. The Albanians, claiming descent from the Illyrians and living mainly to the west, can make a similar claim, as the Romanians have done at times through the Vlachs.

Stuttgart-Tübingen, 1830, referred to in Browning, *op. cit.*
28 Anthony Bryer, 'Greeks and Turks' in Winnifrith and Murray, *op. cit.*

3

GROUP IDENTITY IN
THE OTTOMAN EMPIRE

FROM *MILLET* TO NATION

The Ottoman empire ruled Macedonia for five centuries from the end of the fourteenth century until the Balkan wars in the early twentieth century. The Ottoman conquest saw the arrival in Macedonia and the Balkans of large numbers of Turkish and Turkic-speaking settlers and, with them, Islam. Along with the arrival of new Islamic peoples, there were inevitably many in the Balkans who adopted the religion of the new rulers—in Macedonia these were the majority of the Albanians and Roma, and sections of the Greek- and Slav-speaking populations. Moreover, the arrival of Islam was also especially significant since the Ottoman empire was an empire ruled by Islamic precepts for most of its existence. The duration of the Ottoman rule over Macedonia merits a close look at the way it classified its citizens.

Islam

Islam in its classical form is, in the well-worn adage, more than a mere religion in the Western Christian sense. It encompasses a total way of life, a model for society, a culture and a civilization—in effect it is the state, or should be if the rulers were true Muslims.[1] Whereas from the start Christianity was non-political—'My

---

1 There are many standard books on Islam as a state religion, especially the works of H.A.R. Gibb and Guillaume. A useful introduction is Edward Mortimer's, *Faith and Power: The Politics of Islam*, Faber and Faber, London, 1982.

Kingdom is not of this world', 'Render unto Caesar what is Caesar's' etc.—and there was thus the concept of 'church' as distinct from 'state', the community of believers founded by Mohammed was always closely akin to a state.[2]

Mohammed was an Arab, the divine revelation as revealed to him by God was in Arabic and was transcribed in Arabic in the Quran, and the first Muslim state was an Arab one. Despite this legacy, which has been used by modern Arab nationalists,[3] the central idea of Islam was of a community of believers regardless of race or language. The revelation was valid for all people at all times. As already noted, the concept of the religious law was a powerful force in binding the Islamic community into a single whole reflected in the terminology of the Dar-ül Islam (the world of peace) relating to the Islamic world, and the Dar-ül Harb (the world of war) relating to the rest of humankind. Inevitably, perhaps, significant differences emerged within the Islamic community after Mohammed's death. The main split was between Sunnis and Shias over the succession, with Shias following the claim of Ali, Mohammed's cousin and son-in-law; Ali's defeat in what was a quarrel over temporal power solidified into major doctrinal differences between Sunni and Shias. While this split was important in helping to produce a large degree of differentiation between the Ottoman and the Persian states; the Persian ruler

2 Mortimer, *ibid.*, p. 38.

3 The sense of Islam as a transnational community of believers overriding national differences resulted in the initial Arab nationalists coming from the Christian Arab communities of Lebanon and Syria who were less encumbered with the problems of reconciling universalist Islam with particularist nationalism. However, the secular nationalism of, e.g., Antun Saadeh, which was useful in claiming Arab independence from the Ottomans, fell victim to the overriding need to refer to the Arabic identity of the masses, which was firmly rooted in Islam and Islamic history. Later Arab nationalist ideologues like Sati al-Husri and Abd al-Rahmi al-Bazzaz looked to Islam as an essential component of being Arab, with Mohammed being viewed as the founder of the Arab nation—another typical case of modern nationalists transposing modern concepts backwards into history. An extreme version of this was propounded by Michael Aflaq, himself from a Christian background, who held that Islam *was* Arab nationalism. Thus Arab nationalism saw the redefinition of Islam as a national Arab religion. See Ernest Dawn, *From Ottomanism to Arabism*, University of Illinois Press, 1973; Sylvia Haim (ed.), *Arab Nationalism: an Anthology*, University of California Press, Los Angeles, 1962; Bassam Tibi, *Arab Nationalism*, 2nd edn, Macmillan, London, 1990; Kemal H. Karpat, *Political and social Thought in the Contemporary Middle East*, London, 1968.

Shah Ismail enforced a Shiite homogeneity which became the basis of national sentiment,[4] while in the Balkans and Macedonia Shiism outside of the Bektaşis was not an important factor. The Ottomans and the converted Muslims of Macedonia were mainly Sunni and adhered to the Hanafi school of law.[5]

The Sufi tarikats

Alongside the mainstream legalistic Islam, which was rationalised and codified into a law and systematic theology guarded by the *ulema*, the religious experts, based in the cities,[6] there was the existence of a 'parallel' or 'folk' Islam of the Sufis. Along with

4   See John A. Armstrong, *Nations before Nationalism*, Chapel Hill, NC, 1982. In central Anatolia large numbers of Shiites known as Alevis remained—at present they are estimated to comprise up to 20% of the population of modern Turkey—despite the Ottoman authorities reacting to Ismail's repression against Sunnis by enforcing Sunni orthodoxy by the execution of thousands of Anatolian Alevis; many others fled to Persia. The brunt of this repression fell on the Kizilbaş Shiite dervishes in rural areas whom Ismail hoped to use as a 'fifth column'. Urban Shiites in Anatolia were less receptive to Safavid propaganda and were generally tolerated, if discouraged.

5   The majority of Muslims were and are Sunnis. Their name is derived from the *Sunna*, or words and deeds of Mohammed as recorded in the Hadith—they thus claim to be following the example of the Prophet. They believe the succession to Mohammed passed to the Caliphs. Despite the usual description of Islamic law as attempting to be both all-encompassing and unchangeable, in the early period after Mohammed's death, Sunni Muslims recognised that the 'gates of law' were wider than became permissible later in Islamic doctrine. Each Sunni was obliged to adhere to one of the schools of 'law'—i.e. of religious norms. The four recognised schools—Hanafi, Malakite, Hanbali and Shafi, dating from the ninth century—were named after scholars who founded them (three other schools having died out by 1300). In theory a Muslim could decide to which school to adhere but in practice, with some exceptions, a specific school predominated in a specific area. The Ottomans preferred the Hanafi school, which gave greater flexibility to political rulers, and this school was 'established' throughout the Ottoman empire. Other schools were tolerated in Egypt. However only in the Maghreb portions of the Ottoman empire—viz. Tunisia and Algeria, as the Ottomans did not control Morocco—where indigenous Muslims clung to the Malakite school, did anything approaching ethnic cleavages appear. In the main the different schools in Sunni Islam did not play a part in forming separate group identities in the sense of proto-nations.

6   As Armstrong points out, despite the crucial role played by nomadic warriors from both the Arabian deserts and the Turkic steppes in spreading the faith and the polity, orthodox Islam was essentially an urban religion and the city played a crucial role in Islamic consciousness as the ideal. The sacred centre, Mecca the

the legalistic and formalistic aspects of Sunnism as embodied in the 'Five Pillars'—monotheism, prayer five times a day, keeping the fast, making the pilgrimage to Mecca, and giving alms to the poor—there has from early times been this parallel Islam of the Sufis. A Sufi, so called after the distinctive woollen dress they traditionally wore, is anyone who believes in direct experience of God and is prepared to dedicate time and effort to make this happen. Sufism thus caters to the mystical impulses of individuals. In practice it consists of feeling and unveiling a *ma'rifa* (*gnosis*) reached through a passage of ecstatic states which can not be learned but only attained by direct experience, ecstasy and inward transformation.[7]

While the Seljuk Turks vigorously upheld orthodox Sunnism against any perceived Shiite or other heterodox tendencies, a change came about with Saladin and henceforth there was in Sunni Islam a qualified acceptance and respectability of Sufism.[8] It was not seen as a threat to formal Islam, or a replacement of it, nor was there overt hostility between the different *tarikats* (ways). Each viewed the others as equally valid routes to the end-product of mystic communion. Sufis accepted the law and formal requirements but formed inner coteries and introduced hierarchical structures due to their internal systems of relationships between a master (*murşhid*) and a disciple (*murid*) in the various *tarikats* to achieve the desired mystic communion. In this aspect Sufi orders in one way helped fill the gap left by suppression of Shiite sectarianism as well as aiding conversion of non-Islamic peoples by allowing a certain symbiosis between Islamic and other religious beliefs and practices. As Trimingham points out, Sufi organisations tended to absorb popular movements with Shiites particularly forced to seek asylum within Sufi groups of which the heterodox Bektaşi order gave it its fullest expression.

This also held true of Christian communities in the Balkans which adopted Islam—the Bektasi order was especially prominent among Albanians, Tetovo being one centre. The original Ottoman state was serviced by a 'slave élite' of Christian boys taken from

---

a crucial role in Islamic consciousness as the ideal. The sacred centre (Mecca the vestigial city) was along with the symbolic language of Arabic (often hardly more than a sacred alphabet) and the scriptures encoded in it, indispensable symbols.

7 J. Spencer Trimingham, *The Sufi Orders of Islam*, Oxford University Press, 1971, pp. 1-3.

8 *Ibid.* p. 11.

their homes by the *devşirme* system. There was an obligation on Christian families to supply at intervals a proportion of their most able sons to be educated and raised as Muslims to run the empire in both civilian and military capacities.[9] The civilians often assumed the highest positions in the empire, while the military units, the *Janissaries,* were the élite of the empire until their destruction by Mahmud II in 1826. Partly because of their Christian roots, they were also overwhelmingly Bektaşi.

While in some places there has been a symbiosis of *tarikats* with nationalist movements,[10] this combination of Sufism and incipient nationalism—or at least the preservation of a group identity—appears to have been confined to the Caucasus. As such it can perhaps be seen as a local defence mechanism of predominantly mountainous and thus compartmentalised Islamic communities from attack from an external non-Muslim enemy. Elsewhere the Sufi movements tended to be, like orthodox Islam itself, trans-ethnic and trans-national. Indeed Sufism encouraged direct contact between Bosnia, Albania, Kosovo, parts of Bulgaria and Thrace,

---

9   This levy, unsurprisingly deeply unpopular with the Christian communities despite the opportunities of advancement it afforded to those taken, fell into abeyance in the seventeenth century and had completely disappeared by the eighteenth.

10 This is especially evident in the resistance of Muslim minorities in Russia, and even more under the Soviet Union. Faced with acute hostility from the atheist communist state, Sufism proved a powerful method of resistance. It was made up of closed orders which could remain outside the system and, for example in the Soviet Union, managed to run their own courts, financial systems based on the compulsory levy, and their own secret schools. Their dynamism and organisation proved invaluable in such a hostile climate. In the Caucasus particularly, a symbiosis of Sufi *tarikats* and tribal clans became perceptible in the nineteenth century with the Shamil rebellion the most evident expression of this. This trend continued in the Soviet era and was especially strong in tribal areas of North Daghestan. Sufi orders, especially the Nakşibendi and Kadiri *tarikats,* became heavily involved in the continuing resistance first to Russian and later to Soviet rule in the Caucasus. Indeed the very survival of the Chechen and Ingush peoples as distinct nations after their populations were deported *en masse* to Eastern Siberia and Kazakhstan in 1944 for alleged collaboration with the Nazis, can be seen as in no small part due to the activities of the Kadiri offshoot, the Uis Haji group, in the places of exile. See Alexandre Bennigsen and S. Enders Wimbush, *Mystics and Commissars: Sufism in the Soviet Union,* Hurst, London, 1985; and Marie Bennigsen Broxup *et al., The North Caucasus Barrier: The Russian Advance towards the Muslim World,* Hurst, London, 1992.

the Arab World, Iran and Central Asia.[11] Thus the very universality of the various Sufi movements helped bring about contacts between parts of the Muslim community that diverged geographically and ethnically, and thus helped promote and strengthen unity in the 'imagined' (in Benedict Anderson's usage) Islamic community.

The millet system and the Muslims

The conquest of Byzantium and the advance of the Ottomans almost to Vienna brought large Christian communities under Ottoman control. Although there were inevitably some people —the majority of Albanians, the Torbeši of Macedonia, the Pomaks of the Rhodope mountains, and the Bosnians—who accepted the religion of the new rulers, the Ottomans were non-assimilative and multi-national without the technological and institutional facilities for integrating and unifying the subject peoples. Additionally, communications are difficult in the Balkan peninsula because of its mountainous terrain. This helped to produce communities that tended to be compartmentalised rather than unified. The Christian and Jewish populations were accepted, as traditionally in Islam, as 'people of the book'. The common ancestry of the three religions helped this tolerance—a tolerance illustrated by the acceptance of large numbers of Jews, especially Ladino-speaking Sephardim expelled from Spain after 1492. Many of these people, as we have seen, settled in Salonika, which subsequently developed a pronounced Jewish character.

For Muslims, there was no official differentiation by language or race. The concept of being a 'Turk' as used in modern parlance, was, until the end of the nineteenth century, alien to the Ottoman élites, who saw themselves as Ottomans (*Osmanlı*) rather than 'Turks' which had the connotation of uneducated peasants. The importance of language in group identity has been noted in all studies of nationalism; so we should look at the Ottoman state language. A requirement of high office in the empire was first to be a Muslim, and secondly to know Ottoman Turkish.[12] Ethnicity was not a factor *per se* and many Grand Vezirs and high officials were

11 H. T. Norris, *Islam in the Balkans: Religion and Society between Europe and the Arab World*, Hurst, London, 1993.
12 Modern scholars give credit for the first establishment of Turkish as the base of the official language, at least as far as Anatolia is concerned, to the Karamanids

from originally Albanian or Muslim Slav or other Ottoman Muslim populations; indeed the whole concept of the 'slave élite' and the *devşirme* system worked against an 'ethnically pure' governmental class. Knowledge of Ottoman Turkish was a requisite, and this language was by no means synonymous with everyday spoken Turkish; it was a mixture of Turkish, Arabic and Persian and reflected the importance in Islamic society of men of the sword, men of the pen, and men of religion. Turkish terms predominated in military usage, while Persian words and forms were prevalent in the literary arts, and Arabic—the language of Mohammed and of the holy Quran—naturally featured strongly in religious matters.

As well as the high number of Arabic and Persian words in its vocabulary, Ottoman Turkish also required that when such words were used it should be with the relevant Arabic or Persian grammatical structures. Thus a knowledge of all three languages was needed. In addition the Arabic script was used, which was not suited for writing Turkish with its different vowels (as well as being difficult to learn). All this made the official state language a privileged mystery to the 'common people'. The problem of the script, which did not sign vowels, also resulted in frequent misunderstandings. To cap all this, by the late eighteenth and early nineteenth centuries, Ottoman Turkish had degenerated into bombast with inelastic and tortuous embellished phrases and constructions.[13] Thus the Ottoman empire appears to fit Gellner's paradigm of a trans-ethnic and trans-political élite employing an archaic idiom with no interest in ensuring continuity between its mode of communication and that of the majority.[14]

Large numbers of Muslims fled from the Caucasus in 1859 to the Ottoman empire to escape Russian rule there. A further 5,000 left in 1865. Justin McCarthy estimates that approximately

---

who created in the 13th century a strong polity on the ruins of the Seljuk Sultanate. See M. Önder, 'Türkcenin Devlet Dili Ilanini Yildönümü in *Türk Dili*, vol. X, 1961, p. 507, quoted in David Kushner, *The Rise of Turkish Nationalism 1876-1908*, Frank Cass, London, 1977. However as shown below this was not synonymous with demotic Turkish as spoken by the masses.

13 B. Lewis, *The Emergence of Modern Turkey*, Oxford University Press, 1961, p. 420.

14 Gellner, *op. cit.*, p. 141. Attempts at language reform began in the nineteenth century and remained a major aim until Atatürk's sweeping reforms after the establishment of the Turkish republic.

1.2 million Caucasians emigrated from Russian-conquered territories in this period and that some 800,000 of them moved to the Ottoman empire. Many were settled in the Balkans—indeed the arrival of Circassians into Bulgaria proved a destabilising element which helped provoke the Christian Bulgarian uprisings of the 1870s. These groups progressively become peacefully assimilated into the relevant majority Islamic community there—i.e. the Turkish one in Bulgaria and Northern Greece, the Albanian one in Albania and the Albanian-dominated surrounds of Kosovo and Western Macedonia, and the Muslim Slav community in Bosnia and the Eastern Sandžak.[15] A similar process of Turkification or Albanianisation has also tended to happen—and continues to do so—to small groups of Islamicised Slavs in similar areas outside Bosnia and the Sandžak: Torbeshi in Macedonia or Pomaks in Bulgaria.[16]

An interesting case is that of the Roma (Gypsies) of the Ottoman empire who, like the Vlachs, are a non-territorial ethnic group. The Roma originated in India and moved through Anatolia to Europe. Certain groups became Muslim—most did so in the Ottoman empire—while others became Christian. As such many became assimilated into the Turkish-speaking mass—as illustrated by the second half of the Bulgarian proverb noted above. However, they have been and continue to be subjected to racism and discrimination from all groups in many places. Some—though not all—are easily identifiable by having darker skins. In the Balkans the Roma remain firmly at the bottom of the pile and are subject throughout the region to everyday racism and even attack, although at the time of writing their position in the new republic of Macedonia is currently something of an exception.[17]

---

15 Those who settled in Anatolia have largely become Turkified—a process repeated with later Muslim immigrants from the Balkans. Those who settled in Arab lands of the empire were less easily assimilated however. See Paul B. Henze, 'Circassian Resistance to Russia', pp. 93 ff. in Broxup, *op. cit.*, who also cites Justin McCarthy, *The Fate of the Muslims*, forthcoming.

16 In Bosnia and the Sandžak the problems of nationality based solely on Islam among other groups speaking essentially the same language is graphically illustrated by the tragedy precipitated by the break-up of Yugoslavia.

17 Regarding the attitude to Roma in modern Turkey, the anthropologist Carol Delaney notes that 'Cingene [Roma] are considered subhuman [by the villagers], because they have no book [Quran or Bible] and are thought to be promiscuous: like animals, sharing women in common, see *The Seed and the Soil*:

The Christian millets

While Christians and Jews were tolerated, they were not seen before the *Tanzimat* reform movement as first-class citizens, as were Muslims, and even then in practice they were not. They were forbidden to carry arms or ride horses. They were not eligible for the army, apart from those young Christian boys taken by the above-mentioned *devşirme* system and destined for the élite praetorian guard.[18] While certain avenues of advancement were closed to them as non-Muslims, others, like commerce, which was somewhat looked down upon in Islamic societies, were open. Mardin points out however that the widely-held belief that such commercial activity in the Ottoman empire was always a monopoly of non-Muslims is unsustainable and that the classic non-Muslim 'comprador' type only really appeared after the

---

Gender and Cosmology in Turkish Village Society, University of California, 1991, p 105). This stigmatisation of Roma due to their alleged lack of faith (having 'no book') appears doubly inconsistent. First, many Roma throughout the empire were/are Muslims (and in the Balkans also Christians). Secondly, as Delaney also points out, in the view of the villagers 'not only is humanity unified, but all are essentially Muslim. Humanity is united because all races derive from Adam and Adam was made by God'. (*ibid.,* p. 287). Quite why Roma suffer this racism in an Islamic society remains unanswered. Moreover, despite the self-viewed high status of nomadic groups in areas of south-east Anatolia, this did not apply to nomadic Roma. M. M. van Bruinessen states in his classic work on the Kurds (*Agha Shaikh and State*, Rijswijk, 1978, p. 140) that lineages of Roma-type groups were despised by all, with even the lowliest landless peasants looking down on them, and all Kurdish groups deny any intermarriage with them. The Roma everywhere in the area appeared (and still appear) to be fragmented by occupation with a strict hierarchy between themselves in terms of intermarriage between different groups.

18 Although Christians did fight in the very early Ottoman armies, this quickly ended and the army was a Muslim army of a Muslim state. See Bernard Lewis, *The Emergence of Modern Turkey*, Oxford University Press, 1961, p. 331. The navy however was a different matter. For some time it was a faithful copy of the Venetian and Genoese navies crewed mainly by Greeks, Dalmatians and Albanians. Attempts to replace these by more dependable elements which made up the land army were not successful and there remained a dearth of skilled crew which necessitated up to Mahmud I (1730-54) hiring skilled crewmen from merchant ships who plied Ottoman ports in exchange for remission of customs duty. The navy remained dependent on Greek provincial pilots for navigation as well as Greeks and Arabic-speaking Muslims from N. Africa. Thus it was not an indigenous Ottoman product. See H.A.R. Gibb and H.Bowen, *Islamic Society and the West*, Oxford University Press, 1950-7: vol. I., pp. 88-107.

Crimean war.[19] However in the first half of the nineteenth century the Muslim Ottoman traders (*Hayriye Tüccarı*) all but vanished at the expense of the minority traders (*Avrupa Tüccarı*) who were protected by Western powers—the British also took advantage of the empire's weakness in the 1820s and 1830s to force free trade agreements on it. The Greek Phanariots had by the late seventeenth century acquired a monopoly on providing interpreters for the state—a monopoly that would last until the last Greek *dragoman* at the Porte was executed for treason at the time of the Greek revolt and the decision taken to use only Muslims thenceforward for such positions.[20]

Thus the Ottoman state was an Islamic one, with the population divided by religious affiliation, and the whole system preceding the *Tanzimat* was based on separation of the groups—even down to regulations as to the colour and type of clothing each religious group could wear.[21] As noted above, all Muslims were officially recognised as equal first-class citizens in the Muslim *millet*. Other 'peoples of the book' were organised into separate *millets*—Jews in one, members of the Armenian Church in another etc. Faith and not ethnicity or language was the differentiator.

There remains uncertainty over the origins of the *millet* system. Many trace the system back to the presumed appointment by

19 Şerif Mardin, *The Genesis of Young Ottoman Thought*, Princeton University Press, 1962, p. 167.

20 Lewis, *op. cit.,* pp. 60 and 86.

21 Sultan Mahmud II took the first steps in changing this and thus attempting to end the centuries-old institutionalised separation of his subjects by religious affiliation, by ordering government and army officials to stop wearing the turban and flowing robes habitually worn. These garments by their shape and colours marked both the religion and the status of the wearer. For example only Muslims were supposed to wear yellow shoes and green garments. Henceforth, by a decree of 1829, all officials except those in the religious class were to wear the simple fez and European frock-coat regardless of their status in life. Outside government service, changes in the hitherto rigid dress codes began with the fez becoming universal (despite initial revolts against its imposition—revolts which were to be repeated when Atatürk a century later outlawed it in its turn in favour of the European brimmed hat or cap). The change in dress codes was particularly accelerated by the Crimean war and the corresponding large influx of foreign soldiers and merchants who helped spread European ways and dress codes to all elements of the Istanbul population. Women's clothing however changed much more slowly. See Stanford J. Shaw, *The Jews of the Ottoman Empire and the Turkish Republic*, Macmillan, 1991, pp. 149 and 169; and Lewis, *op. cit.*

Mehmed II, the conqueror of Istanbul, of Patriarch Gennadias, Bishop Yovakim of Bursa and Rabbi Capsali as hereditary leaders of the respective Greek, Armenian and Jewish communities. However, others like Benjamin Braude say that the term '*millet*' really denoted a set of mostly local arrangements which varied from place to place, and that there is much evidence that the authority vested in the leaders was both personal, rather than hereditary/institutionalised, and varied in its territorial extent.[22]

However, despite their origins, perceived or real, the *millets* became accepted and the leaders of the different ones had wide jurisdiction over their flocks, who were bound by their own regulations rather than the *Shariat*. The different *millets* were treated like corporate bodies and allowed their own internal structures and hierarchies—indeed the Ottoman state encouraged this by dealing exclusively with their heads rather than individual members. Included within these structures were the educational systems for the different religious communities. Thus the religious community—the *millet*—was the prime focus of identity outside of family and locality. For the Christian minorities especially, the *millet* system, which left control of the education system and of much of their own internal affairs in the hands of the *millet* hierarchy itself and outside official state control, proved ideally suited to the transmission of the new creed of nationalism penetrating from the West—even if, as shown below, there was often tension between the traditional *millet* leaders and the new nationalist radicals.

It also allowed the subject Christian peoples to retain their separate identities and cultures rooted in their respective churches. Indeed the monophysite churches with Syrian, Armenian and Coptic adherents, as well as the Nestorians, survived mainly in the Muslim lands while vanishing in the more intolerant Christian ones. Along with the Jews expelled from England, France, Spain and Portugal, a variety of heterodox Christians including Protestants, Unitarians and Russian Molokans were able to find refuge

22 E.g. the Greek patriarchates of Jerusalem, Alexandria and Antioch retained their autonomy at least in canon law, while for the Armenians, the see of Istanbul became 'over the centuries..a sort of *de facto* patriarchate, but its ecclesiastical legitimacy was grudgingly recognized, if at all'. See Benjamin Braude and Bernard Lewis *Christians and Jews in the Ottoman Empire*, New York, 1982, pp. 72-82, and the review article 'Remembering the Minorities' by Andrew Mango in *Middle Eastern Studies*, vol. 21, October 1985, no. 4, pp. 118-40. The Jews never had a single patriarch for the whole community (see Shaw, *op. cit.*).

in the Ottoman empire. The *millet* system additionally allowed many of the Christian groups to retain a sense of a former glorious history when they controlled a particular area, which with the national awakenings in the nineteenth century they once more claimed—often at the expense of their neighbours who likewise made historical claims to the territory in question. Thus the national awakenings which saw the first crumbling of Ottoman power in the Balkans by the mid-nineteenth century, with the establishment of the Serbian state in the north around Belgrade and the Greek state in the south around Athens, often gave rise to hostility between the previous Ottoman subject peoples. This was to reach its zenith in the struggle for Macedonia at the beginning of the twentieth century.

For the Orthodox Balkan populations the *millet* was controlled by the Greek patriarchate in Istanbul. Until the nineteenth century and the final establishment of the Bulgarian Exarchate Church, only the Serbs—because of the granting of the autocephalous patriarchate in Peć in 1557[23]—escaped the Greek spiritual tutelage during most of the time under Ottoman rule; the autocephalous archbishopric of Ohrid, demoted from a patriarchate after Samuil's defeat by Basil II, had became a Greek institution and ceased to be head of an autocephalous church in 1772. For centuries the Phanariot Greeks utilised the Istanbul patriarchate to hellenise the Orthodox populations of Macedonia: Slavs, Albanians, Vlachs and Roma.

The importance of the *millet* system allowing control of populations by a church is well illustrated by the case of the Bulgarians. After the Ottoman invasion, the separate Bulgarian church and attendant education system were placed under the control of the Greek Orthodox Church and the Greek Patriarch in Istanbul. Thus, it can be argued that until their national revival in the nineteenth century the Bulgarians faced as great a threat of assimilation from the Greeks who controlled the religious services and education—both of which were in the Greek medium—as

---

23 This was due to the urging of the then Grand Vezir Mehmet Paša Sokullu, a Serb by origin who had been taken in the *devširme* system (showing how some of those taken retained sympathies with their' roots). Banac, *op. cit.*, p. 64. By the time the Patriarchate of Peć had been abolished in 1796 the centre of Serb spiritual life had already shifted northwards with the migration in 1699 of large numbers of Serbs to the area north of Belgrade in the Vojvodina to escape Ottoman control.

they could have done from the Ottoman Turks. This is illustrated in an old Bulgarian proverb: 'Save us Lord from the Bulgarian who becomes a Greek and from the Gypsy who becomes a Turk.' The second half of this proverb illustrates how many islamicised Roma became assimilated into the mass of the Turkish-speaking population. The illiterate peasants in the countryside spoke the vernacular, while the urban educated class spoke Greek and became hellenised.

This is shown in the work of the Miladinov brothers, who were among the best known of that crucial group who helped popularise and spread the idea of Slav or Bulgarian consciousness in Macedonia at this time: the teachers. In a letter written in 1852, D. Miladinov (himself writing in Greek at that time) complained that most educated Bulgarians in Macedonia used Greek, and only in the north had the Slav language made a significant advance. He called for opposition to the hellenisation of Bulgarians, and, with his brother Konstantin, travelled around Macedonia trying to achieve this end. The brothers were eventually denounced to the Ottoman authorities by the Greek clergy and died in prison in Istanbul in 1862. In the twentieth century they were to be claimed by both Bulgaria and by the new Titoist Macedonian regime as their own. They referred to themselves as Bulgarians, yet, as Aarbakke[24] points out, they were better described as Pan-Slavs whose main aim was to oppose Hellenism and the Greek clergy.

Indeed a crucial factor in the growth of Bulgarian national consciousness was the establishment in 1870 of the national church, the Exarchate, by the Ottoman authorities following a long movement which had begun in 1820. In 1867 Patriarch Gregory VI had offered an autonomous Bulgarian Church but one not to be extended to the parishes of Macedonia. The Bulgarians refused and called for the populations of the relevant dioceses to decide. The decree of 1870 gave the Exarchate only seventeen dioceses but allowed parishes by a two-thirds majority vote of all adult Christian males to choose whether to join and whether the liturgy should be in the vernacular or to continue to be in Greek.

This struggle for a national church was patently political rather

24 Vemund Aarbakke, "Ethnic Rivalry and the Quest for Macedonia 1870-1913", unpubl. MA thesis, Institute for East European Studies, University of Copenhagen, Spring 1992, pp. 35-6.

than religious. The parishes which opted for the vernacular comprised the so-called Greater Bulgaria (which included most of geographic Macedonia) of the San Stefano Treaty of 1878 at the end of the Russo-Turkish war of 1875-8. However the Great Powers, notably Britain and Austria-Hungary both of which feared that such a large Bulgaria dominating the Balkans and straddling Turkey-in-Europe would be a client-state of Russia, forced its abandonment at the Treaty of Berlin and its replacement by a severely truncated state. Henceforth Bulgaria would be striving to 'regain' Macedonia and would be almost permanently revisionist and revanchist. Another aspect of the Treaty of Berlin was the administration of Bosnia-Hercegovina and the garrisoning of the Sanjak (Sandžak) of Novibazar, which divided Serbia and Montenegro, by Austria-Hungary. This resulted in Serbia also looking southwards towards Macedonia for future expansion, as her 'natural' territories for expansion (i.e. those territories with large Serbian populations) fell under Habsburg control.

The Tanzimat reform movement

By the end of the eighteenth century, sections of the ruling Ottoman élite had finally become aware of the extent to which the empire had fallen behind its rivals in Europe. Successive military defeats at the hands of the Russian empire rammed the point home. In response, the Ottomans attempted to replace old institutions with new and modern ones—the key one being the abolition of the Janissaries, who had proved themselves repeatedly to be incompetent not only in fighting external enemies but even in settling internal revolts like those of the Serbs and Greeks, and their replacement by a modern army.

The great reforms began during the reign of Mahmud II who firmly reasserted the control of the centre over the periphery. The six-times Grand Vezir, Mustafa Reşid Paşa, led the way in introducing the reforms. At this time the weakness of the empire was plain to see and without the help of foreign powers, notably Britain, it was hard pushed to cope both with the threat from Russia and also that from Mohammed Ali in Egypt, who in many ways was the prototype reformer and one whose success threatened to take over the empire itself. The price of British support was the acceptance of free trade and thus the opening of the empire to British commercial penetration, as well as paying at least lip-service to ending the formal inequality between Muslims and non-Muslims in the empire. Some tend to see the reform movement as due mainly to this Western, predominantly British pressure, and perhaps some aspects, like the Imperial Rescript of 1856, were introduced mainly for foreign consumption (in this case due to the Crimean war). However there is consensus that while in many ways the reform movement attempted to copy institutions and methods from the West, it was mainly a genuine attempt to modernise the empire and try to ensure its very survival.

The *Tanzimat* embodied a whole series of reforms dealing with almost all aspects of interaction between the state and the individual. For our purposes, the aspects dealing with differentiation between the various groups within the empire will be looked at, especially between Muslims and non-Muslims. As noted above, Muslims were seen as first-class citizens and other religious groups—Christians or Jews—were tolerated but not treated as equals. The *Tanzimat*, introduced by Reşid and carried on by the modernist bureaucrats like Ali Paşa and Fuad Paşa who succeeded him, essentially undercut the entire system.

The reforms entailed a gradual and partial secularisation of the state machinery, the judiciary and education. Right from the start with the proclamation in the Rose Garden in November 1839, the concepts of security of life and property, fair and public trial and—most shocking of all to devout Muslims—religious equality in the courts were clearly stated.[25] In May 1840 the new penal code emphasised the equality of all Ottoman subjects and while this was relatively ineffective it was another step in the same direction. In May 1855 the poll-tax for non-Muslims was abolished and henceforth all could bear arms (previously this was allowed only for Muslims). The imperial rescript of February 1856 again emphasised full equality for all subjects. Sultan Abdülmecid (1839-61) clearly expressed the ideas of the reform movement to Albert Cohn, a Rothschild agent, during his visit to Istanbul in 1854: 'My heart knows no difference among the rayas [peoples (literally flock)] of my empire; all rights and privileges will be given to all rayas without distinction.'[26] In practice this meant that Christians, Jews and Muslims were admitted on an equal basis to government

25 Lewis, *op. cit.*
26 Shaw, *op. cit.*, p. 156.

schools and positions in the administration (but not the army), and the Greeks and Armenians in particular took advantage of the new openings in government service.

In the new system the *millet* had become more a religious organisation rather than one dealing with all aspects of the relations between the individual and the state. Now all Ottoman citizens were theoretically to be equal. In line with the gradual bureaucratisation of the Muslim offices of the Şeyhülislam, the 1856 rescript proposed giving fixed salaries to the clergy in the Christian *millets* in place of the previous method of raising dues from the parishes. This would both raise the level of the lower clergy and help to end the corruption resulting from the sale of religious office. It was aimed at providing relief for Slav Macedonian and Bulgarian villagers who previously had to support the Greek clergy. Unsurprisingly the measure was opposed by the latter and therefore the rescript simultaneously proposed commissions for each *millet* to change their administrations to be more in tune with the new system. After a short resistance by the upper echelons of the Istanbul patriarchate, a new constitution for the Greek (as it was now called) Orthodox *millet* was passed in 1862 which saw power within the *millet* pass from the previous all-powerful metropolitans to the lay constituency of the developing urban groups.[27]

New *millets* were created, mostly through outside pressure from the Great Powers, for Catholics and Protestants and crucially the monopoly of the Greek patriarchate was broken with the creation of the Bulgarian Exarchate Church in 1870, the Serbian Orthodox Church in 1879 and the Romanian Orthodox Church in 1885. By 1875 there were nine recognised *millets* of which six were fairly large; by 1914 there were seventeen separate ones.[28] As Shaw points out, the *Tanzimat* reforms did take the first steps towards ending the *millet's* monopolistic control over the lives of their followers by creating secular institutions of education, law and justice side by side with the traditional *millet* ones.[29]

27 Aarbakke, *op cit.*, quoting Kemal H. Karpat, *An Inquiry into the Social Foundation of Nationalism in the Ottoman State: From Social estates to Classes, from Millets to Nations*, Princeton University Press, 1973, pp. 88-9.
28 Figures from Karpat, *op. cit.*, pp. 90-1; and Alexandris, 1983, p. 21 (no further reference) in Aarbakke, *op. cit.*
29 The modern schools were also supplemented by the introduction of a large number of foreign Christian missionary schools, both Protestant and Catholic.

The Jews

As already noted, many Jews from western and central Europe—
Ashkenazim from Germany, France and Hungary, Italian Jews
from Sicily, Otranto and Calabria, and Sephardim from Spain
and Portugal—were already fleeing persecution and emigrating
to the Ottoman empire in large numbers before the expulsion
of all Spain's Jewish population in 1492, and they kept coming
later as well. As a result, the Ottoman Jews formed in the early
seventeenth century both the largest and the wealthiest Jewish
community in the world. They settled in all parts of the empire
but were mostly concentrated in Istanbul, in eastern Thrace at
Edirne, and along the shores of the Aegean at Salonika and in
Palestine.[30] Salonika became the largest Jewish city in south-eastern
Europe. While at the time of the Ottoman conquest the city
had virtually no Jews, there were 23,942 enrolled at synagogues
in 1589. Although new arrivals kept coming, plagues and fires
kept the figure stable until the end of the eighteenth century,
when it was the only Ottoman city where the Jews were in
an outright majority. There were also Jewish communities elsewhere in Macedonia, in Bitola (Monastir) and Skopje.[31]

In Salonika the older Jewish communities formed three con-
gregations: the Greek-speaking Romaniots (Griegos) to which

These were intended for Muslims and Jews as well as Christians, with the aim
of conversion to the particular brand of Christianity propounded. On the whole,
however, Muslims and Jews were forbidden to attend so that only Christian
Greeks and Armenians used them and many of these converted and thus escaped
the traditional *millet* control over them. A result was often that they fell prone
to violent revolutionary activities, using the missionary schools as active bases
against the empire (Shaw, *op. cit.,* p. 157). This highlights an interesting point.
Despite the above-mentioned suitability of the *millet* system for propagating
nationalist ideas due to the system preserving separate group identity, in practice
the *millets* were usually governed by conservative traditional leaders who
preferred the continuance of Ottoman rule, and hence also of their own absolute
power within their own communities, rather than radical change. The *Tanzimat*, by undermining their authority, unintentionally helped the more radical
nationalists who got the (for them) 'best of both worlds'—i.e. the essential
continuance (and even extension by the creation of 'National Churches' in the
Orthodox body) of the *millet* system, whereby the population remained distinct
and unassimilated, but at the same time the undermining of the traditional
centres of authority who had a large stake in keeping the system going.

30 Shaw, *op. cit.,* pp. 33-6.
31 *Ibid.,* p. 39.

were added the emigrants from Bulgaria, the Ashkenazi emigrants from central Europe who made up the largest group until the mass arrival from Spain, and the Italians who were dominant in the late fifteenth century before the Sephardic arrival.[32] The arrival of the Sephardic Jews from Spain and, starting in 1506, of large numbers of Portuguese Marrano fugitives created discord, and promoted various factions and splits among the different groups throughout the sixteenth century.[33] Eventually the community unified around the Castilian Judeo-Spanish (Ladino) community which thenceforward subsumed other groups.[34] Salonika Jews became famous for their skills at weaving and dyeing, and the city, which they know as 'Little Jerusalem', became a centre for all kinds of textiles. It also became a centre of Jewish mysticism.[35]

In the second half of the seventeenth century a number of Salonika's Jews who followed a local Jewish leader named Tzvi joined him in converting to Islam but continued to practise the Shabbatean mystical form of Judaism in secret—these were the so-called *dönmes* (or turncoats). As such they were viewed with mistrust by both Muslims and Jews. This group gradually replaced Ladino with Turkish for everyday speech while maintaining Hebrew for religious purposes.[36]

However the 'golden age of Ottoman Jewry', as Shaw calls it, in the sixteenth and early seventeenth centuries declined along with the general Ottoman decline and Salonika's Jews became subject to repeated attacks in the eighteenth century by unruly *Janissaries* and the local Greek population.[37] Throughout southeastern Europe, growing anarchy as the state declined led to increased blood-libel attacks[38] on Jews by Christians, and rampages by the *Janissaries* and other troops. One result of this increase in

---

32 *Ibid.*, p. 51.
33 *Ibid.*, pp. 52-4. This discord was no doubt amplified by the lack of any real single leader akin to that in the different Christian *millets*.
34 *Ibid.*, p. 56.
35 *Ibid.*, pp. 92 and 100.
36 *Ibid.*, pp. 136-7. Some of them were later to play leading roles in the Young Turk and Atatürk revolutions.
37 *Ibid.*, pp. 122-3.
38 This enduring fiction that Jews kidnapped and sacrificed Christian infants during their religious rites was a prime force behind much of the consistent and appalling persecution and massacres perpetrated on Jews by Christians through the ages and which had often led to the Jews fleeing to the Ottoman empire in the first place.

attacks was an emigration of Jews from Salonika to Izmir were prospects were brighter; in this period Salonika declined. The general decline in their situation saw the escape into religion of most Ottoman Jews who turned their backs on rationalism and enlightenment.[39]

Because of this, the Jews lagged behind initially in the new opportunities afforded by the *Tanzimat* in the nineteenth century. The conservative elements in their *millet* leadership viewed the new educational opportunities with distrust. But by the end of the nineteenth century they had also caught up in the educational stakes.[40] Indeed by the time of Abdülhamid II, the Jews were seen as the only loyal minority subjects of the empire, since they correctly saw repression by Christians as the main threat to them and thus were mostly loyal supporters of the empire.[41]

Despite the loyalty of this most loyal of non-Muslim groups, the failure of the attempt by the *Tanzimat* reform movement to create an Ottoman citizen is amply illustrated by statistics for education for the Jews. Late in the nineteenth century, when the Jewish community had come around to accepting the new opportunities made available by the *Tanzimat* in education *inter alia*, it was reported that out of some 300,000 Jews then in the empire, as many as 100,000 knew French but only 1,000 understood Turkish. So, as Shaw writes, just as the traditional schools had cut young Jews off from Ottoman society by teaching only Hebrew, the modern schools were doing the same by emphasising French at the expense of Turkish.[42]

*   *   *

39 *Ibid.,* pp. 129-31.
40 *Ibid.*
41 The exception to this solidarity between Muslim and Jew in the face of Christian hositility—the newly emerging national Orthodox Christian movements in the Balkans repeatedly slaughtered Muslims and Jews together at almost any opportunity—came over the movement by Theodor Herzl and his supporters for a Jewish national state in Palestine. This movement, which many Ottoman Jews initially opposed, had many similarities with the Christian national movements in that it aimed at independence for a portion of the empire—for the Muslims, an historically and religiously important portion. This movement tended to be fuelled by Jews who fled to the empire from persecution in Europe and Russia. The numbers settling in Palestine quickly grew from 24,000 in 1882, to 47,000 in 1890, 80,000 in 1908 and 85,000 in 1914. *Ibid.,* p. 217.
42 *Ibid.,* p. 165.

Thus the Ottoman system—until the need for change became too intense to resist, due mainly to outside weakness especially *vis-à-vis* Russia—followed a policy of classifying its citizens using religion as the criterion—the *millet* system. Despite welcoming converts to Islam who were then seen as first-class citizens along with all its other Muslim subjects, the Ottoman empire was essentially non-assimilative and allowed the separate Balkan peoples to retain their individual cultures and identities—this aided by the geography of the region. In this the empire seems to have fitted Ernest Gellner's paradigm of a pre-modern society where the mass of the general population lived according to the precepts of their own local 'low' cultures. Conversely, the 'high' culture of the state was a minority achievement of privileged specialists, differentiated from the fragmented, uncodified majority folk cultures, and tending—by design—to be trans-ethnic and trans-political, employing an élite idiom with no concern whatever to ensure continuity between its mode of communication and that of the masses. The majority were excluded from power and from the 'high' culture and were tied to a faith and a church rather than to the state and a single pervasive culture.[43] In Benedict Anderson's terminology, the 'real' community was the family and the village or city quarter, while the 'imagined' community was the religious group and not those who made up the state or even a geographic part of it.

Despite the gradual decline of the empire's internal structure, which continued apace through the eighteenth and nineteenth centuries and saw a progressive breakdown and rise in violence against sections of the population, the Ottoman empire for much of its existence was characterised by a greater tolerance towards religious groups than Western Europe and became a haven especially for Jews fleeing intolerance and persecution, many of whom settled in Macedonia. As noted in Chapter 2, the Ottoman *millet* system, which till the late nineteenth century put Macedonia's Orthodox population under the control of the Istanbul patriarchate, both aided the definition of a Greek identity after the blurring of it in the Byzantine period, and helped to propagate this to other sections of the Orthodox community.

The nineteenth century and the rise of nationalism in Western Europe saw a profound change. On one hand, the Ottoman

---

43 Gellner, *op. cit.,* p. 59.

state began to change its fundamental basis and treat all its citizens as equal regardless of religion and thus move towards creating an Ottoman citizen; a category which would include non-Muslims—the attempt resisted by many sections of the Muslim population both within and outside the governing élites—on the other, the impact of Western nationalism profoundly affected the way the Christian groups identified themselves. The *millets* became progressively identified with national groupings. At the same time, the new radical nationalists were competing with the old traditional leaders within the *millets*. On top of all this was the interference by the Great Powers in the internal affairs of the ailing empire which saw them at times encourage and at other times discourage particular emerging national groups, depending on what the powers perceived their own interests to be at any particular time.

The beginning of the nineteenth century saw the empire's Balkan holdings beginning to crumble at the periphery. The Serb revolt in the north led by Karageorge was initially not so much a nationalist liberation struggle as a local revolt against the collapse of the old system and the ensuing hardships which this collapse had brought to the population. Although defeated, the Serb revolt eventually led to the formation of a Serb statelet around Belgrade in 1830. Meanwhile the Greek revolt of 1820 had again shown the Ottoman weakness not merely *vis-à-vis* the might of imperial Russia now on its northern border, but even against internal revolts, and a fledgling Greek state was formed in the southern end of the peninsula. Both these new states were from the start expansionist and aimed to include within their future borders all their fellow-nationals, real or perceived. The Greek state was at first at a particular economical disadvantage since it controlled only a small amount of mainly barren land.[44] The Treaty of

44 This led to the anomaly whereby after the introduction of the *Tanzimat* reforms in the remaining Ottoman empire, considerable numbers of Greeks migrated out of the new Greek state to take advantage of the new opportunities afforded them, and it was only in the nineteenth century that the west coast of Anatolia came to be dominated by Greeks—classic nationalist theories would indicate that the reverse should have happened and that Greeks should have migrated in to take ethnic advantage of the new national state. Moreover, as Clogg points out, while the Balkan wards led to many Muslims fleeing Macedonia to Anatolia, the Greeks in Anatolia stayed put, and there remained some 2 million Greeks in the remnants of the Ottoman empire at the start of the Great War. Richard Clogg in Braude and Lewis, *op. cit.*

Berlin resulted in a truncated Bulgaria similarly looking to expand, as well as Serbia being forced to look south for expansion as Austria-Hungary closed other avenues to it. All three looked to Macedonia where all three had historical claims. As we see in the next chapter, the mostly Muslim Albanians also began to loosen their allegiance to the empire and look to a possible national state to protect them from their rapacious neighbours. Over all this was the despotic rule of Abdülhamid II, a centralist who attempted to use Islam and pan-Islam as the cement to hold the empire together but whose extension and expansion of the *Tanzimat* education system led to the education of a group of Muslims, Turks and others, who asked themselves the question: 'How is this state to be saved?' They were also centred in Macedonia. Given all these internal and external factors, inter-ethnic violence was perhaps inevitable.

4

FROM BERLIN TO VERSAILLES

THE APPLE OF DISCORD—
PROPAGANDA, VIOLENCE AND WAR

Local uprisings

The Russo-Turkish war, which saw the emergence of a Bulgarian principality which in the aborted San Stefano treaty would have included much of Macedonia, was accompanied before, during and after by local uprisings in Macedonia. The April uprising in Bulgaria which led to the war spread into eastern Macedonia but was quickly suppressed by the Ottoman forces. The Bulgarian supporters were at this time apparently unable to organise west of the Vardar, where Greek uprisings were planned by the national societies *Ethniki Amina* (national defence) and *Adelfotis* (brotherhood) which were to link up with the Greek army.[1]

The Greek insurrections met with some success, and provisional governments were set up in the Olympus and Kastoria regions in expectation of the arrival of the Greek army. However, by the time the Greek army moved into Thessaly, a ceasefire between the Russians and the Ottomans had been concluded and the uprisings, which had a large brigand element, were also quickly suppressed, as the Bulgarian ones had been, often with aid from Muslim (mostly Albanian) *başıbozuk* irregulars.

Notwithstanding this, there was already a perceptible if fragile

---

1 Aarbakke, *op. cit.,* pp. 53-4. Much of this chapter up to the time of the Young Turks is indebted to Aarbakke's work, which is particularly good on Greek and Bulgarian sources.

alliance of Greeks and Muslims against the Bulgarians due to the threat of being included in a future Bulgaria of the type envisaged by San Stefano. The relationship between the large Muslim element—an element which became more concentrated in Macedonia as the Ottoman empire progressively lost its European territories to the new expanding Balkan states and Muslims fled to what remained of Ottoman territory—and the main protagonists (the Bulgarians and the Greeks) depended on which of them was currently in the ascendant. Before the establishing of the Exarchate Church, the Bulgarians were relatively weak in relation to the Greeks and thus were not seen as the danger they later became. Thus the Muslims in the population were not so antagonistic to them and in Veles in the late 1860s they took the Bulgarian side against the local Greek bishop.[2] This was a typical divide-and-rule policy which became more pronounced with the reign of Abdülhamid. The existence, after the founding of the Exarchate, of two rival Orthodox institutions also gave great leeway to the Ottoman authorities as mediators as well as wielders of power in permitting Bulgarian bishoprics. These were only granted in late 1874 for Skopje and Ohrid after Russian pressure and, for Bitola, as late as June 1897.

A major Bulgarian uprising took place in October 1878 in the north-east of the Razlog-Kresna region. Committees had appeared in the new Bulgaria at the end of August to achieve Bulgarian unity along the lines of San Stefano, and these planned the uprising which began at Kresna. The insurrection was initially successful, with the capture of the town of Kresna, and it was followed by another in November in the Bansko-Razlog valley which held Bansko for seven days before the Ottomans retook it. They also quickly retook Kresna, and the uprising petered out. There are conflicting interpretations of the uprising: Bulgarians, stressing the unity of the Bulgarian people, claim it as a protest against the Berlin Treaty; for modern Skopje historians it was an expression of Macedonian independence from Ottoman rule. Almost every Slav action in Macedonia from this time onwards has been similarly contested between these two conflicting viewpoints. In the Kresna case, the Macedonian side is based on Article 145 of the 'rules of the Macedonian rebel committee' which states: 'After the liberation of our fatherland, the Central Committee

2   See Aarbakke, *op. cit.,* pp. 39-40.

will prepare a Constitution for the organisation of the state of Macedonia as either autonomous or with political and cultural autonomy within the Ottoman empire, or outside it, should the European Great Powers allow this.'[3] While at first sight this appears to point to a striving for outright Macedonian independence, it would also have been a first step to separating the area from Ottoman control, which could also be a first step to possible later incorporation into Bulgaria. The reference to the Great Powers is instructive, since they had already vetoed the immediate creation of a 'Greater Bulgaria'.

The struggle for church control and the Bulgarian advance

In the immediate aftermath of the Russo-Turkish war, the proponents of the Bulgarian case and the Exarchate church in Macedonia were in a weak position. After the failure of 'San Stefano' Bulgaria, many leading Bulgarians emigrated to the new principality, which left a dearth of natural leaders. The Exarchate's organisation outside the principality was shattered after the authorities called the Bulgarian bishops back to Istanbul during the war and kept them there. Most of the lower clergy had also departed in the course of the war, and the Porte now viewed the Exarchate with great suspicion and many of its churches and schools were closed. The Porte also attempted—without success—to oust the Exarchate from Istanbul. If the Exarchate had been moved to the new principality of Bulgaria it would have lost its rights and influence over the population remaining in the Ottoman territories proper. While in this period it seems that the Porte favoured the Patriarchate over the Exarchate, it also tried in the 1880s to limit the Patriarchate's privileges, most crucially in the field of education.[4]

3 *Documents on the Struggle of the Macedonian People for Independence and a Nation-State*, vol. 1, Skopje, 1985, pp. 267-84.
4 P. B. Kiril, *Bâlgarskate ekzarchija v Odrinsko i Makedonija sled Osvoboditelnata voyna (1877-1978), Tom 1 (1878-85), Kniga 1-2,* Sofia, 1969-70, p. 66, in Aarbakke. *op. cit.,* p. 63. At this period Abdülhamid implemented strict centralisation, his personal dictatorship, Islam and pan-Islam and his own role as Caliph as cement both to create loyalty to himself personally and to keep the Islamic elements in the empire unified. He was also to a large degree continuing and expanding the *Tanzimat* education programme with a large extension of the state schooling

After the war, the Greeks were especially strong around Salonika and had success in hellenising the surrounding villages. However, the bulk of the Slav Macedonian population still looked towards the Exarchate and there were conflicts with the Greek clergy in a number of places including Strumica, Bitola and Edessa. The period from 1884-94 saw a great expansion of Bulgarian influence throughout the whole area, to the extent that in the early 1890s more than 150 towns and villages in the Salonika *vilayet* went over to the Exarchate from the Patriarchate.[5] At this period Stambolov was in power in Bulgaria and pursued a policy of conciliation to the Ottoman authorities and opposition to internal revolt. At this time the Bulgarian camp also scored dramatic gains and extended its influence steadily southwards. The policy of peaceful proselytising for the Bulgarian cause rather than helping armed insurrection paid dividends. This was aided by the work of the Uniate and Protestant missions, backed by Austria-Hungary and Britain, which helped to promote the spread of the Bulgarian language.

Education was the key. In the empire, schools were typically of three types : state schools dependent on the Ministry of Education; *millet* or community schools under the control of the religious community; and those opened by private individuals and answerable directly to the Ottoman authorities. To open a community school there had to be at least thirty households of the relevant community. The Bulgarians chose Salonika as their educational centre and opened a gymnasium there as early as 5 October 1881. By the mid-1890s they had 600-700 schools in Macedonia mostly under the aegis of the Exarchate.[6] However, as Aarbakke points out, the development of a Bulgarian school system was not easy; even an important centre in the north like Skopje did not have a

---

His regime also attempted to make the empire more homogeneous though the compulsory use of demotic Turkish—the decree of 1894 required the use of Turkish in all schools of the empire. The decree further stipulated the use of clear, simple language, devoid of Arabic and Persian words not commonly used as well as the use of proper textbooks. See Levend, *Türk Dilinde Gelişme ve Sadeleşme Evreleri*, Ankara, 1949, pp. 143-5, and the circular to this effect to a high school in Monastir reproduced in M.F. Köprülü, *Milli Edebiyat Cerayanın Ilk Mübeşşirleri, Istanbul, 1928*.

5   Aarbakke, *op. cit.*, p. 67.
6   L.S. Stavrianos, *The Balkans since 1453*, New York, 1958.

well developed school system, and prospects for those who finished Bulgarian secondary education in Macedonia remained poor.[7] An illuminating picture of the situation around 1890, in Bitola— second in importance after Salonika and the commercial centre of western Macedonia as well as the administrative centre of the Monastir *vilayet*—is given by Kânchov.[8] The Muslim population of 8,500-9,000 was made up of Albanians and Turks between whom there was no clear differentiation. The Jews numbered just over 5,000 while the Christian community was made up of Slavs (about 9,500), Vlachs (about 6,500), Albanians and Roma (about 1,500 together), and a few Greek and Armenian households. The Orthodox were split three ways between the Exarchate community comprising about three-quarters of the Slav population and all the Christian Roma, the Patriarchate community including four-fifths of the Vlach population, the Christian Albanians and the remaining Slavs, and the Romanians headed by Apostol Margit which accounted for the remaining Vlachs. The Vlachs were the wealthiest element of the population, and the Albanians were mostly skilled workers, while the Slavs were farmers on the outskirts of the city or involved in trade.

The surrounding villages were fairly evenly split between the Exarchate and the Patriarchate. Bitola became a centre for competing propaganda claims. The position of the Vlachs shows the success of the Greek side in hellenising this strong element, and indeed many of them played a leading role in the general Greek liberation struggle. The Patriarchate's hold over the Christian Albanians and a sizeable portion of the Slavs is also noticeable, while the Roma identification with the Exarchate—given the current situation (described in Chapter 9)—is interesting. The Bulgarians however were making inroads into the Greek side, and after 1890 the Vlachs in south-west Macedonia were changing sides. Towards the end of the century, contemporary observers like Kânchov and the German ethnographer Weigand viewed the Bulgarian case as irresistible.

---

7 Aarbakke, *op. cit.*, pp. 70-2, referring to Vasil Kânchev, *Izbrani proizvedenija*, vols I-II, Sofia 1970 (first publ. 1924), vol. I, p. 386.
8 Kânchov, *op. cit.*, vol. I, pp. 375-6, in Aarbakke, *op. cit.*, pp. 72-3.

VMRO

With Stambolov being replaced as premier in 1894, Bulgaria's position of opposition to internal revolt changed. Henceforth, until the failure of this strategy became evident, the Bulgarians pursued the policies which had worked in the initial uprisings in 1876 and resulted in the founding of the Bulgarian principality. These were local uprisings which were designed to attract Ottoman reprisals and consequently Great Power intervention.

Within Macedonia the Internal Macedonian Revolutionary Organisation (VMRO)[9] had already been formed on 23 October 1893 in Salonika with D. Gruev, director of the Bulgarian school in Štip, in the leading role opposing any partition of Macedonia. In March 1895 another organisation, 'The Supreme Macedonian Committee',[10] was set up in Bulgaria by Macedonian associations to direct the liberation movement. The failure of San Stefano Bulgaria had seen many inhabitants of Macedonia emigrate to Bulgaria and this was to be a continuing feature. Indeed by 1903 almost half the population of Sofia were Macedonian refugees or immigrants. This mass of refugees, as well as destabilising Bulgaria internally for many years, provided a pool of support for this second organisation. While both aimed at autonomy for Macedonia as a first step, the latter Sofia-based organisation openly favoured eventual annexation to Bulgaria, and was supported by the Bulgarian government. The IO on the other hand was more ambivalent, with some factions more pro-Bulgarian than others.

Thus almost from the outset, VMRO was fatally divided in its aims between protagonists of Macedonia for Bulgaria, and of

9 This organisation repeatedly and confusingly changed its name, often as a reflection of the balance between pro-Bulgarian and pro-Macedonian autonomists (see below). It appears to have originally been called the Bulgarian Macedonian-Adrianopolitan Committee (BMORK—the 'O' standing for Odrin or Adrianopole). In 1902 it changed its name to the Secret Macedonian Adrianopolitan Revolutionary Organisation (TMORO) while from 1905 it was first known as VMORO and then simply VMRO, where the 'V' stands for 'inner' in Bulgarian.

10 This was also called the External Organisation (EO) as opposed to the 'internal organisation' of VMRO on the ground in Macedonia. The members of the Supreme Committee were often later referred to as 'Supremacists'. For convenience's sake, in this chapter the Supreme Committee will be referred to by the acronym EO, and VMRO within Macedonia by the acronym IO standing for the 'Inner Organisation'.

a separate Macedonian state, existing either within some form of federation or independently. Later, faced with differing situations, VMRO veered one way and then the other. The nuances between the two camps have fuelled endless polemics in recent times between the Bulgarians, who naturally stress the former view, and the post-Second World War Yugoslav Macedonian regime and its successors who as naturally stress the latter.

The IO at this time consisted mainly of teachers recruited from Bulgarian schools (showing again the importance of education in the struggle for influence) rather than from the rural population.[11] It decided on a long preparatory phase to lay the foundations for a successful uprising. A key figure in the IO strategy was Gotse Delchev (1872-1903), born in Kilkis, who had been dismissed from the military academy in Sofia because of his radicalism and who returned to Macedonia as a Bulgarian teacher in Novo Selo near Štip. In 1896 he, along with G. Petrov, was given the task of writing the organisation's statutes which divided Macedonia into seven regions, each with a regional structure and a central committee in Salonika as the supreme organ. Below the regional committees were district and village ones. Article 10 provided for each committee to have its own secret police empowered to punish enemies and those who damaged the cause.[12] In several instances this involved death sentences.

Almost immediately, in the summer of 1895, the EO attempted an uprising in the vicinity of Melnik with four special units led by young Bulgarian army officers and Macedonian leaders attempting without success to stir up the local rural population.[13] This set the pattern of failed attempts at uprising, mixed with brigandage, with the populace having to face the consequences from the Ottomans. A similar failed EO excursion in November 1897—the Vinitsa affair—saw the Ottomans finding arms and ammunition of the IO in the ensuing searches, and thus for perhaps the first time seeing the danger of internal revolts as opposed to those originating in Bulgaria. This in turn put pressure in the IO to speed up their preparations.

This, along with the precedent of the 1897 Greco-Turkish

11 Duncan M. Perry, *The Politics of Terror: The Macedonian Revolutionary Movements, 1893-1903*, Durham and London, 1988, pp. 41-2.
12 Aarbakke *op. cit.,* pp. 96-7.
13 *Ibid.,* p. 95.

war, which despite Greek defeat saw autonomy obtained for Crete and thus seemed to confirm that an uprising with Great Power backing could gain results, saw the IO accelerate its timetable. In summer 1898 it decided to go all out for forming armed bands in each district. Delchev was again the key figure. A problem of funding these bands often led to brigandage—an activity which many of the bands had practised for a long time anyway—and this in turn tended to alienate the local population.

There was also tension between the IO and the Exarchate. Given the radical-intelligentsia nature of the IO leaders and the influx of socialist ideas among them, this was perhaps inevitable. The change was reflected in the revised IO statutes of 1902 which dropped 'Bulgarian' from the title; this was now TMORO, and appealed to all dissatisfied elements in Macedonia, not merely Bulgarian ones. As such the IO now even attracted Patriachists as well as Exarchists. While it seems that only a small group of left-wingers was actually opposed to the Exarchate, such developments were enough to lead to the emergence of a counter-group in the Exarchate who opposed an early uprising. This was the 'Evolutionist' group led by Ivan Garvanov, who founded his 'Revolutionary Brotherhood' in the late 1890s against a premature uprising. The IO responded with factional violence, and Garvanov become an open EO supporter (he later became an advocate of an early uprising).[14] In the main however the Exarchate supported the IO and *vice versa*.

The shifting position of the EO in relation to the IO is reflected at the VI Macedonian Congress in 1899 when the IO, with Delchev and Petrov to the fore, effectively took over the EO and installed Boris Sarafov (1872-1907), a former Bulgarian army officer, as EO leader. This saw a period of close co-operation between the two organisations which lasted till 1901—a period ignored by Skopje historians who stress the differences between the two.[15] However the old divisions soon became evident with General Ivan Tsonchev and fellow Bulgarian army officers organising a faction against the Delchev/Petrov line. Weakness and division within the IO following arrests saw the Tsonchev line come to the fore, and another EO uprising—the Dzhumaya uprising—was organised in north-east Macedonia in September 1902,

14 See Perry, *op. cit.*, pp. 89-95, for details of the Brotherhood.
15 Aarbakke, *op. cit.*, p. 101.

which again elicited little local support and even saw resistance from local IO leaders like Yane Sandanski.[16]

The strategy, as noted above, was to get the Great Powers moving due to Ottoman reprisals. To some extent this did happen with the reform programmes which now came into operation. One aspect of this was that Bulgaria, as a sign of good faith in the reform proposals, temporarily closed down the EO and arrested its leaders. The failure of the Dzhumaya uprising led the IO to reappraise its options. At the Salonika Congress of January 1903 the pros and cons of an early uprising were fiercely debated, and despite Macedonian leaders in Sofia now calling for delay, it was decided to stage one in the spring of 1903. Delchev and Petrov also decided to step up confrontation with the Ottomans, and special terror units were created. These had links with the anarchist organisation, the 'Macedonian secret revolutionary committee', which called for a Macedonia independent of the other Balkan states incorporating all the population groups including the Turks. A leading member was Mihail Gerdzhikov who advocated sabotage and terror rather than an uprising. Such tactics however tended to be counter-productive. A series of bomb attacks in Salonika—perpetrated mainly by the *Gemidzhi* group—led to Muslim, and to some extent West European, outrage and censure. The increased tension led to the death of Gotse Delchev, killed on 4 May in a skirmish with Ottoman troops.[17]

The Ilinden uprising

And so we come to the biggest uprising and one which occupies a leading place in Macedonian mythology—the Ilinden ('St Elijah's day') uprising of 2-3 August 1903. It was decided to follow Gruev's ideas of starting the uprising in the countryside, and the revolt began around Bitola. However, foreign observers aver that the majority of the population did not support the uprising and in some instances even denounced the bands to the Ottomans. For the EO the goal of the uprising appears to have been to provoke the Great Powers to intervene against Ottoman misrule. However when it came, it seems to have surprised both Bulgaria and the

16 For more on the Tsonchev faction see Perry, *op. cit.,* pp. 86-8.
17 See Aarbakke, *op. cit.,* pp. 106-7, for details.

Great Powers, the latter determined to continue their policy of maintaining the *status quo*. Bulgaria went to the brink of war but no further. The Ottomans responded with the usual repression, mostly by Muslim irregulars, and the uprising fizzled out in October.

However it did manage to take over Kruševo for a week—aided by the absence of most of the Ottoman troops in Kosovo to deal with Albanian resistance to the reform movement—and declare a republic there. There was even an attempt to form a kind of revolutionary government led by the socialist Nikola Karev. The Kruševo manifesto was declared, assuring the population that the uprising was against the Sultan and not against Muslims in general, and that all peoples would be included. As the population of Kruševo was two-thirds hellenised Vlachs and Patriarchist Slavs, this was a wise move. Despite these promises the insurgents flew Bulgarian flags everywhere and in many places the uprising did entail attacks on Muslim Turks and Albanians who themselves organised for self-defence.[18]

Despite the revolutionary rhetoric of the uprising and the somewhat confused and uncoordinated declarations which have been so extensively used by the Macedonian Communists to legitimise their own historical perspectives, the Ilinden uprising was yet another major failure for VMRO. Thenceforth the IO was seriously weakened and split between a wing led by Hristo Matov, Hristo Tatarchev and Garvanov which looked to Bulgaria, and the revived EO now known as the 'Supremacists', and the Sandanski wing which espoused a more independent line that would embrace all ethnic groups. A great loss was the death of Gruev, killed by Ottoman troops at the beginning of 1907, and ensuing internal strife saw VMRO begin its long descent into internal factionalism. Sarafov and Garvanov were killed by Sandanski supporters in December 1907 in Sofia. In the spring of 1908 VMRO killed more 'traitors' in its own ranks than Greeks.

Additionally the tactic of armed bands was copied by the Greeks and Serbs, and their armed bands came to the fore after 1903. The result was that the unfortunate Christian population, which by most accounts had been most sympathetic to one of the wings of VMRO up till the late 1890s, was subjected to repeated visits by armed gangs. These were from both wings

18 Aarbakke, *op. cit.*, pp. 108-9.

of VMRO, Serbs and Greeks as well as the Ottoman authorities; from 1905 the latter began to organise small mobile units which were more effective against the armed bands, many of which were more traditional Balkan bandits than national liberators. The violence led to a drop in Bulgarian support, with many people wanting merely to be left alone. With hindsight it appears that the decisions made in the late 1890s by the Bulgarian camp to opt for violent activity and armed uprisings was a major mistake.

The IO seemed oblivious to all this and in 1904 embarked on a campaign of forcing Patriarchate villages to recognise the Exarchate. Thus, despite Petrov's objections, the VMRO movement became more overtly Bulgarian-nationalistic. However, a contrary approach was called for by Krste P. Misirkov (1874-1926), who in his book *Za Makedonskite raboti* (On Macedonian Matters) which appeared in Sofia in December 1903 overtly called for a Macedonian identity separate from the Bulgarian and for a Macedonian language based on the Veles-Prilep-Bitola-Ohrid dialects.[19] The book was confiscated by Bulgarian police and he was expelled to Russia. The Young Turk revolution led to further divisions within VMRO, with the Sandanski wing most fervent in its support of the new authorities. His wing now formed the National Federation Party and began to propagate socialist ideas in the Serres region. The Supremacists responded by forming the Bulgarian Constitutional Clubs.

The declaration of formal Bulgarian independence and the assumption of the title of Tsar by Prince Ferdinand of Saxe-Coburg-Gotha, who had been offered and accepted the Bulgarian throne in 1887, allowed the Ottomans to use this to try and cut links between the Exarchate in Istanbul and Sofia. Hitherto, since Bulgaria was not technically independent of the Ottomans, all the Exarchate sees were technically in Ottoman territory and the Exarchate had resisted pressure to move it out of Istanbul; this had now changed with the Bulgarian church established in an indisputably independent state. The Ottomans set up a new synod which inevitably quarrelled with that in Sofia. The Russians used these disputes to call for the ending of the Orthodox schism in the Ottoman territories, i.e. bringing Macedonia back under the Patriarchy now that Bulgaria was independent.[20] All these

19 The book was republished in English in 1974 in Skopje.
20 Crampton, *op. cit.,* pp. 58-9.

factors led the Bulgarian government to abandon the strategy of internal uprisings and go for outright war with the Ottomans.

The Greeks organise

Despite the hegemony of the Greek Patriarchate before 1870 and the founding of the Exarchate, there were few Greek schools in Macedonia till after the founding of the Greek state. Expansion of the new state was from the start seen as essential and the Greeks evolved a coordinated effort to this end. On 17 April 1869 the Society for the Dissemination of Greek Letters was founded in Athens, and together with the Greek Philological Society, founded in Istanbul in 1861 and reorganised in 1871, it set up similar organisations in Serres in 1870 and Salonika in 1872.[21] By 1880 these societies had been founded throughout Macedonia. Reorganisation in 1882 saw a unified system with close cooperation between the Patriarchate, the Greek Foreign Ministry and the Greek state school system.[22]

In November 1894 the secret *Ethnike Hetairia* (national society) was founded with the aim of liberating all Greeks still within the Ottoman empire. The incorporation of Macedonia into the Greek state would be the first step. It was supported by three-quarters of the officers in the Greek army and had many wealthy patrons. This body, as well as organising armed bands, also helped the spread of the Greek education of Slav peasants. The result was a dramatic rise in the number of Greek schools in Macedonia. There were 574 schools in 1878 and 610 in 1885. By 1895 the Greeks were claiming 1,400 schools and were spending proportionally more on education in Macedonia than in Greece itself.[23] Despite this concerted and coordinated effort which saw the Greeks handing out free meals in 1903 in some areas like Kastoria, in competition with Bulgarian measures of a similar kind to win over locals, as noted above the tide appeared to be definitely moving in Bulgaria's favour as the new century approached.

21 Stephanos I. Papadopoulos, *I Paideia sti Makedonia kai ī sumbolī́ tīs stī́ dīmiourgia tōn proupotheseōn gia tīn epituhia ton Makedonikou Agona*, Simposio, Salonika, 1987, pp. 23-6, in Aarbakke, *op. cit.*, p. 76.
22 N. Vlachos, *To Makedonikon ōs fasis tou Anatolikou Zitimatos, Athens, 1935, pp. 103-9, in Aarbakke, op. cit.*, p. 76.
23 Figures from Aarbakke, p. 77, and Stavrianos, *op. cit.*

In response to the growth of VMRO bands, the *Ethnike Hetairia* began to organise its own bands. The first appeared in April 1900 in the Kastoria region under the local leader Kota.[24] In May 1903 the Greek government supplied Cretan fighters to the growing number of Greek bands which to some extent were tolerated by the Ottomans as a counterweight to those of the VMRO. After Ilinden the Greek movement moved up a gear and a Macedonian committee organised by newspaper editor D. Kalapothakis managed the armed groups. Local bands were not deemed particularly trustworthy, and others were sent in from Greece under the command of Pavlos Melas—a Greek army officer killed by the Ottomans in late 1904. The Greek consul in Salonika, L. Koromiles, played a key part in the growth of Greek bands. However because the VMRO had a head start on them, they were at something of a disadvantage. The arrival in Salonika of another Greek officer, Athanasios Suliotis-Nikolaidis, in March 1906 led to the build-up of a secret organisation which encouraged the display of Greek signs in shops, where previously they had been in French or Turkish. Compared to the Bulgarian side, the Greek effort was far more under government control and thus more unified.

The Great Power reform programmes

As the conflict became increasingly more violent, the Great Powers progressively interfered. The 1897 agreement between Austria-Hungary and Russia led in February 1903 to the 'Vienna Reform Programme' concerning Macedonia. Abdülhamid tried to pre-empt this with his own reform proposals, and made Hüseyin Hilmi Paşa General Inspector to the three *vilayets* in December 1902. He did however accept the Vienna programme, among the terms of which were: the power to use troops without prior permission from the Porte in support of the general Inspector, who was to have the tenure of his post fixed in advance (article 1); the reorganisation of the gendarmerie by foreign officers, with Christians being recruited as well as Muslims (article 3); measures against Albanian offences (article 5); an amnesty for all political

24 For this and other references in this paragraph see Aarbakke, *op. cit.,* pp. 120-8.

prisoners (article 6); and separate budgets for all three *vilayets* and the abolition of the tax-farming tithe (article 7).[25]

The Ilinden uprising followed. Britain now called for a Christian provincial governor or *vali*, and the Porte agreed on 9 October 1903 to the Mürzsteg Reform Programme, a compromise between the Russian and Austrian emperors, who met in Mürzsteg in September 1903. This saw control split three ways between Hilmi Paşa and one Russian and one Habsburg civilian official, and the institution of foreign control of the gendarmerie under an Italian general who would have the assistance of officers from the Great Powers (Germany did not agree to collaborate in this). Great Power pressure was evident: in 1903 Austrian and Italian fleets sailed to Salonika, and when the Porte demurred at a further proposal to add more Russian and Habsburg officials to control the finances in 1905, five German boats landed parties who occupied postal and customs offices on two of the Aegean islands.[26]

The Vlachs and the Romanian efforts

Romania, while not contiguous with Macedonia, could and did make claims regarding the Vlach community. In this the main aim was to mobilise the community with a view to obtaining concessions from the Bulgarians in the Dobrudzha. However, as noted above, the Vlach community was mainly hellenised, and in many Macedonian towns the Greek Patriarchate element consisted almost entirely of Vlachs. As such the main conflict was with the Greek Patriarchate over the Vlach community. The wealthy urban Vlachs tended to be hellenised and continued to support the Greek cause, but the transhumant shepherds in the hills were another matter. They had not been subjected to hellenisation and in the violence which followed in the early twentieth century they were not especially pro-Greek and often supported Bulgarian bands or acted as guides to the Ottoman forces. These people became susceptible to Romanian propaganda.

However, the Romanian effort was in no way comparable with that of the Greeks or Bulgarians; for example, there was not a Romanian national clergy. It appears to have mainly revolved around the personality of Apostol Margit (1832-1902) who became

25 Aarbakke, *op. cit.* p. 105.
26 S. Akşin, *Jön Türkler ve ittihat ve Terrakki*, Istanbul, 1987, pp. 50-1.

the general inspector of Romanian schools in the Ottoman empire (although the Ottomans did not officially recognise him as such).[27]

Romanian activities against the Patriarchate were at their height in the 1880s, mainly in the Bitola area, and the Ottomans, pursuing the policy of 'divide and rule', favoured the Romanian cause. In December 1903 the Romanian minister in Istanbul began to appeal for Arumanian (Vlach) ecclesiastical autonomy and eventually in 1905 an effective Arumanian *millet*—not actually referred to as a *millet* and without a leader (*millet-i başı*)—was established.[28] However, by the 1890s, in the face of the seemingly inexorable Bulgarian advance, the Romanian gains were falling to the Exarchate, and by the end of the decade the Romanian government had decided to scale down its efforts and funds were decreased— despite which it was still subsidising more than thirty schools in Macedonia in 1912.[29]

One of the main Vlach organisations was the Macedonian- Romanian Society for Intellectual Culture with headquarters in Bucharest. During the Balkan wars, it called for the setting up of an autonomous Macedonia as the most equitable solution to the 'Macedonian problem'. The society also sent a delegation to the Versailles peace conference at the end of the First World War to reiterate the call for an autonomous Macedonia in which there should be an independent Vlach canton of the Pindus—which, it declared, the local population had already proclaimed. For the rest of Macedonia the society called for complete autonomy for all the nationalities, including the Vlach/Romanians. [30]

The Serbs

One result of the Treaty of Berlin was that thereafter Serbia would also look towards Macedonia for expansion. To some extent the Serb claims can be seen to have predated the Treaty; for example, Serbian rather than Bulgarian was spoken by the Macedonian Slavs in Kičevo, Debar, Gostivar and Tetovo. A

27 Aarbakke, *op. cit.,* p. 82.
28 Aarbakke, *op. cit.,* p. 131.
29 Stavrianos, *op. cit.*
30 Dr I.D. Ghiulamila, Dr P. Pucera, N. Papahagi and C. Papacostea, *Le Problème Macédonien. La solution la Plus Equitable*, Bucharest, July 1919, reprinted in *Zborlu a nostru*, year IX, 1 (33), 1992, Freiburg im Breisgau, pp. 5-7.

Belgrade newspaper in 1852 reported that 'pure Serbian' was spoken in and around Skopje.[31] However there was little apart from some common grammatical features to back up these claims, the main plank of which seems to have been the 'Slava' festivals which the Macedonia Slavs shared with the Serbs. Unlike the other contestants, the Serb case was especially weak with barely any indigenous local support except in the Skopska Crna Gora hills north of Skopje. What little support there was for the Serb cause appears to have come from those who went to Serbia for seasonal work or from outright bribery or force.

Indeed, as early as 1866 Stojan Novaković, the leading Serbian politician and historian who was instrumental in developing Serbian strategies towards Macedonia, saw that Serb linguistic claims were so weak compared with those of Bulgaria that he called for the financing of those Macedonians who preached national and linguistic separateness from Bulgaria[32]—an interesting parallel with the policies of Tito. Such policies, however, would have to wait till the twentieth century when Serbia pursued the policy of claiming the Macedonian Slavs as its own. Moreover, Novaković admitted that the adoption of the 'Ekavian' dialect (which was closer to Bulgarian than other Serb dialects) as standard Serbian after 1878 was in part motivated by the possible expansion into Macedonia.[33] As early as 1868 a cultural committee was set up in Belgrade to open Serbian schools in Macedonia and Kosovo; Serb sources claimed over sixty such schools by 1873 but other sources show that they had little success. Most disappeared after the Serbian-Turkish war of 1876.[34]

The Society of Saint Sava was founded in Belgrade in 1886 to promote Serbian nationalism, especially in Macedonia where the Serbs undertook extensive propaganda efforts. By 1889 they were attracting young people away from Bulgarian schools by scholarships to Belgrade and were propagating as far south as Salonika and Halkidiki, which brought them directly up against the Patriarchate Greeks as well as the Exarchate Bulgarians. The Bulgarians countered this threat with the Brotherhood of Mercy,

31 Banac, *op. cit.,* p. 107.
32 Klime Džambazovski, 'Stojan Novaković i makedonizam', *Istoriski časopis*, vols 14-15, 1963, p. 141 in *ibid.*, p. 112.
33 See Stjepan Ivšić, 'Etimologija i fonetika u našem pravopisu', *Hrvatski jezik*, vol. 1 (1938), no. 1, pp. 12- 13, in *ibid.,* footnote to p. 107.
34 See Aarbakke, *op. cit.,* pp. 84-5.

founded in March 1897 in Salonika, which succeeded in stemming Serbian influence.[35] Again it seems that the Ottoman authorities supported the Serbs against the Bulgarians so as further to divide and weaken the non-Muslim populations.

By the mid-1890s it was claimed that there were 100 Serbian schools in Macedonia,[36] but attendance figures were low and the Serbs were no match for the Bulgarians in the educational struggle for control and influence over the Slav Macedonian population. The situation in Skopje where the Serbs exerted much effort is illuminating. Intense effort to open a Serbian school there eventually resulted in one being founded in 1892, but the Bulgarians complained that the requisite thirty households within the relevant city quarter (see above) were lacking and the school was therefore closed—the same thing occurred in Kumanovo. Two new schools were opened in 1893 but as private and not as community schools. The Serbian influence reached its peak about 1896 and had waned by the turn of the century.[37]

However, like the Greeks, the Serbs copied the Bulgarian strategy of violence and their armed bands became active in the Kičevo area by February 1904. In the summer of 1905 the Serb armed movement was reorganised, and a supreme committee was set up in Belgrade under the leadership of the general staff of the defence department with main committees in Skopje and Bitola. In 1906 the Serb cause, which from the start was weaker than its main rivals, appeared to be gaining in the Skopje area with some support from Slav Muslims. This however was not strong, and internal strife in 1907 hampered the cause further. The Young Turk revolution had two main effects on the Serbs. On the one hand it saw most Slavs revert to one of the VMRO wings, and on the other it averted the immediate risk of an autonomous Macedonia which would lean towards Bulgaria.

The rise of Albanian nationalism

In the Ottoman empire, the Muslim Albanians had been regarded as especially loyal to the empire; the majority of the population

35 See Perry, *op. cit.*, pp. 89-90.
36 Stavrianos, *op. cit.*
37 See Aarbakke, *op. cit.*, pp. 88-90, for a detailed description of the Serbian efforts in Skopje.

were Muslim with a large Orthodox minority in the south of the Albanian inhabited lands, and a smaller Roman Catholic one in the more mountainous and tribal north. Many senior Ottoman officials were of Albanian descent. However expansion of the Greek state to the south and the Serbian state to the north raised fears among the Muslim Albanian community that the Ottoman empire might not prove strong enough to protect their interests from their rapacious neighbours. In 1878 a group of Albanian intellectuals founded the League of Prizren, which aimed to assert Albanian national consciousness by promoting the use of the Albanian language, and to combat the threat of the country's partition between Serbia and Greece and possibly Bulgaria as well. In the early 1880s, under the guidance of intellectuals like Naim Frasheri, a number of schools were opened in southern Albania using the Albanian language as a medium of instruction. While this was still confined to some intellectual circles and not a mass movement, it was still an important new factor.

Abdülhamid clamped down on this and, as we have seen, pushed pan-Islamic solidarity instead. Anyone in possession of written material in Albanian faced punishment, and the Greek Patriarchate backed this up by threatening the excommunication of any Orthodox believer so convicted. The League of Prizren was banned and its leaders fled abroad. However the pressure for greater cultural recognition continued within the empire. In 1896 Christian and Muslim Albanians combined to send a joint appeal to the Great Powers demanding a single administrative unit of Albanian-inhabited lands with its capital in Monastir, as well as the establishment of Albanian schools. In this, the Muslim Albanians in the north faced with Serbian expansion were on the whole the most prominent. The two clashed during the Greco-Turkish war, while the Orthodox Albanians to the south in the regions of Korçë and Kastoria remained faithful to the Greek cause. There was however some Albanian co-operation with Vlachs around Bitola and Korçë leading to inter-communal strife with hellenised Albanians there.[38]

The first Albanian guerrilla movement with a political motivation (actually resistance against the activities of Bulgarian revolutionary groups) was founded in 1899 by Haji Mulla Zeka. By 1905 so-called

38 N. Vlachos, *op. cit.,* pp. 202-6, and Wayne S. Vucinich, *Serbia between East and West*, New York, 1968, p. 27, in Aarbakke, *op. cit.*, pp. 92-3 and 147.

Albanian Revolutionary Committees were being formed in numerous towns in Albania with the aim of staging an uprising against the Ottoman authorities. In the run-up to the 1908 Young Turk revolution, contacts had been established between some members of the Committee of Union and Progress (CUP—see below) in Macedonia and their opposite numbers in the Albanian Revolutionary Committees. In Debar the two actually amalgamated. In Skopje the CUP consisted largely of Albanians, and Midhat Frasheri in Salonika issued an appeal for all Albanians to support the revolution. Indeed the Albanian Muslims were to the fore in the initial period of the Young Turk revolt, and Ahmad Niyazi Bey's flight from Resen into the mountains on 3 July 1908 with 200 men was seen as the first real move. Under his influence, Albanian groups around Lake Ohrid all joined the movement, although in Korçë support was only forthcoming on condition that Albania be granted autonomy after the revolution. Contrarily, the more conservative religious Albanian Muslims of Kosovo would only support the revolt if the Sultan remained on the throne—again illustrating the problems of nationalism in Islamic communities.

Thus for a short period the growing Albanian national movement was allied with, and essential for, the CUP. However when it became apparent that the Young Turks' real agenda was to promote Turkish nationalism, this further stimulated Albanian nationalism and resulted in the creation of an independent Albanian state in November 1912. The Albanians came out in an open rebellion centred on Kosovo demanding their own educational facilities. A further rebellion broke out in May 1912, and before the outbreak of the Balkan wars (see below) the Albanian revolts were the biggest problem for the Young Turk governments. By the beginning of August the rebels had occupied as far east as Skopje and the government met many of their demands, granting of an amnesty on 19 August 1912.[39] The change in consciousness brought about by the influence of Western nationalism on the Albanians is graphically illustrated by the major contemporary figure, Ismail Kemal Bey. In his memoirs it is clear that at first he saw himself mainly as an Ottoman and a Muslim, and later

---

39 Akşin *op. cit.,* pp. 185-6, 198-9 and 210.

as an Albanian—a seemingly effortless change due in no small part to the emphasis by the CUP on Turkishness.[40]

The Turks and the CUP

It was still too early to differentiate clearly between different Muslim groups and there was still no real mass concept of being a Turk as opposed to other Muslim groups. Even the Albanian national movement already mentioned was confined mostly to a small intellectual circle. All figures of the time group the Muslims together. However, Turkish sources state that of the 1.5 million Muslims in the three *vilayets* of Kosovo, Salonika and Monastir at the turn of the century, the majority were Turks while the rest were Albanians, with smaller numbers of Muslim Greeks, Slavs or Roma.[41]

However, all sources agree that the Muslims were the largest group, making up about half the total population. As the Ottomans progressively lost control of the Balkans, Muslims and Jews (see below) moved to Macedonia, thus swelling their respective populations. Additionally, a Greek source states that in 1904 the Porte decided to prevent soldiers who had finished their seven-year service in Macedonia from returning to Anatolia so as to boost the Muslim element of the population.[42] The vast majority of the land was owned by Muslims with the Slav or Greek populations mainly sharecroppers.[43] Indeed some like Hüseyin Kazım Bey,

---

40 Ismail Kemal Bey, *Memoirs*, Constable, London, 1920. For more details on the Albanian movement see Stavro Skendi, *The Albanian National Awakening, 1878-1912*, Princeton University Press, 1967.

41 Sina Akşin, *op. cit.*, Istanbul, 1987, p. 49.

42 P. Arjiropulos, 'O Makedonikos Agon—Apomnimoneumata' in *O Makedonikos Agonas Apomnimoneumata* (IMXA 199), Salonika, 1984, quoted in Aarbakke, *op cit.*, footnote 21, p. 18.

43 The Ottoman empire in its classic form did not have a feudal class. After the conquest, private estates and most church lands were taken over by the state which had divided the best lands into non-heritable fiefs, *timars*, usually under a Muslim military leader—the *askeri* class. However, many of the lower nobility were able to keep their earlier ownership, and most converted to Islam in the second generation. The tenure of the *askeri* class was subject to revocation at the whim of the centre. The peasants had the right to hereditary plots provided that they paid the tax-farming tithe. The system changed in the eighteenth century when weakness at the centre allowed the *timars* to change into *chiftliks* where landlords broke the non-hereditary right as well as the legal limits. The result

a senior Ottoman official who served as *mutaş arrif* of Serres and later as *vali* of Salonika, viewed the whole Macedonian question as really one of land ownership (or lack of it) by peasants.[44] As noted above, Abdülhamid had undertaken an extensive expansion of the education programme. One result of this was that a new breed of junior officials emerged who both chafed at the constraints of his autocratic rule and looked for ways to defend what remained of the empire in the Balkans. The pressure from the Great Powers in the form of naval contingents despatched to force issues and the presence of foreign officers in the country influenced the reforms and accelerated the growth of patriotism among young Ottoman officers and officials in Macedonia. The proximity of well-dressed and well-paid foreigners inevitably affected their Ottoman counterparts. In addition, these men could learn from the nationalism of the Christian groups.[45]

Macedonia became a school for nationalism for young officers from the war academy as well as members of the bureaucracy. In contrast to the Christian Balkan nationalists who were often teachers and intellectuals, these harbingers of Turkish nationalism were army officers and junior officials and were the nucleus of the Committee of Union and Progress (CUP), which overthrew Abdülhamid in 1908 and 1909.[46] Akşin gives the typical profile of a CUP cadre in Salonika in 1906 as predominately Turkish

---

44 was that the peasants' lot declined, which in many ways provided the real spur to the initial revolts which saw the establishment of the new Balkan states (see Stavrianos and Aarbakke, *op. cit.*).

44 See his memoirs, *The Revolution of 10 July and Its Consequences*, published after the First World War, pp. 66-72.

45 In addition Turkish Muslims in the new Bulgaria led the way in imbibing nationalist ideas. See Serif Mardin, *Jön Türklerin Siyasî Fikirleri 1895-1905*, Ankara, 1964, pp. 99-100. Such people were suddenly minorities having previously been majorities. Similarly the leaders in propagating a Turkish national consciousness were often Turks from Russia like Yusuf akçura whose position as numbers of a minority faced with strong nationalism from the majority caused them to adopt Western ideas more quickly than the Ottoman Turks who, because of their position of power within the empire, did not see themselves as being so immediately threatened.

46 The whole Young Turk period is still fairly obscure due to a dearth of sources. By far the best account of the CUP is in Akşin, *op. cit.* Mardin, *op. cit.*, is also good on the source of their ideology. For English readers the best is Feroz Ahmad's somewhat confusing *The Young Turks: The Committee of Union and Progress in Turkish Politics, 1908-1914*, Oxford, 1969.

(rather than from other Muslim groups—despite the close involvement of the Albanians in the initial stages of the Young Turks period), young, connected with the administrative class, a product of Abdülhamid's schooling system, and of a 'bourgeois' mentality.[47] Thus, along with the inter-Christian struggles, Macedonia was the centre of the new breed of Young Turks.

The revolution began in Macedonia on 3 July 1908 with Niyazi taking to the hills and appealing to Slavs living around Resen for support. The Porte's countermeasures forced the CUP to act, and Şemsi Paşa, sent to quell the rebellion, was assassinated on 7 July. His replacement, Osman Paşa, arrived in Monastir on 12 July but by then his troops were in rebellion and the CUP was taking over. The Slavs sided with the rebellion from the start, and Muslims were also coming over. But on 20 July the Muslim population of Monastir rose in support and the 1876 Constitution, which Abdülhamid had replaced with his personal autocracy, was proclaimed there. Other places quickly followed, and finally Salonika, the CUP centre but the last important place in Macedonia to move, declared for the Constitution on 25 July. With the Albanians in Kosovo threatening to march on Istanbul if the Constitution was not brought back into force, Abdülhamid conceded. A reaction occurred in April 1909 with a counter-revolution in Istanbul, but troops from Salonika including Mustafa Kemal (Atatürk) and 1,200 Macedonian revolutionaries under Sandanski marched to Istanbul to restore the revolution. Initially the revolution was greeted with delight from almost all sections of the population, but the new rulers' secret agenda of Turkicisation soon saw a return to the old inter-ethnic violent rivalries.

As well as adopting nationalism from their Christian Balkan counterparts, the Young Turks also adopted the bloodletting of the Balkan bands, and thereafter violence and assassination were to be part of Ottoman government business. However, their Turkish nationalism had to be kept hidden, initially in order not to antagonise the other nationalities of the empire. But despite this, the Turkish nature and extreme centralising tendency of their government quickly become apparent and helped to stimulate Albanian nationalism. This was further aggravated by the Young Turk provisions for compulsory Turkish in Albanian schools, along with the arrival of many Muslim and Jewish emigrants from Bosnia-

47 Akşin, *op. cit.*, p. 78.

Hercegovina and Bulgaria who were given land and settled in Albanian territories.[48]

The CUP continued to some extent with the previous Ottoman policy of 'divide and rule', and collaborated with Sandanski's faction, which had helped put down the 1909 counter-revolution in Istanbul against the Supremacists who favoured unification with Bulgaria. This policy met with fierce criticism from Hüseyin Kazım who pointed out that the violence in Macedonia had become chronic and that what was needed was not collaboration with any one side of the Bulgarian factions, but to stamp them out at source.[49] The new rulers did initiate more effective measures against the bands, and reliance on foreign officers was ended. On 16 August 1909 the 'Law of Association' banned political organisations based on ethnic or national basis, which saw the closing of Greek, Bulgarian and other minority clubs in the capital and elsewhere. On 27 September the 'Law for the Prevention of Brigandage and Sedition' against the Balkan armed bands was enacted[50] and special 'pursuit battalions' were created. These mobile units proved more effective than previous Ottoman measures, and the Young Turks also formed local Muslim irregulars. These measures, however, merely increased the general bloodshed. In 1910, 400 were killed—a quarter by the authorities. In the first half of 1912 more than 500 were killed, often by Ottoman units in the villages.[51]

On 3 September 1910 a law on the founding and opening of schools and churches in the European provinces was passed, stating that if, in a place with two communities (i.e. Greek or Bulgarian), one of these communities accounted for less than one-third of the population, then one had to hand any school or church that it owned over to the other side. If there was no school or church, then financial help would be given to build them. If there were several schools or churches then they should be divided between the two groups.[52] However, the real aim of the Young Turks was to modernise and Turkify the state.

48 Akşin, *op. cit.*, pp. 206-7.
49 Kazım, *op. cit.*
50 Lewis, *op. cit.*, p. 215.
51 Aarbakke, *op. cit.*, p. 146.
52 Akşin, *op. cit.*, p. 206, quoting from Hilmi Kâmil Bayur, *Sadrazam Kâmil Paşa*, Ankara, 1954, pp. 320-1.

The old Ottoman system of *millets* and populations classified by religion was to go.

The Jews

The aborted San Stefano Treaty imposed by the Russians left the Jews of the Balkans—both inside and outside the would-be 'Greater Bulgaria'—in the same sorry state as those of the Pale in Russia, namely with no formal equality, freedom of religion or representation in the parliaments of the new states. However, the Treaty of Berlin rectified this and it was agreed that the newly-independent Balkan countries should provide equal rights and protection to Jews and the remaining Muslims, giving them access to all public offices and full religious freedom—this despite the anti-Semitic objections of the Russian delegate Gorchakov.[53]

Despite these provisions many Jews did not look forward to losing the mantle of the Ottoman empire, especially if this meant falling under Greek control. While there are those, like Shaw,[54] who see the whole course of the Greek nationalist revolution and the expansion of Greece as being marked by massacres of Jews and Muslims, such massacres of Jews were really only prominent in the 1820s. Many Ashkenazi Jews in Athens supported the Greek revolt, and there were Jewish supporters of the Greek cause elsewhere in Europe. In 1889 they were recognised by the Greek government as citizens of the Jewish faith. However the Sephardic Jews of Macedonia were very different. They had come to the empire to escape Western persecution and had helped replace the Greek-speaking populations of Thrace and Macedonia whom the Sultan had forcibly deported to Istanbul after the conquest of the city so as to repopulate it. These Jews feared the Greek advance and fled to Anatolia and Salonika for protection. Salonika's Jewish population rose from 28,000 in 1876 to 90,000 in 1908 making it the outright majority there. Relations in Salonika between Greeks and Jews were bad in consequence and clashes were frequent.[55]

However, relations between Jews and Muslim Turks were helped by the role of the Salonika *Dönmes* in the Young Turk revolution

53 Shaw, *op. cit.*, p. 193.
54 *Ibid.*
55 *Ibid.*, pp. 204–5.

of 1908; Emmanuel Carasso (Karasu), who was close to Talat Paşa in the forefront of the movement, used his Masonic contacts to further the cause.[56] In the first Balkan war (see below), the Jews of the empire fought for the Ottomans, especially in Edirne against the Bulgarians. The Ottoman defeat saw general attacks on Jews and synagogues by both Greeks and Bulgarians. Two contemporary reports graphically describe the Jewish predicament in Salonika:

> All the self-interested justifications of the newspapers of Europe, all the lies which they have used to cover up the truth, can never destroy the impression of the terrible anguish which marked the entry of the Greeks into Salonika. A week of terror and horror one can never easily forget....[57]
>
> It wasn't only the irregulars [*Comitacis*] who massacred, pillaged and burned. The soldiers of the Army, the Chief of Police and the high civil officials took an active part in the events at Serres. Out of 6,000 houses, 4,000 were burned. Almost 1,200 shops were consumed by flames and destructive bombs. The [Jewish] population lost all, and without even anything to wear are in despair. Everyone wants to emigrate.[58]

The Balkan wars

By the turn of the century a new factor had arisen in the already hopelessly complicated Balkan situation. Before 1890 the new Balkan states were small and weak, effectively controlled by and dependent on, outside Great Power patronage. Now this situation was changing and the new states themselves began to play the diplomatic game themselves by changing patrons and, more important, building up their own military strength. By the early twentieth century Greece had a large navy and Bulgaria had the largest army in proportion to population in Europe—around 1900, Abdülhamid's military advisers predicted that a Bulgarian invasion

56 *Ibid.,* p. 217-18.
57 A. Cohen, Ecole Secondaire Moïse Allatini, Salonika, to AIU, Paris, no. 7745/7, 4 December 1912, in AIU Archives (Paris) I C 49, quoted in Shaw, *ibid.,* p. 195.
58 Mizrahi, President of AIU at Salonika, to AIU (Paris), no. 2704/3, 25 July 1913. In AIU Archives (Paris) I C 51. Quoted in Shaw, *ibid.,* p. 195. Shaw also graphically details similar Bulgarian atrocities outside Macedonia.

of Macedonia might reach Salonika in seven days. Additionally the change of dynasty in Serbia in 1903 increased Serbian military potential.

This new situation opened up the prospect of the new states allying themselves against the ailing Ottoman empire. The failure of Ilinden had led the Bulgarians to believe that the best way of gaining their objectives was actual war. Ferdinand declared formal independence following the 1908 Young Turks Revolution, adopting the title *Tsar* (hitherto he had merely been a prince) and as well as coveting Macedonia he looked towards possibly taking the grand prize of Constantinople/Istanbul as well. An impetus to this was provided by the Italian invasion of Tripoli in the Italo-Turkish war of 1911 which further encouraged the Balkan states.

However, Macedonia remained as a great stumbling block to concerted action. In 1912, however, Serbia and Bulgaria, while agreeing on an autonomous Macedonia, secretly agreed to a division of influence in northern Macedonia. Serbia recognised Bulgarian ascendancy south of a line stretching from just north of Kriva Palanka to just north of Ohrid. The territory north of this line— which included Struga, Debar, Kičevo, Gostivar, Tetovo, Skopje and Kumanovo—was to be subject to arbitration by the Russian Tsar. Bulgaria and Greece came to no similar arrangements but the way was now clearer for agreements between the new Balkan states against the Ottoman empire, and a flurry of alliances in 1912 were made—between Serbia and Bulgaria in March, Greece and Bulgaria in May, and Montenegro, Bulgaria and Serbia in October—paving the way to the first Balkan war which broke out in October.

The new allies were at first triumphant, with Bulgarian forces leading the way, mostly engaged in Thrace and driving towards Istanbul. Despite the Bulgarians being held up at the Catalca defence line at Edirne, the Ottomans sought an armistice on 3 December. However, CUP elements led by the adventurer Enver advocated a continuation of the fighting and after a coup on 23 January 1913 the war continued until Edirne fell to the Bulgarians and a new armistice was declared on 26 March 1913. By the Treaty of London of 30 May the Ottomans lost all mainland European Turkey except Istanbul and its environs.

Inevitably there followed problems among the victors over

how to divide up the spoils, with Bulgaria largely at odds with the others. Geography played its part. Bulgaria had borne the brunt of the fighting on the Edirne front and consequently suffered most casualties, while the conquest of Macedonia, the main aim, had been left more to Greek and Serbs. The Great Powers, especially Austria-Hungary and Italy, insisted on the formation of an Albanian state; this necessitated the Serbs giving up some conquered territory, and they consequently wanted compensation in Macedonia at Bulgaria's expense. Salonika was contested by both Greeks and Bulgarians, and Romania claimed parts of the Dobrudzha from Bulgaria as its price for remaining neutral. While Russia tried to mediate between the different camps, Greece and Serbia formed an alliance against Bulgaria.

Faced with this, the Bulgarians made the colossal blunder of attacking Greek and Serbian lines on 19/20 June. This was the start of the second Balkan war, in which all the other parties including the Ottomans and the Romanians, combined against Bulgaria which was soundly thrashed. By the 31 July armistice the Ottomans retook Edirne, the Romanians occupied the Dobrudzha, and Macedonia was mostly split between Serbia and Greece. The Bucarest Peace Treaty of 10 August inaugurated the three-way division of Macedonia—there was no mention of its being autonomous—which with some minor alterations has continued to this day. Greece won most of southern Macedonia including the prize of Salonika as well as Kavalla and most of the Macedonian coast, Serbia won Vardar and was now contiguous with Montenegro and Greece, while Bulgaria was left with merely a small part of Macedonia and had lost much of Thrace including Edirne to the Ottomans.

Both during and immediately after the second Balkan war, both Serbia and Greece subjected the Bulgarian communities under their control to heavy repression. The Serbs expelled Exarchists and closed as many as 641 Bulgarian churches and 761 Bulgarian schools. The population was put under pressure to renounce Bulgaria and take oaths of Serbian nationality. Thousands fled to Bulgaria. VMRO sources claim that in 1912-15, the Serbian terror killed 1,845 people, while 285 'disappeared'; 1,221 houses were burnt. The worst repression was in western Macedonia where many Muslim Albanians, perhaps as many as half the total, were among the victims; in eastern Vardar Macedonia from Kočani and Štip to near the Bulgarian border; and on the west bank of the Vardar from Prilep to Negotino. Twenty-three Exarchist priests were killed and in Kičevo the Serbs crucified Hieromonach Teofan and two villagers.[59]

Similar atrocities of a kind that has become familiar again in late twentieth-century Bosnia occurred in the areas under Greek rule. The Greeks burned the Bulgarian centre of Kilkis as well as much of Serres and Drama. The use of Bulgarian and Slav dialects were forbidden.[60] Letters home from Greek soldiers make the policy clear: 'We are to burn the villages, massacre the young, and spare none but the old people, children and minors.'[61] Rape was common. Along with the purely ethnic component of the atrocities, contemporaries like the Balkan expert H. Brailsford, who was a member of the Carnegie Endowment commission on the Balkan wars, noted: 'The accumulated hatreds, the inherited revenge of centuries...gave the opportunity of vengeance to every peasant who cherished a grudge against a harsh landlord.'[62] As a result about 15,000 Slavs left for Bulgaria while many Greeks from Thrace and both Bulgarian and Yugoslav Macedonia moved in order to be under Greek control. With both Bulgaria and the Ottoman empire losing in the Balkan wars, there was some scope for rapprochement, and the CUP entered into dealings with VMRO to try jointly to subvert Greek and Serb Macedonia.

The First World War

The pattern for the two world wars was now set. Serbia, Greece and Romania now favoured the *status quo* and would support the Western allies,[63] while Bulgaria remained revanchist and there-fore supported the Central/Axis powers who wanted revision. As Stavrianos points out, the First World War was in Balkan

---

59 See Ivan Mihaylov, *Spomeni, Osvoboditlena borba, 1919- 1924*, Brussels, 1965, pp. 383-524 in Banac, *op. cit.*, p. 317, and footnote 25 where he breaks down Mihailov's figures.

60 Banac, *op. cit.*, p. 317.

61 See the Carnegie Endowment *Report on the International Commission to Inquire into the Causes and Conduct of the Balkan Wars*, Washington, DC, 1914.

62 *Ibid.*

63 Romania wavered and actually fought for both but always ended up on the Allied side and sitting at the victors' table.

terms a continuation of the second Balkan war.[64] In 1915 the Bulgarians, on the side of the Central powers, returned and administratively occupied most of Vardar Macedonia as well as eastern Aegean Macedonia. This appeared to have been popular with most of the Slavs there, the majority of whom would probably have identified themselves as Bulgarians. Greeks and Serbs, however, were dislodged and persecuted, but as Banac points out, the persecution in Vardar was nothing compared to that imposed on the parts of Serbia proper and Kosovo which were also under Bulgarian control—the suppression there was directed by General Aleksandâr Protogerov and his Supremacist bands.[65]

In eastern Aegean Macedonia, the Bulgarian occupation was harsher than in Vardar because of the greater number of Greeks and Patriarchists there, and this was aggravated by a famine which the Inter-Allied Commission accused the Bulgarians of propagating deliberately. In their report,[66] the Commission, which studied 339 towns and villages in eastern Macedonia, concluded that the total population of 305,000 had dropped during the two-year Bulgarian occupation to 235,000 (some 32,000 died in the territory, 30,000 from 'hunger, blows and disease'); the areas of highest mortality being Kavala, Serres and the region of Pangaion. Some 42,000 were deported to Bulgaria. The Bulgarians also allowed the Ottoman army forcibly to enlist Macedonian Muslims, whether Turks, Albanians or Slavs. Many were also enlisted into the Bulgarian army where they were employed at the rear and later returned to their homes. Those who entered the Ottoman army, however, did not return; this was the case with 8-10,000 of the total of 18,000 Muslims enlisted in the two armies.[67]

Thus in this crucial time between the Congress of Berlin and the end of the First World War, the initial period up to the end of the nineteenth century saw the Bulgarian side advancing with no apparent resistance in most of Macedonia. However the change to violent tactics led to an undermining of the incipient Bulgarian hegemony as well as a debilitation of the population

64 Stavrianos, *op. cit.*
65 Banac, *op. cit.,* p. 318.
66 *Report of the Inter-Allied Commission in Eastern Macedonia*, part I, London, 1919.
67 *Ibid.*

who were subjected to outrages from the rival armed bands—indeed from the mid-1890s to the end of the First World War, they were subjected to repeated atrocities from different camps as the pendulum of power swung back and forth. With the Young Turks coming to power in Istanbul, the Ottoman regime toughened its resistance to ceding more territory, but in terms of military power the new Balkan states were becoming independent of Great Power patronage. They engaged in war with the Ottoman empire and without great difficulty succeeded in driving the Ottomans effectively out of Europe.

How to divide their winnings, however, proved a difficult problem, and Bulgaria made the fatal blunder of attacking Greece and Serbia with the result that it lost most of Macedonia. The three-way split that followed the second Balkan war has essentially continued until the present. This is because the new states would make the ethnic and national territories co-terminous by force, migration and state-sponsored homogenisation, as we see in subsequent chapters. Of the three main external contestants—Greece, Bulgaria and Serbia—the one with the least indigenous support, Serbia, found the greatest difficulty in forcibly assimilating (i.e. Serbianising) the population under its control.

5

THE INTER-WAR YEARS

REPRESSION AND VIOLENCE

Albania

The partitioning of geographic Macedonia in the Balkan wars, and the creating of the new state of Albania in November 1912 saw a small portion of Macedonia going to that state. Within this area, as elsewhere in Macedonia, a variety of different peoples lived: Albanians, Slavs, Vlachs, Gypsies and Greeks. As well as the ethnic mix, there was also—again as elsewhere in Macedonia—a religious split between Christian Orthodox populations and Muslims. Thus there were both Muslim and Christian Slavs, Albanian Roma and so on. The actual numbers of the different groups remain unclear, especially where the ethnic-religious breakdown was concerned. Complications arise from the tendency of Greek sources to claim resolutely that all Orthodox Christians in Albania are of Greek descent—as a result of the *millet* system which continues up to the present.[1]

At the turn of the century, according to the British vice-consul

[1] This is clearly shown in the polemics over the size of the Greek minority in Albania with émigré Greek sources claiming, on the basis of historical accounts of Orthodox church schools etc., that some 400,000 Greeks live there (see Poulton *op. cit.,* p. 193-201). The issue has recently come to a head over the expulsion from Greece of an Orthodox bishop who was accused by the Albanian authorities of 'irredentist activity', and the insistence by the Albanian authorities that the Autocephalous Church of Albania should at least be run by Albanian citizens and ideally ethnic Albanians. While all, or at least the vast majority of, Albania's Greek population are Orthodox, the Orthodox community is not made up of Greeks alone. At the end of the Second World War, while 70% of the total population was Muslim, approximately 17% were Orthodox mainly in the south and central areas (and about 10% in the mountainous north were Roman Catholic).

in Bitola (Manastir), C.C. Blunt, there were some 11,000 Orthodox and Muslim Slavs in the area of 'Bilishta, Korcha [Korçë], Borbot and Golo Brdo [Gorni Debar]'.[2] In the 1930s, the Macedonian National Committee in Sofia estimated that 27,000 Slav Macedonians (called Bulgarians by the native Albanians) were living in Albania.[3] In contrast to the Greek and Serbian authorities, those in the new Albanian state after 1912 did not attempt to assimilate the Slav minority or forcibly change the Slav names of villages and towns. As in other former Ottoman territories, the battleground for national identity tended to be ecclesiastical, with the Greek Orthodox Church and its attendant educational facilities instrumental in checking Slav Macedonian/Bulgarian tendencies. Significant in this connection was the founding of the Autocephalous Albanian Orthodox Church in 1925, which placed the religious hierarchy under Albanian control. The pro-Bulgarian orientation of the Slav-speaking population in Albanian Macedonia was shown by the fact that VMRO had contacts and bases in Albania from which it launched armed raids into western Vardar Macedonia.[4]

However, the minority situation in inter-war Albania, especially that concerning the strip of Macedonia, is unclear—the more so because of the country's internal problems which caused it to become increasingly a vassal state of Mussolini's Italy. As Banac points out, there were many similarities between the armed activists —Albanian *kaçaks* and Macedonian *komitas*—against Great Serbianism in the southern regions where Yugoslavia met Albania. Indeed the two groups co-operated with each other, as is shown below, and both had dealings with Mussolini's Italy as well as with Croat anti-Yugoslav parties like Ante Pavelić's Ustašas.[5]

Bulgaria

In Bulgaria, the 'Macedonian Question' played a key role in internal politics from the end of the First World War till the

2 H. Andonovski, *The Socialist Republic of Macedonia*, Skopje, 1974, p. 203.
3. *Makedoniya*, no. 8, III, Sofia, 1932.
4. Glogor Todorovski, 'Nekolku podatoci za aktivnosta na vrhovističkata VMRO vo Albanija i Bugarija pomeģu dvete svetski vojni' *Institut za nacionalna istorija: Glasnik*, vol. 15, no. 1, pp. 137-56, referred to in Banac, *op. cit.*, p. 322, n. 37.
5. Banac, *op. cit.*, p. 326.

mid-1930s—a role that was often destructive and explosive. As detailed in Chapter 3, Bulgaria was the loser over Macedonia in both the Balkan wars and the World War (after which it also lost part of Thrace and its direct access to the Aegean sea), and for most of the ensuing period retained an attitude of resentment and irredentism. The situation was not improved by the presence of a huge number of refugees from 'the lost territories', especially after the population exchanges with Greece. By 1934, Macedonian and Thracian refugees accounted for more than 10 per cent of Sofia's population, and Macedonian activists caused much instability by continuing their feuds and violence within Bulgaria.[6] As well as this internal destabilisation, VMRO effectively established its own control over an area in the south-west of Pirin Macedonia around Petrich from which it launched numerous armed raids mainly into the territory of the new kingdom of Serbs, Croats and Slovenes (later Yugoslavia), but also into Greece. In this a pattern for the future was established: Bulgarian Macedonians saw Serbia/Yugoslavia as the main enemy and to some extent acquiesced in population exchanges with Greece, which lessened the feeling of loss over Aegean Macedonia (although the claims to Greek Macedonia remained—if not as strong as for Vardar Macedonia).

For a long time the Bulgarian monarchy and authorities appeared to acquiesce in this blatant lawlessness on the part of VMRO. The great exception to this was the government of the peasant leader Aleksandâr Stambolisky.[7] At the end of the World War, a revolt by soldiers and others led by Stambolisky's fellow-Agrarian Raiko Daskalov—the Radomir Rebellion—had been put down by two German divisions and a Macedonian unit led by General Protogerov, the VMRO-Supremacist. When Stambolisky took power after the elections of August 1919, the new government's first act was to arrest previous leaders including the prominent Macedonians Protogerov and Todor Aleksandrov. Both escaped from prison on 13 November 1919 after being detained for little more than a week. Aleksandrov soon eclipsed Protogerov and

6   Richard Crampton, *A Short History of Modern Bulgaria*, Cambridge University Press, 1987, p. 92.
7   For Stambolisky's extraordinary career and for the Bulgarian Agrarian Union in general, see John D. Bell, *Peasants in Power: Aleksander Stambolisky and The Bulgarian Agrarian Union, 1899-1923*, Princeton University Press, 1977.

became the outright leader of a single Macedonian paramilitary organisation, now definitely called VMRO.[8]

However VMRO remained riven by feuds and, despite Aleksandrov's pre-eminent position, contained other currents especially from those with more left-wing views such as Bulgarian Communist members like Dimo Hadzhi Dimov and those of the more anarchic and unorthodox left. The latter elements viewed Aleksandrov as too pro-Bulgarian and distrusted his espousal of autonomy.

The successors or survivors of Sandanski's Serres faction, led by Todor Panitsa, also favoured a Macedonia within a Balkan federation—a plan outlined by Dimov in a pamphlet of 1919 entitled 'Back to Autonomy' which called for a Macedonian republic modelled on the Swiss federation within a wider Balkan federal context.[9] In 1920 the Bulgarian Communist Party rejected such ideas but some left-wing sympathisers remained loyal to them, which led to a split at the Second Congress of Macedonian Fraternities in late 1920. As Banac points out, the federalists' programme was highly impractical with its somewhat bizarre formulation of a Macedonia organised as a vertical union of communities, led by a governing council which would have to convene abroad in Western Europe or even the United States, and using Esperanto as a neutral language.[10] However the idea of a wider Balkan federation did to some extent fit in with Stambolisky's wider foreign policy visions as well as serving him as a possible rival to Aleksandrov's VMRO. After Stambolisky's visit to Belgrade in May 1921 his Defence Minister, Aleksandâr Dimitrov, was entrusted with the job of smashing VMRO, and a bloody struggle began which saw several VMRO leaders killed including the émigré Macedonian leader Petrov, who favoured co-operation with Stambolisky, as an act of retaliation. In pursuing this policy against VMRO's 'state within a state' in Petrich and its surrounding area, the government now turned to Panitsa and the federalists.[11] Stambolisky also purged the army and border guards of VMRO supporters and tried to reduce and control VMRO's influence,

8 Banac, *op. cit.,* p. 321.
9 See Banac, *op. cit.,* pp. 324-5 and footnote 44 referring to excerpts cited in Ljubiša a Doklestić (ed.) *Kroz historiju Makedonije: Izbrani izvori,* Zagreb, 1964, pp. 214- 15.
10 Banac, *ibid.,* p. 324.
11 Banac, *ibid.*

banning its publications and even setting up a special force against it in the Petrich district.[12]

Stambolisky, in line with his policy of Balkan co-operation, had also gone out of his way to mend bridges with the new Yugoslav state; he denounced VMRO while on a visit to Belgrade in November 1921 and this policy culminated in the Treaty of Niš of March 1923. To VMRO this was the final treachery, and it responded with customary violence. In October 1921 Dimitrov was assassinated. In response to Stambolisky's visit to Belgrade in December 1922, VMRO occupied Kyustendil and even passed death sentences on the 'traitors' who were betraying Macedonia (and/or Bulgaria) to the new Yugoslav state; the government reacted and VMRO forces retreated to Petrich. VMRO staged physical attacks on both Daskalov and Stambolisky, and joining forces with other sections that were alienated by Stambolisky's somewhat bizarre domestic policies, it overthrew him on 9 June 1923. The VMRO leader Aleksandrov's men, led by Ivan (Vancho) Mihaylov, oversaw the torture and murder of Stambolisky; his hand which had signed the hated Niš treaty was cut off while he was still alive.[13] Thus ended for the next decade any serious attempt to control VMRO within Bulgaria. It also ended Stambolisky's sincere attempt to implement internationalist policies at the expense of narrower ones (i.e. a change from trying to undo recent history and gain at least Vardar Macedonia), which cost him his life.

VMRO, now relatively unchecked in its stronghold in Petrich, was free to grow into a full-scale organisation, and throughout most of the 1920s it was the only real authority in Pirin Macedonia. In Sofia it derived its influence from its collaboration with the coup leaders against Stambolisky as well as through the influential Macedonian émigré societies there. In Pirin itself its paramilitary units, mostly made up of peasants, had become by 1923 a veritable army of over 9,000 men with main bases of 3,000 men in Gorna Dzhumaya (Blagoevgrad), 2,100 in Petrich and 1,800 in Nevrokop (Gotse Delchev). In these areas it fulfilled all the functions of government—collecting taxes, administering justice and passing laws.[14] Secure in its base, it could also engage in its habitual

12 Crampton, *op. cit.,* p. 93.
13 Kosta Todorov, *Stamboliski,* Belgrade, 1937, p. 152, and Bell, *op. cit.*
14 Banac, *ibid.,* p. 322.

activity of violence and internecine fighting. Daskalov was murdered in Prague in August 1923, and in 1924 a splinter group called for co-operation with the Communists—who along with the authorities had reacted by initiating their own cycle of bloody violence—and issued a manifesto in April 1924 in Vienna signed by the VMRO central committee of Aleksandrov, Protogerov and Petâr Chaulev. Before the abortive September 1923 uprising by the Communists, Aleksandrov had signed an agreement with them to stay neutral if in return the uprising did not take place in Pirin Macedonia—an agreement which the Communists violated.[15]

Aleksandrov also contemplated an agreement with the Soviet Union to gain an independent Macedonia with Communist help but then repudiated the agreements with the Communists, which led to further splits within VMRO. The 'Old Man', Aleksandrov himself, was assassinated on 31 August 1931. Officially, VMRO blamed a pro-Communist faction within it, led by Aleko Vasilev-Pasha, but others blamed circles round the Bulgarian throne. Either way the Comintern now tried to build on the pro-Communist elements within VMRO and formed VMRO United (VMRO-ob) led by Dimitâr Vlahov,[16] but this, despite obtaining some influence, never really challenged VMRO on the ground. VMRO now moved to the right under the leadership of Protogerov who was assassinated in 1928—Chaulev had only survived until 1927—and then under Ivan Mihaylov, who survived the continuing feuds to live to a ripe old age and publish his memoirs in exile.[17] Mihaylov became the undisputed VMRO leader from this time. Meanwhile VMRO continued to launch attacks on neighbouring countries from Petrich, which resulted in Greece occupying some areas in retaliation in October 1925, and being obliged by the League of Nations to pay 30 million leva damages.[18]

In January 1926 Andrey Liapchev, who was from Macedonia, became prime minister and the ensuing period saw even more government largesse towards VMRO and the Macedonians despite the continuing domestic killings and violence. As Crampton notes,

15 Crampton, *op. cit.,* and Banac, *op. cit.,* p. 325.
16 See Stephen Palmer and Robert King, *Yugoslav Communism and the Macedonian Question,* Hamden, Conn., 1971, and Paul Shoup, *Communism and the Yugoslav National Question,* New York, 1968.
17 Ivan Mihaylov, *Spomeni,* Brussels, 1965.
18 Crampton, *op. cit.,* p. 102.

it was not just the murders that upset public opinion, the Macedonians also demanded and got well-paid easy jobs in the public sector—more than 100 were employed in the Pernik mines alone. In the Petrich 'state within a state' VMRO continued to levy 'taxes' and, like many other such armed bodies, claimed the status of a 'national liberation movement' and for a long time controlled an area as a non-governmental entity, degenerating more and more into a mere gangster organisation that terrorised its own population. The relationship between the 'Macedonians' and the other Bulgarians in this period is complex. Although Bulgarians saw all Slav Macedonians as their fellow-nationals, many were alienated by the continued lawlessness and violence. There was a clear differentiation between the two. The situation was confusing: to the outside world VMRO portrayed Macedonians as part of the Bulgarian nation, while to Bulgarians it manifested a fierce autonomy bordering on independence

In October 1927 Yugoslavia reacted to the raids into its territory by closing the border. There was also in 1930 the case of Marinopolski, an army officer who confessed that he had given false testimony against a senior officer—a leading VMRO critic—after being tortured by VMRO. This greatly affected the officer corps and fostered connections between the army and *Zveno*, an above-party pressure group founded in 1927 which was disgusted both with inept politicians and with the VMRO outrages.[19]

The 'Macedonian Question' and VMRO's continuing actions made attempts at any form of Balkan unity in the early 1930s impossible—this at a time when Mussolini's influence in the area was growing. Rather, Bulgaria was seen as a problem, and by the Balkan *entente* of 9 February 1934 Yugoslavia, Turkey, Romania and Greece—the second Balkan war allies—guaranteed their existing borders. Moreover these countries declared that they saw potential threats not from outside the Balkans but from inside: although Albania was coming increasingly under Italian domination, this could really only mean Bulgaria and the 'Macedonian Question' once more.

Meanwhile a shift had taken place in the perennial struggle within VMRO between 'federalists' and 'autonomists'. At its 1932 congress, it voted to change its objectives from Macedonian autonomy to independence. Moreover the area defined as

19 Crampton, *op. cit.,*pp. 103-6.

'Macedonia' included Dupnitsa, Kyustendil and areas close to Sofia. All this fed the general discontent felt by the pro-*Zveno* officers, led by Damian Velchev and Kimon Georgiev, who launched the coup of 19 May 1934. This time the new authorities were not prepared to tolerate further trouble from VMRO within Bulgaria, and the army was sent into Petrich in a popular and successful mission to subdue it. Indeed the ease with which the new authorities tamed VMRO suggests complicity on the part of previous governments. While VMRO would continue to be involved in spectacular outrages like the assassinations of the Yugoslav King Aleksander, together with the French Foreign Minister, in Marseilles in October 1934, its influence had been severely curtailed. In the ten years up to 1934 VMRO violence had claimed at least 884 lives within Bulgaria and bedevilled Bulgarian politics.[20]

Greece

As noted above, the Greek authorities ever since the founding of the modern Greek state have consistently denied the existence of the Slav Macedonians as a separate people from the Greeks. Instead they have referred to them officially as Slavophone Greeks while the Bulgarians claimed them to be Bulgarians—in common speech the Greek population referred to them as Bulgarians and the notion of them as a separate people, the Macedonians, only came later, as we see in the following chapters. Assessing population figures is problematic due to the tendency for the Greek or the Slav population figures to be exaggerated depending on who is making the assessment—Greeks, Bulgarians or Yugoslavs. One of the most detailed assessments is a Yugoslav one,[21] using Bulgarian and Greek sources, made just before the Balkan wars of 1912 which resulted in the liberation of the areas from Ottoman rule: it established that in Aegean Macedonia there were 326,426 Macedonians, 40,921 Muslim Macedonians (Pomaks), 289,973 Turks, 4,240 Christian Turks, 2,112 Cherkez (Circassians), 240,019 Christian Greeks, 13,753 Muslim Greeks, 5,584 Muslim Albanians, 3,291 Christian Albanians, 45,457 Christian Vlachs, 3,500 Muslim Vlachs, 595,960 Jews, 29,803 Roma, and 8,100 others, making

20 Figures from Crampton, *op. cit.*
21 Todor Simovski, 'The Balkan Wars and their Repercussions on the Ethnical Situation in Aegean Macedonia', in *Glasnik*, vol. XVI, no. 3, Skopje, 1972.

a total of 1,073,549. However, this is merely one among many rival assessments of the population at that time. Some Greek sources put the figure of Greek-speakers as high as 44 per cent with Slav-speakers as low as 9 per cent.[22]

However from 1913 to 1926 there were large-scale changes in the population structure due to ethnic migrations. During and immediately after the Balkan wars, about 15,000 Slavs moved from the new Greek territories into Bulgaria while many Greeks from Thrace, Bulgarian and Yugoslav Macedonia resettled themselves in order to be under Greek rule. More significant was the Greek-Bulgarian convention of 27 November 1919 allowing a voluntary population exchange, as the result of which some 25,000 Greeks left Bulgaria for Greece and between 52,000 and 72,000 Slavs (depending on which estimate is used[23]) left Greece for Bulgaria, mostly from Eastern Aegean Macedonia which from then onwards remained virtually Slav-free. Most Slavs living west of the Vardar-Axios river, especially in the area bordering on Yugoslavia, chose to remain. However those who were seen as actively pro-Bulgarian were deported and settled far away in the islands, especially in Crete.

Larger population exchanges took place between Greece and Turkey following the war between those countries in 1920-2. Attached to the peace treaty of July 1924 was a convention stipulating that the Greek and Turkish populations of Turkey and Greece respectively were to be exchanged, except for the Greeks of Istanbul and the Turks of Western Thrace. Again, as so often in the Balkans, religion was the criterion used to define 'Greek' or 'Turk', which resulted in many non-Turkish Muslims (Slavs and Greeks) emigrating to Turkey and conversely Turkish-speaking Christians to Greece.[24] In this exchange some 390,000 Muslims (mostly Turks) emigrated to Turkey and more than 1,200,000 Greeks left Turkey, of whom some 540,000 settled in Greek Macedonia along with about 100,000 more Greek refugees who had come

22 Dimitri Nicolaidis, 'Penser l'identité nationale', *Temps Modernes*, no. 548, March 1991.

23 Hristo Andonovski, 'Macedonian National Minorities: Greece, Bulgaria and Albania' in Mihailo Apostoloski and Harampie Polenakovich (eds.) in *The Socialist Republic of Macedonia*, Skopje, 1974, and Barker, *op. cit.*

24 The 'Dignity' organisation in Skopje claims that some 40,000 Muslim Slav Macedonians, mainly from the Meglen region, were thus moved to Turkey—see their *Petition* to the Human Rights Conference in Denmark (no date given).

before 1920. Thus there was an influx of more than 600,000 Greek refugees into Greek Macedonia while most of the Turkish and Pomak populations outside Western Thrace emigrated. The official Greek census of 1928 recorded 1,237,000 Greeks (almost certainly an exaggeration), 82,000 Slavophones and 93,000 others. These intensive population changes and the settlement of Aegean Macedonia by Greeks from Asia Minor, which so greatly contributed to the cementing of Greek control over the area, perhaps explain why the repression against Slav Macedonians in Greece immediately after the First World War period was less than that by the Serbian authorities of the new Yugoslav state. Mihaylov mentions in his memoirs that in 1918-24 there were thirty-three recorded killings, three disappearances and 724 arrests in Greece— considerably fewer than in Vardar Macedonia (see below) in this period.[25]

A schism took place in the Greek Orthodox Church after the Greek state adopted the Gregorian calendar in place of the Julian one in the 1920s, and the Slavs tended to be 'Old Calendarists'—i.e supporters of the Julian calendar. The Serbian Orthodox Church, which at that time held sway in Yugoslav Macedonia, still retained (and retains to this day) the Julian calendar, and hence many Slavs crossed the border to Yugoslavia to celebrate religious festivals—an activity which caused the Greek government concern over possible foreign penetration.[26]

While the repression of Jews by the Greeks, which had been acute while the fledgling Greek state expanded, decreased in this period, the continuing Greek emphasis on religion as an essential component of Greek citizenship made the position of the Jews, who were mainly concentrated in Salonika, uncertain.[27] However the Greek authorities used the great fire which devastated the Jewish quarter of the city in 1917 to further the process of attempted national homogenisation. The bulk of the former Jewish areas were taken over by the authorities and kept for historical excavation and for the new planned city which emerged, so that even as

25 Mihaylov, *op. cit.*, p. 692.
26 I am indebted to Father Kallistos Ware for this information. For more on the 'Old Calendarists', see *The Old Calender Orthodox Church of Greece* by Archimandrite Chrysostomos (the schismatic Bishop of Florina) and Hieromonks Ambriosa and Auxentios (the 'Old Calendarists' 'gang of three'), California 1985.
27 Shaw, *op. cit.*, p. 206.

late as the eve of the Second World War up to half the Jews made homeless were still living in temporary accommodation financedbyforeign—mostlyUS—aid.[28] Furthermore, the rebuilding process obliterated all traces of the former Ottoman multiculturalism by wiping out mosques and synagogues while keeping Greek Orthodox churches even where their position did not fit in with the new modern urban plan. The University of Salonika was built on the site of the old Jewish cemetery—Jewish tombstones used as paving-stones can be seen in the walkways. The new Salonika was built to reflect the new national myth that the city was and had always been Greek by culture, although the University had a chair for Jewish studies.

Greece was obliged to protect its Slav minorities, and these obligations were further stipulated in the Agreement at Sèvres in 1920 with educational rights and guarantees for the use of their mother-tongue for official purposes. In September 1924 Greece and Bulgaria signed a protocol known as the Kalfov-Politis agreement placing the 'Bulgarian' minority in Greece under the protection of the League of Nations, which prompted the Yugoslavs to renounce the Greek-Serbian treaty of 1913 in protest. On 15 January 1925 Greece announced that it would not follow the protocol and thereafter treated the Slavs as Greeks. The Greek government ordered, in decree no. 332 of November 1926, that all Slavonic names of towns, villages, rivers and mountains should be replaced by Greek ones.[29]

However, the Greek Ministry of Education commissioned a primer for Slav Macedonians in Greece, and this, called *Abecedar*, was published in Athens in 1925. It used the Lerin-Bitola dialect printed in the Latin alphabet, and was ostensibly to be used in new schools in Aegean Macedonia and was submitted by Greece to the League of Nations to show how well its minority obligations were being complied with. The Bulgarian representative described it as 'incomprehensible' but the Greek representative to the League, Vasilis Dendramis, defended it on the grounds that the Macedonian Slav language was 'neither Bulgarian, nor Serbian, but an independent language' and produced linguistic maps to back this

---

28 I am indebted to Professor Steve Bowman for this information.
29 Tosho Popovski, *Makedonskoto Natsionalno Maltsinstvo vo Bulgarija, Grtsija i Albanija*, Skopje, 1981, p. 72.

up.[30] Needless to say, *Abecedar* was not used by the Greek authorities but was immediately confiscated and destroyed.[31]

Up till the Balkan wars, Greek Macedonia had, under the control of the Exarchate Church, nineteen primary schools in towns and 186 in villages, with 320 teachers catering for 12,895 pupils in the Bulgarian medium. In addition there were four Serbian schools and some 200 other Slav primary schools supported by village communities. All these Slavonic schools were closed and the inventories destroyed, while in the Slavonic churches the icons were repainted with Greek names following a decree of 15 July 1927.[32]

The position of the Slav minority worsened between 1936 and 1941 under the Metaxas regime, which viewed the minority as a danger to Greece's security, and large numbers of Macedonians (Yugoslav sources allege over 5,000) were interned from the border regions with Yugoslavia, and night schools were opened to teach adult Slavs the Greek language.[33] The Macedonian PEN organisation in Skopje claims that in this period the use of the Macedonian language was forbidden not only in the street but also in the family, and detailed the penalties—for 'every Macedonian word uttered publicly or in the confines of the family, punishments resulted...the forced eating of salted fish, monetary fines, the drinking of castor oil, the plucking of moustaches and imprisonment' and even 'piercing of the tongue with a needle and cutting off part of the ears'.[34] Despite the repression the inhabitants continued to use the Slav language, and a grammar of the Macedonian language was even written in the detention camp on Akronapvlia.[35]

30 Türkkaya Ataöv, 'Macedonia in Cophenhagen', in *Review of International Affairs*, 5-20 August 1990. *Abecedar* was reprinted in 1993 by the Macedonian Information Centre in Perth, Western Australia.
31 Macedonian PEN Newsletter, Skopje, May 1986.
32 Andonovski' *op. cit.,* p. 198-9, and *Petition* to the Conference on Human Rights in Denmark by 'Dignity organization, Skopje (no date).
33 *Istorijata na Makedonskiot Narod*, Kniga III, published ny NIP Nova Makedonija, Skopje, 1969, p. 271-5.
34 Macedonian PEN Newsletter, *op. cit.*
35 *Ibid.*

Yugoslavia

In the kingdom of Serbs, Croats and Slovenes, Serbian was compulsory in schools and for official purposes in both Macedonia (referred to as South Serbia) and Kosovo. The Macedonians (or Bulgarians) were not recognised and Serbianisation of the population was attempted. In September 1920 the unification of the new state's Orthodox churches was proclaimed and henceforth the Vardar Macedonian Orthodox community fell firmly under the jurisdiction of the Serbian Orthodox Church—the Istanbul Patriarchate was prepared to sell out its control for a payment of 800,000 francs on 19 September 1919.[36]

The restoration in 1918 of the rule of Serbia (which now included the Strumica district which Bulgaria lost due to having backed the losing side in the war) saw a re-run of the immediate post-Balkan war period. Once more Bulgarian clergy and teachers were ousted, all Bulgarian signs and books removed, societies closed etc. Names were once more compulsorily Serbianised and there was the inevitable wave of repression although this time there appear to have been fewer killings, the authorities preferring arrest, detention and internment. Mihaylov claims in his memoirs that in 1918-24 there were 342 killings, forty-seven disappearances and 2,900 political arrests—with the Kratovo area especially affected with sixty-two killings, six disappearances and more than 1,100 arrests.[37]

Albanians. The situation of the ethnic Albanians of Macedonia is intimately connected with events in Kosovo. The first Yugoslav state was from its inception bitterly hostile to ethnic Albanians. Yugoslavia of course literally means 'land of the south Slavs' and thus while the Slav Macedonians were not included in the initial formulation of the 'kingdom of Serbs, Croats and Slovenes', they at least were south Slavs, whereas the more numerous Albanians of course were not. The Serbs in particular harboured bitter recent memories of Albanian attacks on them during their epic retreat in the First World War over the mountains of Montenegro and Albania to Corfu, as well as intense rivalry over possession of Kosovo—the Serbian 'Jerusalem'. The second Serb occupation of

36 Banac, *op. cit.,* p. 221.
37 Mihaylov, *op. cit.,* p. 680.

Kosovo and the Albanian inhabited provinces of western Vardar Macedonia was as brutal as that of 1912-13. Irregular Serbian troops, the Četniks, were created to keep the majority Albanian population down and an estimated 40,000 Orthodox Slav peasants (mostly Serb-Montenegrins) were moved into Kosovo and given good land and benefits, while over half a million ethnic Albanians were forced to emigrate from the region.

Like Kosovo, Vardar Macedonia was also seen as ripe for Serb settlement and colonisation, and the authorities hoped for 50,000 families to move in. In the event only 4,200 had been placed in 280 colonies by 1940.[38] While Serb speculators bought land and in many ways extended the Ottoman system of owner-peasant relationships, and the state systematically undercut local agricultural earnings, Slav Macedonians moved out in large numbers—26,000 in 1938 alone.[39]

All schools now officially promoted Serbian in place of Albanian, Bulgarian or the local dialects. After 1918 all Albanian schools (with the exception of the Great Medresse of King Aleksandar in Skopje, which was opened in 1924 and used Albanian as a medium of instruction) were shut down in the 'southern regions' (i.e. Kosovo and western Macedonia). Assimilation through Serbian education was the policy, and the predominantly Muslim religious schools, known as 'Turkish' schools, were seen as useful in keeping the Albanians in a state of ignorance until this could be achieved. As Banac notes, this policy proved a failure, and despite an appalling illiteracy rate of 90 per cent, the Albanians embarked on self-education and even the Skopje *medresse* founded to train loyal Albanian imams with a carefully screened intake became a centre of nationalist activity.[40] Albanian landholdings in the Šar Planina, as in Kosovo, were restricted to 0.16 acre per household member unless ownership could be proved. The clear aim of the authorities

38 Banac, *op. cit.,* p. 320.
39 *Ibid.* E.g. the purchase prices of agricultural products subject to state monopolies like opium, silk and tobacco were systematically reduced while the export prices fell less far. The new Serb business speculators however, arranged tax-free status for their new estates. One such colonists was Milan Stojadinovic, Minister of Finance for much of the post-1922 period and Prime Minister in 1935-9 who bought, in association with a group of business associates, over 7,00 acress of land including all of Kruševica village in the wine-growing district of Tikveš.
40 *Ibid.,* pp. 298-9. The official line was summed up in a Ministry of Foreign Affairs document of 1929, which stated that there were no national minorities in 'our southern regions'.

was either to assimilate the Albanians or persuade them to emigrate, which many did, mainly to Turkey.

While the Society for the Preservation of Muslim Rights (*Cemiyet*) legally represented the Muslim Albanians and Turks, it was largely controlled by the small Muslim landowning élite. For ordinary Albanians in both Kosovo and Vardar Macedonia, armed resistance was the norm. From the start, armed Albanian bands reacted to Serbian efforts to disarm them and impose control, and in Macedonia and Kosovo they attacked government offices and trains and stole cattle. In 1918 some 10,000 cattle were stolen in the Debar area alone and Albanian fighters, *kaçaks*, were active around Ohrid and Bitola.[41]

VMRO. Since both Albanians and Slav Macedonians were faced with the same state-sponsored repressive assimilation policies, there was naturally much in common with their positions, and in 1920 Protogerov for VMRO and Hasan Bej Prishtina for the Albanians signed an agreement for the 'liberation of Macedonia in her ethnographic and geographical frontiers' with only Debar to be decided by a future plebiscite.[42]

The alienation of the Slav Macedonians from the new state was shown by their rejection of the mainstream parties and the large protest vote for the Communists working for the overthrow of the existing system. In reality VMRO remained among the most potent forces in Vardar Macedonia, if not the most potent. In 1923 it commanded 1,675 active *komitas* and its main zone of operations was the east bank of the Vardar—the west bank, leading into Albanian-dominated territory, remained mostly outside its control; a central zone stretched from Tetovo to Kyustendil in Bulgaria and Radoviš, while a southern zone operating from Bitola to Pirin oversaw operations in Greece.[43] According to Yugoslav sources of the years 1919-34 there were 467 attacks by VMRO

41 Banac, *op. cit.*, p. 303 in a footnote, cites a report of 31 October 1918 in Bogumil Hrabak, 'Reokupacija oblasti srpske i crnogorske države s arbanaškom većinom stanovištva u jesen 1918. godine i držanje Arbansa prema uspostavljenoj vlasti', *Gjurmine albanologjike*, 1969, no. 2, pp. 268, 278, 267-9, 271.
42 Ivan Mihaylov, *Spomeni*, vol. 2, p. 159.
43 Ivan Katardžiev, *Vreme na zreenje: Makedonskoto nacionalno prašanje meǵu dvete svetski vojni (1919-1930)*, vol. 1, Skopje, 1977, pp. 176-7 and 203, quoted in Banac, *op. cit.*, p. 322.

activists in which 185 Yugoslav officials were killed and 235 wounded, and 268 civilians were similarly killed or wounded by VMRO actions; VMRO casualties were 128 dead, thirteen wounded and 151 arrested in the same period.[44] The most pronounced outrages by VMRO in this period were the massacre in January 1923 of some thirty Serb settlers in the Ovče Polje region with the object of scaring other settlers out of Macedonia, and the killings of Spasoje Hadži Popović, a Serb newspaper director in Bitola, in 1926 and of General Mihailo Kovačević in 1927 in Štip.[45] Violent Serb counter-measures like the killing of all males from Garvan (Radoviš) village in March 1923 and the excesses of the Association Against Bulgar Bandits, founded in 1922 in Štip, tended merely to cement local support for VMRO.

However, in the 1930s there was something of a change. With VMRO's effectiveness severely curtailed by the clampdown on it within Bulgaria and its degeneration into mere gangsterism, it began to lose its support among the young in Vardar Macedonia. A clearer call was heard for separate Macedonian recognition within Yugoslavia, which Tito was to build upon so skilfully after the Second World War. As an official Serbian report to Prime Minister Stojadinović stated in May 1938,

....[the] liquidation of the Bulgar revolutionary committee [VMRO], our good relations with Bulgaria, and finally our relations with Italy and Austria (ending their aid to Croat separatism)—all of that contributed to a certain reorientation of Macedonians, who are manifesting [preferences for] a reformed autonomy without conspiracies, or rather Macedonia for Macedonians...
[Their] slogan is: come to the parliament in the greatest possible numbers regardless of party, and fight there for separatism within the frontiers of Yugoslavia.[46]

However, this can be overstressed. Many Slavs in Vardar Macedonia, perhaps the majority, still harboured Bulgarian consciousness

44 Aleksandar Apostolov, 'Specifičnata, položba na makedonskiot narod vo kralstvoto Jugoslavija', *Institut za nacionalna istorija: Glasnik*, vol. 16 (1972), p. 55, in Banac, op. cit., p 323.
45 Banac, *op. cit.*, p. 323, using Mihailov (p. 141) and Apostolov (p 56) as sources.
46 Cited in Aleksandar Apostolov, 'Manifestacije makedonske nacionalne individualnosti u Kraljevini Jugoslaviji', *Jugoslovenski istorijsku časopis*, 1970, nos 3-4, p. 84, in Banac, *op. cit.*, p. 327.

and this once again came to the fore in the Second World War in the initial period of the Bulgarian occupation.

Vlachs. Studies in the 1930s recorded 3–4,000 Vlachs in Bitola, 2–3,000 in Skopje and 1,500 in Kruševo which at the time was predominately Vlach, but recent studies, especially those by Jovan Trifonoski, show a pattern of gradual assimilation. Using the Ovče Polje area in the east of Vardar Macedonia as a case study[47] he shows how the Vlachs there originated from Gramos on the border between Greece and Albania but emigrated to Macedonia at end of the eighteenth century to escape the tyranny of Ali Pasha of Janjina. They were nomadic cattle-breeders and maintained an extended family under a dominant headman, summering in the mountains of Osgovo, Pljačkovica and Ogražden, and wintering in the plains of Strumica, Kočani, Ovče Polje and as far as Salonika. After the First World War, the disintegration of the old Turkish estates and the narrowing down of pastures induced a shift from nomadic flocks to farming. A gradual assimilation into the Slavic majority took place, aided by the shared Orthodox religion. Even in 1938 it was noted that nomadic Vlachs living in the Ogražden mountains, including the women, could speak Slav well and some children were attending schools.

The Comintern

In view of the importance of Communism in the Balkans during and after the Second World War, one should look briefly at the twists and turns of the policy of the Comintern—the international Communist movement orchestrated from Moscow—towards Macedonia and the 'Macedonian Question'. The initial euphoria of Lenin and his compatriots after the successful Bolshevik coup and their expectation of imminent world revolution soon faded. Thus, while it was still held that questions like that of Macedonia—concerning nationality—were products of the 'bourgeois' order and that their importance would recede and eventually disappear after the advent of Communism, it became

---

47 For a recap of Dr Trifunoski's findings in Ovče Polje and other references see Dragoslav Antonijević, 'Tzintzari in Ovče Polje in S.R. Macedonia' in *Balkanica*, V, Belgrade, 1975.

more apparent that the 'bourgeois' order was going to last longer than had at first been expected. However, in line with Lenin's nationality policy which saw national liberation movements as natural allies against advanced capitalism and imperialism, the Comintern viewed the obvious dissatisfaction with the post-1918 political set-up felt by large sections of the population in all parts of Macedonia as a tool to help bring about the desired end—revolution. The new Yugoslav state was seen as a creation by the Western imperialist forces, and the obvious discontents of the Croats and others like the Slav Macedonians were seen as potentially useful. In line with this the Comintern was revisionist regarding Yugoslavia's borders and it specifically called for an independent united Macedonia. However, it took some time for this policy to be firmly impressed on the local parties in Bulgaria, Greece and Yugoslavia (Albania did not even have a Communist party at this time).

As the new regime in the Soviet Union stabilised and it became clear with the overthrow of Bela Kun's regime in Hungary and the defeat of the Red Army in Poland that attempts to export the revolution would prove premature, the Comintern became more and more dominated by the successful Russians and became an adjunct of Soviet foreign policy. While this process became completely cemented by Stalin after his rise to power in the late 1920s, it was evident even before that. For the Slav Balkan countries and Macedonia this was not as problematic as in other places where anti-Russian feeling was endemic (e.g. Poland). The south Slavs, especially the Orthodox, had historically looked to Russia as the Orthodox Slav Great Power. Pro-Russian feeling was evident among many, especially in places like Montenegro.

In the initial period, however, the discipline was not so strong and in the new Yugoslav state the Communist Party, which grew out of Serbian Social Democratic currents, ignored the national question at the start. Despite this its greatest success in the November 1920 elections came in Macedonia, Kosovo and Montenegro. In Macedonia it won 36.72 per cent of all votes cast, with especial success in the districts of Kumanovo, Skopje and Tikveš where it polled respectively 44 per cent, 44.11 per cent and 45.9 per cent of the vote. This seems to have had nothing to do with its policy (or lack of it) on the national question and everything to do with the discontent of the local population with the new set-up. Denied the possibility of voting for a national party (which the Croats for example could and did do) the voters went for the avowed revolutionary option of the Communists. The head of the party in Skopje was a Serb, Dušan Čekić, who had moved there from Leskovac after the Balkan wars. He supported an autonomous Macedonia within a Balkan federation; this was also the Comintern line, but that fact did not seem to have been a determining factor.[48]

At the Unification Congress of the Communist Party of Yugoslavia (KPJ)[49] the national question was alluded to in just one sentence. The party favoured 'a single national state with the widest self-government in the regions, districts and communes' while at the Vukovar Congress it was briefly mentioned that 'the KPJ will further remain the bulwark of the idea of national oneness [*nacionalno jedinstvo*] and equality of all nationalities in the country.'[50] Thus the national question was not seen initially by the KPJ as meriting any great attention, but was viewed rather as something which had bedevilled the Habsburg monarchy but would not be as important in the new Yugoslav state. As Banac points out, the KPJ at first had a similar view to the arch Serb unitarist, Svetozar Pribičević, denying separate nationhood for the different Slav peoples in Yugoslavia and insisting on national unity (*narodno jedinstvo*) based on a common (in practice, Serb) nationhood. The KPJ believed that with the advent of socialism the 'tribal' idiosyncrasies of different national characteristics among the Yugoslavs would disappear.[51] The first head of the new Communist Party, Filip Filipović, while grudgingly admitting to the 'assertion' that Serbs, Croats and Slovenes were different people, would not accept the same for the Slav Macedonians and the

---

48 Banac, *op. cit.*, p. 321.

49 The party was actually called the Socialist Workers' Party of Yugoslavia (Communist) until June 1920.

50 *Istorijski arhiv Komunistiške partije Jugoslavije, vol. 2: Kongresi i zemaljske konferencije KPJ, 1919-1937*, Belgrade, 1949, pp. 14 and 42 respectively. While the phrasing of the second quote at first sight bears striking similarities to Tito's later espoused policies, Lukač stated firmly that 'The phrase "all nationalities" means the equality between the Yugoslavs on one hand and the Hungarians, Albanians, Germans and other ethnic groups on the other.'—*Radnički pokret*, quoted in Banac, *op. cit.*, p. 333.

51 Banac, *op. cit.*, p. 335.

Montenegrins; he denied that they were nations and stated that to recognise them would be unpopular.[52] Thus the KPJ initially ignored the national question. Instead, buoyed up by Lenin's success in Russia, it displayed over-confidence both in its own strength and in the strength of the international Communist movement, and went for open confrontation. This led to government repression, and after some members without authorisation killed the former Minister of the Interior and attempted to assassinate Regent Aleksandar on 2 August 1921, the authorities clamped down on its activity with a vengeance and the organisation was almost completely smashed. Within three years its membership was down to a mere 688 activists for the whole country—less than 2 per cent of the membership in 1920.[53] Following this débâcle, the party slowly regained ground and at the same time the Comintern's control was strengthening. The national question was now to the fore, and thus the concept of an independent autonomous Macedonia within a Balkan federation was the official line. Not unsurprisingly, this policy was unpopular with many Serbs. Similarly in Greece, where there was not the benefit of pro-Russian Slavic solidarity, such a revisionist policy was seen by many as anti-national and thus treacherous, and this was to be clearly demonstrated in the Greek civil war. In both cases, while it may have been expected to gain support from Slav Macedonians in both Yugoslavia and Greece, in fact, as we have already seen, VMRO was seen by those sections of the population as more attractive.

Bulgaria of course was also for the most of this period revisionist, and thus the Communist line could possibly have appealed more to Bulgarians than to Serbs or Greeks. However, as noted above, the Bulgarian Communist Party—like the KPJ—initially viewed the 'Macedonian Question' as a bourgeois problem. Later, while there were links and agreements between the Communists and the Macedonians, the population of Pirin remained firmly under VMRO control. The Comintern attempted the methods (which Stalin's acolytes were to use so skilfully after the Second World War) of infiltrating and splitting VMRO by setting up VMRO-ob

52 Nikola Grulović, 'Jugoslovenska komunistićka revolucionarna grupa 'Pelagić', *Matica srpska Zbornik za društvene nauke*, vol. 22 (1959), p. 116, quoted in Banac, *op. cit.*, pp. 335-6.
53 See Paul Shoup, *op. cit.*

as a Communist-controlled rival under Vlahov. By now the Stalinist formulation that a 'nation is not merely a historical category but a historical category belonging to a definite epoch, the epoch of rising capitalism' was the Communist orthodoxy. Vlahov records the 1934 Comintern thinking on the 'Macedonian Question':

> I mentioned earlier that the Comintern itself wanted the Mace-
> donian question considered at one of the consultations of its
> executive committee. One day I was informed that the consult-
> ation would be held. And so it was. Before it convened, the inner
> leadership of the committee had already reached its stand, includ-
> ing the question of the Macedonian nation, ... It was concluded
> that the Macedonian nation exists.[54]

The Bulgarian Communists had reservations about this procedure and feared that many Macedonian militants would defect to the 'Macedonian fascists' (VMRO). In fact some like Vasil Hadzhi Kimov did, thus illustrating how unsure Bulgarians as well as Serbs and Greeks were of the Comintern line, which is now blamed by all sections of Bulgarian mainstream political opinion for 'inventing' the whole idea of a Macedonian nation.

However, Yugoslavia was the arena where debate and action were perhaps most fierce in the late 1920s. Comintern policy at that time called for the complete break-up of Yugoslavia, and in this the 'Macedonian Question' was merely one aspect along with calls for independence for Croatia and Slovenia. The rise of Hitler changed all this. While Vlahov mentions in 1934 the decision by the Comintern to recognise a Macedonian nation, this was already to some extent a thing of the past. Hitler's Germany was now the leading revisionist power in Europe, and this new threat gave rise to a change in Comintern policy to that of the Popular Fronts. This entailed a scaling down of hostility towards the West and their allies and calls for the break-up of Yugoslavia and the truncation of Greece by the separation of Aegean Macedonia and Thrace. In Greece the Communist Party (KKE) gratefully adopted a new resolution in 1935 whereby the slogan 'a united

54 Dimitar Vlahov, *Memoari*, Skopje, 1970, p. 357. Vlahov states that the resolution
    was done by a Pole who knew nothing of the intricacies of the whole problem.
    This, along with the statement that 'the inner leadership had already reached a
    stand,' gives an illuminating illustration of how the Comintern functioned under
    Stalin's dominance. Banac, *op. cit.,* p. 328.

and independent Macedonia' was changed to 'complete equality for the minorities', the Stalinist principle of 'self-determination' of national minorities was reaffirmed and the 'definite' solution to the Macedonian question was left until 'after the victory of Soviet power in the Balkans'.[55] With Tito's rise to leadership of the KPJ in 1937 there was a further change: to the adoption of a federalist solution for Yugoslavia—one which would include Macedonia.

55 Alekos Papapanagiotou interview in *Anti*, Athens, 19 June 1981, p. 35; Pavlos Nefeloudis, *Stis Piges tis Kakodaimonias*, 2nd ed, Athens, 1974, pp. 93-7; texts in KKE, *Deka Chronia Agones*, Athens 1945, pp. 45, 75, 76. All cited in Evangelos Kofos, *The Impact of the Macedonian Question on Civil Conflict in Greece (1943-1949)*, Athens, 1989, p. 5.

6

WAR AND CIVIL WAR

From uneasy neutrality to war

In the initial phase of the Second World War, the three states which were the main actors in the unfolding Macedonian drama— Bulgaria, Yugoslavia and Greece (Albania was by this time under the control of Mussolini's Italy)—attempted to remain neutral. All were under pressure from the two opposing sides in the conflict, each seeking to recruit them as allies. Bulgaria, as we have seen, was the one state with strong irredentist feelings over the perceived loss of Macedonia. Mussolini made the first move with his self-aggrandising invasion of Greece from Albania in November 1940, which Metaxas's troops easily repulsed. By early December the Greeks had humiliated the Italian troops and moved into southern Albania itself. An embarrassed Mussolini turned to Hitler for support. Hitler had already decided on Operation 'Marita' to send troops into Romania and Greece to forestall any attempt at an Allied landing in the Balkans which could threaten his coming campaign against the Soviet Union.[1] Thus by the end of 1940 King Boris of Bulgaria had effectively run out of room for manoeuvre and the Bulgarians were being forced into the Axis camp under extreme German pressure.

Bulgaria of course wanted Macedonia in return, but Hitler could not promise Yugoslav Macedonia to Bulgaria while he was still putting pressure on the Yugoslav government to join his camp. However, the 27 March 1941 coup in Belgrade changed all this and provoked Hitler to launch a *Blitzkrieg*, in the face

1 Crampton, *op. cit.* p 124.

100

of which the first Yugoslav state rapidly collapsed. Nazi efficiency proved too much for Greece also and Macedonia was once again carved up between the new victors. The Bulgarians, while getting the lion's share of Vardar Macedonia, eastern Aegean Macedonia and Thrace, and a small part of western Aegean Macedonia, was not however allowed to have any of the Macedonian coast: the Germans controlled Salonika and the Italians the rest.

Vardar and Pirin Macedonia

Despite the slight change of attitude among some sections of the younger generation in the late 1930s—reflected in the slogan 'Macedonia for the Macedonians' (within the Yugoslav state)—anti-Serbian and pro-Bulgarian sentiment still prevailed. Even 'Macedonia for the Macedonians' signalled in many ways an acceptance of the state of Yugoslavia and an attempt to gain autonomy within it. The collapse of the state changed all this. There is little doubt that the initial reaction among large sections of the population of Vardar Macedonia who had suffered so much under the Serbian repression was to greet the Bulgarians as liberators. While Hitler did not allow the Bulgarians formally to annex the parts they now controlled, and the new border between the Italian and Bulgarian controlled portions was not defined, leading to periodic tensions between the two, Bulgaria was given a free hand in the areas which it controlled.

At first Bulgaria pursued policies, especially in education, which the population welcomed. More than 800 new schools were built and a university was established in Skopje.[2] However the honeymoon period did not last long as the Bulgarians soon fell into the old Balkan trap of centralisation. The new provinces were quickly staffed with officials from Bulgaria proper who behaved with typical official arrogance towards the local inhabitants. In March 1942 the central government in Sofia took absolute control over the new territories, ushering in the classic Balkan governmental vices of bureaucracy and corruption which further alienated the population. Particularly insensitive, in view of the long and close association in the Balkans between religion and nationality, was the influx of Bulgarian Orthodox bishops who

2   Crampton, *op. cit.*, p. 125.

displayed the same negative features as the government bureaucrats. The result was resentment and the growth of autonomist feelings.[3]

Tito and the Partisans. Tito had taken over the helm of the KPJ in 1937 and espoused the line that Macedonia should exist within a federal Yugoslavia. The attractions of the initial Bulgarian occupation is shown by the local Communist cadres led by Metodi Shatorov who tended to view it as natural and looked to the Bulgarian Communist Party (BCP)—which, after being banned, resurfaced in 1927 as the Bulgarian Workers' Party (Communist) or BWP(C)—in preference to the KPJ. As such, while they still saw the Bulgarian authorities as 'bourgeois-fascists', they tended not to see them as foreign occupiers. Even staunch KPJ supporters admitted that in May 1941 the Yugoslav Macedonian party attempted to unite with the BWP(C).[4] The Comintern, on the other hand, favoured the KPJ over the BCP in Vardar Macedonia.[5]

Resentment against the Italians and the Bulgarians led to a number of uprisings in 1942 and to certain areas being temporarily liberated. By 1943, the local resentment against the Bulgarians was such that Tito turned his attention to Macedonia and sent his dynamic trouble-shooter Svetozar Vukmanović-Tempo to the area to start organising for a Macedonia under Tito's Communist auspices. Tempo was also entrusted with the task of making contact with the Greek Communists and with contacting and aiding the fledgling Albanian Communist movement. Tito's aim seems already to have been a united Slav Macedonia—not merely the pre-war Yugoslav section—under his control. However, the time was not yet ripe for Tempo's dynamism and he was brought back in September 1943.[6]

While a communiqué from the Macedonian Communist command of October 1942 did mention the Macedonian nation,[7]

3   *Ibid.*
4   Mihailo Apostolski, 'The Antifascist Council for the National Liberation of Yugoslavia and the Macedonian Question', *Contemporary Macedonian Statehood*, Skopje, 1994.
5   Stevan K. Pavlowitch, *Tito: Yugoslavia's Great Dictator*, London, 1992, p. 42.
6   For his own detailed account of his Balkan trouble-shooting for Tito; see Vulkmanović-Tempo, *Borba sa Balkanot*, Skopje, 1982 (or published in Serbo-Croat under title *Borba za Balkan*, Zagreb, 1981).
7   It began with 'The Macedonian nation, which cannot endure the fascist slavery, arranges itself in wide ranks alongside the peoples of Yugoslavia and all other

the first Congress of the Anti-Fascist Council for the National Liberation of Yugoslavia (AVNOJ) held at Bihać on 26 and 27 November 1942 did not specifically mention the Macedonians. However, the crucial step was taken at the second AVNOJ congress in Jajce on 29 November 1943. Here the Macedonian nation was affirmed and given status equal to that of the other five federal units: Serbia, Croatia, Slovenia, Montenegro and Bosnia-Hercegovina. However this equality was at this stage still somewhat qualified. As Barker points out,[8] Macedonia was not at Jajce given any wider autonomy than Bosnia-Hercegovina, and it only had a Central National Liberation Committee while the other units already had full-blown Anti-Fascist Councils of National Liberation. Moreover, perhaps showing the weakness of the KPJ in Macedonia at this time, Macedonians were thinly represented on the central bodies of AVNOJ—there was not one on the seventeen-member supreme executive body or provisional government (the National Liberation Committee). Dimitâr Vlahov—the old Comintern VMRO-ob leader, who had by now abandoned his previous line of advocating an independent Macedonia in a Balkan federation and thrown in his lot with Tito—was one of the five vice-presidents. On the 556-member central Anti-Fascist Council in 1943 there were only three Macedonians: Metodije Antonov-Chento, Vladimir Poptomorov and Mihajlo Apostolski.

The weakness of the KPJ in Macedonia compared with the BCP is amply shown by the subsequent fate of the first two. In August 1944 Chento became president of the newly-formed Anti-Fascist Assembly of National Liberation of Macedonia (ASNOM)—Macedonia had by now joined the ranks of the other five federal units in the formal struggle. However, he resigned from the government in the summer of 1946, having been caught reportedly trying to cross to Greece in order to call for an independent Macedonia at the Paris Peace Conference, and was sentenced to eleven years' hard labour. Poptomorov showed his more 'supremacist' Bulgarian sympathies by going to Bulgaria in 1944 and becoming the country's Foreign Minister in August 1949.[9] Thus for Tito there was a real problem of reliability at

---

enslaved peoples, in order to fight together with them for the destruction of that great enemy of freedom—German-Italian fascism and its faithful servants, the Bulgarian fascists.' Quoted in Apostolski, *op. cit.*, p. 22.

8 Barker, *op. cit.*, pp. 94-5.

the top of the Macedonian party—this was not helped by the fact that at this time one of the leading young loyal Titoist cadres, Lazar Kolishevski, was in detention.

Meanwhile on the world stage the tide of the war was beginning to turn and after Stalingrad it became ever more evident that the Allies were going to win. Partisan activity was stepped up in 1943, and this increase also saw the formation of new brigades in Macedonia, especially Vardar Macedonia where Tempo was gaining more success in mobilising support for the KPJ and liberating territories. However, as in other parts of Yugoslavia, the main priorities for the Germans were keeping control of the main communication axis of Belgrade-Niš-Skopje-Salonika; fighting over barren hills in Macedonia was much less urgent. Still, the propaganda value of liberating areas under Communist control was high, as was that of fighting on what was now clearly the winning side.

Defections began from Bulgarian army units, and Bulgarian partisan groups were also set up but their numbers and activity were small compared to that of the Yugoslav and Greek partisans. The highest estimate for the number of partisans active at any one time in Bulgaria was 18,000, mostly concentrated around Plovdiv, Varna and Burgas.[10] There were however some partisan forces fighting in Pirin. On 1 May 1943 the 'Yane Sandanski' brigade was formed under Krum Radinov and in the spring and summer of 1943 there were armed actions around Gorna Dzhumaya (Blagoevgrad). On 7 November they managed to free prisoners from a detention camp near Hârsovo village.[11] This was all relatively small-scale, and the partisan movement in Pirin suffered from the death of two of its leaders there—Nikola Parupanov on 9 December 1943 and Arso Pandurski on 27 January 1944. At the end of 1942, the BCP had begun to try to form Fatherland Front organisations—the Communist-dominated front—in Pirin, but Yugoslav sources state that these were unpopular as they were seen as being too pro-Bulgarian in their orientation.[12]

This again raises the issue of the relations between the Yugoslav and Bulgarian Communists over Macedonia. As we have seen, in the initial stages of the war the Bulgarian Party appeared to

9   Barker, *op. cit.*, p. 101, and footnote to p. 95.
10 Crampton, *op. cit.*, p. 129.
11 *Istorija na Makedonskiot Narod*, vol. III, Skopje, 1969, p. 373.
12 *Ibid.*, p. 374.

have the stronger hand, and the local Vardar Communists tended to look to the Bulgarian rather than to the Yugoslav party. However, over this issue the Comintern had supported the KPJ. The Bulgarian Communist leader and figurehead of the Comintern, Georgi Dimitrov, both of whose parents were from Macedonia, was somewhat atypical of Bulgarian Communists over the 'Macedonian Question'. Also, as the war progressed the prestige of Tito and his troops steadily grew and the Bulgarian Communists certainly suffered from something of an inferiority complex over their efforts in the partisan struggle compared to the successes of the former. It was becoming ever more apparent that Tito was the Communist force in the Balkans, and his lieutenant Vukmanović-Tempo was increasingly active in helping to organise fellow parties in the whole region—so much so that for example the Albanian Communist Party was little more than an appendage of the KPJ at this time.

As regards Vardar Macedonia, while the movement there lagged behind other parts of Yugoslavia, by mid-1944 Tito was confident enough to set up ASNOM. On the symbolic date of 2 August (Ilinden) 1944, the first ASNOM assembly was convened at the Prohor Pčinski monastery. This proclaimed 'Macedonia as a federal state in the new Democratic Federation of Yugoslavia' and issued a 'manifesto' which described its position under the old Yugoslavia as that of a colony and then went on to proclaim, in what was to become standard Titoist phraseology, the brotherhood with the other peoples of Yugoslavia. The manifesto also stated that it stood for equality for all the nationalities in Macedonia and called on Albanians, Turks and Vlachs to join the national liberation struggle.[13] A crucial decision by ASNOM was the introduction by a special resolution to make Macedonian the official language of the 'federal state'.[14] But what was the 'federal state' to be? The manifesto made this clear:

Macedonians under Bulgaria and Greece!
The unification of the entire Macedonian people depends on

13 *ASNOM: A Collection of Documents*, Skopje, 1964, referred to in Alexander Hristov, 'The Construction of Macedonia as a State in the Yugoslav Federation', in *Contemporary Macedonian Statehood, op. cit.* The absence of any mention of the Roma is noticeable especially in comparison to current statements by President Gligorov.

14 *Ibid.*

your participation in the gigantic anti–Fascist front. Only by fighting the vile Fascist occupier will you gain your right to self-determination and to unification of the entire Macedonian people within the framework of Tito's Yugoslavia, which has become a free community of emancipated and equal peoples. May the struggle of the Macedonian Piedmont incite you to even bolder combat against the Fascist oppressors![15]

A proclamation of 4 August 1944 was even more explicit:

People of Macedonia!
In the course of three years of combat you have achieved your unity, developed your army and laid the basis for the federal Macedonian state. With the participation of the entire Macedonian nation in the struggle against the Fascist occupiers of Yugoslavia, Bulgaria and Greece you will achieve unification of all parts of Macedonia, divided in 1915 and 1918 by Balkan imperialists.[16]

Thus the Tito line had become more ambitious. Flushed with success, he had moved on from the minimal programme of the late 1930s for a Vardar Macedonia within a federal Yugoslavia, and now saw a united Macedonia within the new Yugoslavia under his control. This new federal state was also to include Bulgaria and probably Albania—where the Communists, who were very much under Tito's shadow, were the main force ready to take over after the collapse of the Axis powers—and even Greece as well.

It is clear that despite the Stalinist formulation of national self-determination up to and including the right to secession (although in reality this was empty verbiage as long as the Communist Party wielded the real power), Tito, though still at that time a faithful Stalinist, was not prepared to go as far as the Soviet formulation for the new Yugoslavia.[17] From the start of the post-war Yugoslav state, constitutions were carefully worded so that while the 'right to self-determination, including the right to secession'

15 *Documents on the struggle of the Macedonian people for independence and a nation-state,* vol. II, Skopje, 1985, quoted in *Memorandum of Greece concerning the application of the former Yugoslav Republic of Macedonia for admission to the United Nations,* Hellenic Foundation for Defence and Foreign Policy, 25 January 1993.
16 *Ibid.*
17 Milovan Djilas, then one of Tito's closest collaborators, spells this out in his book *Vlast.*

of each of the 'nations of Yugoslavia' was mentioned, it was asserted that during the Second World War these nations had united 'on the basis of their will freely expressed'. This meant that constitutionally the 'nations' had made a decision that was binding for all time, and the right of secession no longer applied. Thus the new Macedonia was seen clearly as remaining under Tito's control.

Dimitrov was receptive to the proposed plan of unifying the constituent parts of Macedonia, and signed the Bled agreement of August 1947 between Yugoslavia and Bulgaria which was tantamount to union of Pirin with Vardar Macedonia. The agreement abolished entry visas and envisaged a customs union. However, Dimitrov opposed immediate formal union until after the proposed Yugoslav-Bulgarian federation had been realised.[18] This proved something of a stumbling block as Tito wanted Bulgaria to join on a basis of equality with the other constituent republics of Yugoslavia (e.g. Serbia) while the Bulgarians wanted equal status with Yugoslavia. Meanwhile under the Bled agreement there was a flood of communication between Vardar and Pirin Macedonia with the Skopje authorities very much taking the initiative and seizing the opportunities. The Macedonian language as adopted by ASNOM was also to be the official language in Pirin, and to achieve this ninety-three teachers from Yugoslav Macedonia arrived in Pirin and a flood of books arrived. A Macedonian newspaper *Pirinski Vestnik* was published and a 'Macedonian Book' publishing company set up. Additionally there were scholarships for Pirin students to come to Skopje, and a course was attended by 135 teachers from Pirin.[19]

The Stalin-Tito split. The aggressive Yugoslav actions in Pirin caused great unease among many Bulgarians, both Communists and non-Communists. More crucially Tito's obvious ambitions, his general activism and his independence inevitably raised Stalin's suspicions. Communist power in neighbouring Hungary, Romania and Bulgaria was speedily being consolidated, and Stalin floated a number of possible federal options for the new Communist eastern Europe.[20] However, in the famous 'back-of-an-envelope deal' he had promised

18 Barker, *op. cit.*, p. 103.
19 *Ibid.*, p. 104.
20 See Milovan Djilas, *Conversations with Stalin*, London, 1962.

Churchill Greece, and thus was against helping the KKE in the ensuing Greek civil war. Moreover Tito's expansionist aims around Trieste was raising the cautious Stalin's fears of the Soviet Union becoming embroiled in outright hostilities with the West. He decided to bring his overmighty lieutenant to heel.

The Comintern, which had been quietly wound up during in the war, was relaunched as the Cominform and Stalin tried his usual tactics of using this as a proxy to maintain discipline and rein Tito in. The attempt was one of Stalin's major miscalculations and Tito, though temporarily traumatised at being excommunicated by the communist 'church', managed to keep the KPJ behind him despite Stalin's efforts at ousting and replacing him. Thus Tito survived the anathema of June 1948, but the split marked the end of Yugoslav-Bulgarian co-operation and any plans at uniting Vardar and Pirin Macedonia. The death of Georgi Dimitrov in July 1949 further underlined this since future Bulgarian Communist leaders were not at all sympathetic to any manifestation of Macedonian—as distinct from Bulgarian—consciousness.

However, the full-scale cultural assault on Pirin Macedonia by the new authorities in Skopje obviously met with considerable success among the local population, as is made clear by the bitterness of the Bulgarian leaders' speeches after the rapprochement between the two countries had collapsed. Similarly the new authorities in Yugoslav Macedonia suffered defections to Bulgaria and had to resort to considerable repression to control pro-Bulgarian support by arresting and even killing large numbers. This once again highlights the problematic nature of the relationship between Slav Macedonians and Bulgarians.

Aegean Macedonia

The war. The repression by the Metaxas regime against Slav Macedonians was further stepped up after the beginning of the war between Greece and Italy in October 1940, despite the numbers of them fighting loyally in the Greek army. According to Yugoslav sources, some 1,600 Macedonians were interned on the islands of Thasos and Kefallinia (Cephalonia).[21]

It has already been noted that after the defeat of Greece

---

21 *Istorijata na Makedonskiot Narod*, vol. III, Skopje, 1969, p. 274.

by the Axis powers in 1941, Bulgaria occupied the eastern portion of Greek Macedonia, except for Salonika which was occupied by the Germans, and a small part of the western portion. The rest was under the Italians. In their own portions the Bulgarians imported settlers from Bulgaria and acted in such a way that even a German report of the time described their occupation as 'a regime of terror which can only be described as "Balkan"'. In Kavalla alone more than 700 shops and enterprises were expropriated and large numbers of Greeks were expelled or deprived of their right to work by a license system that banned the practice of a trade or profession without permission from the occupying authorities.[22] Many of the Greeks subjected to what is now known as 'ethnic cleansing' had themselves previously been émigrés from Turkey and were now understandably hostile to being once more ruled by a foreign power, and thus bitterly anti-Bulgarian. They also became more violently opposed than ever to the idea of a 'United Macedonia' which, up until the change of line of the Comintern in the mid-1930s to that of the Popular Fronts following Hitler's rise to power, had been the KKE's line. It is thus not surprising that, feeding on this, the non-Communist Greek nationalist forces were unremittingly hostile to any concessions over Macedonia.

While the occupation caused the hostility to Bulgaria among the ethnic Greek population to grow, the Slav-speaking population remained at first split between a pro-Bulgarian wing and a smaller faction which espoused Hellenism even though their mother-tongue was Slav.[23] The post-1935 KKE position was one of equality for minorities in Greece and as such Slavs were allowed into

22 Hans-Joachim Hoppe, 'Bulgarian Nationalities Policies in Occupied Thrace and Aegean Macedonia', *Nationalities Papers*, spring-fall 1986, vol. XIV, no. 1-2, pp. 89-100.

23 See Kofos, *Impact of the Macedonian Question...*, *op. cit.* Just how strong this pro-Hellenic wing of the 'Slavophone' population in Aegean Macedonia actually was remains contentious. However, as is common among people of one ethnic group who actively espouse another, they were somewhat fanatical in their adherence to Hellenism. Some were armed by the anti-Communist National Army and held out against both Bulgarian and ELAS forces in so-called 'village-fortresses of Macedonia'. Again on 2 June 1949, in the 'third round' of the civil war (see below), NOF leader Keramidzhiev complained: 'We had to struggle against the Great Idea chauvinism of many Greek cadres...who were united with the most fanatic anti-Macedonian elements, i.e. Macedonians from villages who said they were Greeks.' Quoted in Kofos, *op. cit.*, p. 21.

the KKE ranks. The 'United Macedonia' line was always unpopular with rank-and-file Greeks, and the KKE flirtation with it was to prove an important factor in the civil war which followed. The Communist-controlled resistance movement, the National Liberation Front (EAM), and its military wing, ELAS, while less dynamic that Tito's partisans, was nevertheless the main force fighting the German occupiers. In 1943 EAM/ELAS tried to organise resistance in Aegean Macedonia. Tito's aide Vukmanović-Tempo, who, as shown above, was very successful in Yugoslav Macedonia, arrived in the summer of 1943 with plans both to curb Bulgarian influence among Slavs in Aegean Macedonia and to push Tito's line. To achieve this, free movement of bands across the border and access for political instructors from Yugoslavia to propagate the Tito Macedonian line were organised. Crucially Tempo called for the setting up of Slav Macedonian military units. This led to the creation of the political organisation SNOF—the Slav National Liberation Front—as well as armed Macedonian Slav partisan units allied to ELAS.

Inevitably there was prolonged resistance from non-Communist Greeks, especially a movement called the 'Protectors of Northern Greece' (YVE), and relations between ELAS and SNOF were strained. However, by the beginning of 1944 Tito's line—pushed energetically by Tempo—of a Slav Macedonian consciousness separate from Bulgaria was beginning to take root so that from now onwards in Greek Macedonia there was a trichotomy between self-identified Greeks, Slav Macedonians and Bulgarians, and Kofos points to the 'considerable opposition in accepting nationalist-minded Slavo-Macedonians into the Greek resistance'.[24] Tempo and others later claimed that EAM/ELAS had agreed in 1943-4 to the secession of Macedonia, but this is contentious.[25] As in Pirin after the war, the new language and alphabet were used, a Macedonian primer was printed, and Macedonian newspapers appeared. Additionally the church liturgy was in Slav Macedonian for the first time since 1913.[26]

By 1944 EAM/ELAS was in the ascendant over its internal

24 Kofos, *op. cit.*, p. 7.
25 Kofos refutes this chapter and verse, see *op. cit.*, p. 38, footnote 22.
26 Newsletter of the Macedonian PEN Centre, Skopje, May 1986. All these concessions were later formally revoked after the treaty of Varkiza in February 1945.

rivals in most of Aegean Macedonia with the exception of some south and east-central parts where Bulgarian or nationalist forces under Anton Tsaous held sway. Here Bulgarian influence remained strong among the Slav populations and the Tito line only really began to impinge in late 1944 when the German withdrawal was imminent.[27] Despite the military success, the KKE position on Macedonia remained torn between the need on the one hand to collaborate with the dynamic Yugoslav partisans and on the other to retain popular Greek support which viewed concessions over Macedonia as little short of treason. As a result KKE policy was confused and went through a succession of changes. In the late spring of 1944 SNOF was shut down by party orders, to be followed three months later with the formation of 'pure' Slav Macedonian units within ELAS under the command of Naum Peyov.[28] Tensions between these units and those of ELAS came to a head in October 1944 and the Slav units were driven out of Greece. On October 30 1944 Salonika was taken by ELAS and the Greek-Yugoslav border was manned by 'loyal' troops—i.e. non-Slavs.[29] Refugees streamed across the border into Yugoslavia, where some were formed into the '1st Aegean Macedonian Brigade' in Bitola, possibly to be used to aid ELAS against the 'imperialist' British.[30]

The Vlach 'Principality'. The rise of fascism in both Italy and Romania led to attempts, especially during the Italian occupation of parts of Greece and western Macedonia during the war, to harness the Vlachs to the fascist cause. To this end, Alcibiades Diamandi, a Vlach extremist, even declared a so-called autonomous 'Principality of the Pindus', consisting of Epirus, Macedonia and all of Thessaly, with himself as prince and a compatriot as head of the 'Roman Legion'—an army of Vlach fascists.[31]

But this was merely a brief interlude in the real struggle between

27 Kofos, *op. cit.*, pp. 11–12.
28 *Ibid.*, p. 10.
29 *Egejska Makedonija vo NOB*, Skopje, 1971–85, vol. I, pp. 520–1, cited in Kofos, *op. cit.*, p. 13.
30 Brigadier Maclean to FO, FO 371/48181, 1 February 1954, in Kofos, *op. cit.*, p. 16.
31 See E. Averoff-Tossizza, *The Call of the Earth*, Caratzas Brothers, New Rochelle, NY, 1981, and review of same by N. Balamaci in *Newsletter of the Society Farsarotul*, vol. II, issue 2, August 1988, pp. 19–22.

Slavs and Greeks, and Communists and non-Communists. After
the end of the war, the new Romanian authorities quietly chose
not to continue financing its schools and churches in Greece
which had been allowed under an agreement with Venizelos officially to allow Romanian schools and churches for Vlachs in
Greece.

Genocide against the Jews. The German military invasion and
Bulgaria's formal entry into the Axis camp brought Macedonia's
Jewish population, especially the large community in Salonika
which was under German control, face to face with Hitler's genocidal policies. Many Jews had earlier sought refuge from intolerance
and persecution in Western Europe in the then more tolerant
Ottoman empire. However, their descendants were now faced
with intolerance from the West of a nakedly genocidal character
and implemented with modern methods of mass extermination
and Teutonic thoroughness.

In Bulgaria proper, the government was pressured as early as
October 1940 to place legal restrictions on the country's Jews
but, in contrast to German Nazi laws, religious rather than racial
criteria were applied. In addition King Boris delayed signing what
was obviously an unpopular law until the end of January 1941.
With the by now inevitable entry of Bulgaria to the Nazi camp,
stiffer legislation followed, including an obligation on Jews to
wear the Star of David, in early 1942. In August a Commissariat
for Jewish Affairs (KEV) was set up in Sofia under Aleksandâr
Belev, to prepare the transfer of Jews to the death camps in
Poland. However massive opposition from prominent Bulgarians
in all walks of life, including the King, parliamentarians and leading
church figures, helped to save the Jews of Bulgaria from deportation
and death and instead they were settled temporarily in the provinces
and assembled in labour camps.[32]

While this defence of the Jews by Bulgarian society in the
face of Nazi pressure was admirable, the treatment of Jews in
Macedonia in areas under Bulgarian control was less so. Here

32 As a result nearly all of Bulgaria's estimated 51,500 Jews survived the war. However
   almost 40,000 emigrated to Israel in the period 1946-56 and the country's Jewish
   population has dwindled to about 5,000 (some say only 3,000) with Sephardic
   Jews still more numerous than Ashkenazim. For Bulgaria's treatment of its
   Jewish population in the Second World War, see Hoppe, *op. cit.*

responsibility for their transfer to Nazi authority and inevitable mass murder rested with KEV, and it appears that despite Bulgarian claims to the contrary, or claims that these transfers were all the work of the Nazis and that the Bulgarian authorities had no hand in the matter, the Jews of Macedonia and Thrace were knowingly transferred to their deaths by the Bulgarians—possibly sacrificed for the sake of the Jews in Bulgaria proper. The investigator into Nazi crimes, Simon Wiesenthal, confirmed on Skopje television in February 1986 that Aleksandâr Belev and Bulgarian ministers who signed documents on the liquidation of the Macedonian Jews in February and March 1943 were included in his list of war criminals.[33]

For the Jews of Salonika under direct German control there was no hope. Deportations began in March 1943. Bulgaria was ordered to provide 20,000 Jews for slave labour of which 8,000 came from Yugoslav Macedonia and 4,000 from Aegean Macedonia and Thrace. This was followed by deportation and extermination of the entire community. The overwhelming majority died in concentration camps in Poland[34] with only some 2,000 returnees for all of Greece to join those who managed to avoid the genocide—some by actively taking part in the Greek resistance movement. Of the total of some 30,000 EAM-ELAS fighters in Greece in 1943, 600-1,000 were Jews.[35] The Jewish population of Greece, which had officially numbered 63,200 in 1928 and was almost entirely Ladino-speaking and concentrated in Salonika, was only 6,325 in 1951. In Yugoslav Macedonia the 1953 census recorded only 55 Jews. While many had emigrated to Israel after the war, as they did from Bulgaria, the huge majority were victims of the holocaust.

33 Tanjug, 20 February 1986, in BBC SWB EE/8190 A1/2, 22 February 1986.
34 Hoppe, *op. cit.*, states that most were deported to Treblinka but according to Bowman, while the initial deportations ended up there, the main ones which followed ended up in Auschwitz. Some question whether Treblinka was actually a final destination. Using newly available wartime reconnaissance photographs of the camp retrieved from the US National Archives in Washington, Mark Weber expressed scepticism regarding the widely held view that Treblinka was a mass extermination camp, and instead postulated that from the visual evidence it was more likely a transit camp—see Marin County Historical Society, California, news release, 7 January 1991. Either way this is a somewhat academic point since thousands were actually murdered.
35 I am indebted to Steve Bowman for this information.

The Greek civil war. The Greek civil war began in earnest (after a brief "First Round" in the winter of 1943/4) in December 1944. It was fought between the Communist-controlled ELAS and non-Communists, supported by Britain and later the United States, and saw the exodus of many Slavs and Greek Communist Party members to Yugoslavia.

The last round of the civil war, which lasted until 1949, saw SNOF reformed as NOF (National Liberation Front) and up to 40 per cent of the Communist forces comprising Slav Macedonians.[36] However the struggle at the top of the KKE between Nikos Zachariades and Markos Vafiadis (who had close links with Tito) which even survived the initial Stalin-Tito break of 1948, which ended in Markos's retirement due to "ill-health" on 31 January 1949 was followed by an attempt by the KKE to set up an anti-Tito NOF. The KKE, of course, sided with the Cominform in the Stalin-Tito split and in the second half of 1948 removed all pro-Tito factions from NOF. As Kofos points out,[37] this at a stroke freed the KKE leadership from both avowed Titoists and extreme nationalists looking to Yugoslav Macedonia. In view of this the next twist in KKE policy must appear somewhat surprising at first sight but surely reflects the dependence of Zachariades and the KKE on the Macedonian contingents at this late stage in the struggle. At the fifth plenum of the KKE in January 1949 Zachariades oversaw the re-introduction of the 1924 Comintern-inspired platform of a united and independent Macedonia within a Balkan federation which had proved so unpopular with rank-and-file Greeks before.

Even former KKE fellow-travellers and sympathisers condemned the new policy, and the government was able to appeal directly to Greek nationalism and portray the Communists not just as class enemies but as national traitors.[38] But the war was by now virtually lost for the Communists and only gestures remained. On 1 March 1949 'Free Greece', the Communist radio station, broadcast the declaration of an Independent United Macedonia which was not recognised by the Soviet Union or its allies and

---

36 Some give a figure as high as 50%—see E. Kofos, *The Impact of the Macedonian Question on Civil Conflicts in Greece, 1943-49*, Hellenic Foundation for Defence and Foreign Policy, Occasional Papers 3, Athens, 1989, pp. 20-2.

37 *Ibid.*, p. 27.

only caused further alarm in the rank-and-file of the KKE. In July 1949 Tito closed the Yugoslav-Greek frontier.

During the Second World War and the ensuing civil war the Slavs of Aegean Macedonia enjoyed language rights such as education in a Slav language, which had been denied them before except for the brief appearance in September 1925 (or rather non-appearance) of the language primer, *Abecedar*, using the Latin script. During the war, as we have seen, the Slavs came more and more to look towards the glamorous success of Tito and his espousal of a Macedonian nation and to turn away somewhat from support for incorporation into Bulgaria—an illustration of the fickleness of self-identification. The newly-arrived Bulgarians unintentionally aided the growth of a separate Macedonian consciousness among Slavs by alienating the local people in Vardar Macedonia. An enduring legacy of this profound shift was the widespread use of the terms 'Macedonia' and 'Macedonian' by the Tito regime to convey concepts which had no connection with Greece. This has caused great offence to Greeks ever since, because of the powerful historical connotations which Macedonia and the term 'Macedonian' have for Greeks, antedating the arrival of Slavs (whoever they may have been) into the area; the terms 'Bulgaria' and 'Bulgarian' of course do not have connotations that are in anyway the same. The apparent appropriation of this name by a Slavic people outside the country was bound to offend Greek sensibilities.[39] Similarly, the use by Yugoslavia of the adjectives 'Vardar' and 'Aegean' to describe the Yugoslav and Greek portions of Macedonia respectively, offended Greeks although the reasoning behind their offence was less apparent.

---

38 The government's emergency legislation (Compulsory Law 509) in June 1946 which provided for court-martials etc., initially only for northern Greece, allowed life imprisonment or execution for either the violent overthrow of the existing order or the detachment of part of the whole of the state. In this way the government clearly tried to tar the KKE with the anti-national brush, but had to wait till the fifth plenum for complete justification of this charge. Kofos, *op. cit.*, p. 23.

39 See Kofos, *The Macedonian Question: the Politics of Mutation*, Institute for Balkan Studies, Salonika, 1987.

7

MACEDONIANS AS THE MAJORITY

Ethnogenesis

Language and education. In Yugoslav Macedonia the new authorities quickly set about consolidating their position. The new nation needed a written language, and initially the spoken dialect of northern Macedonia was chosen as the basis for the Macedonian language. However, this was deemed too close to Serbian and the dialects of Bitola-Veles became the norm.[1] These dialects were closer to the literary language of Bulgaria but because the latter was based on the eastern Bulgarian dialects, it allowed enough differentiation for the Yugoslavs to claim it as a language distinct from Bulgarian—a point which Bulgaria has bitterly contested ever since.[2] In fact the differentiation between the Macedonian and Bulgarian dialects becomes progressively less pronounced on an east-west basis. Macedonian shares nearly all the same distinct characteristics which separate Bulgarian from other Slav languages— lack of cases, the post-positive definite article, replacement of the infinitive form, and preservation of the simple verbal forms for the past and imperfect tenses—but whether it is truly a different language from Bulgarian or merely a dialect of it is a moot point.

The alphabet was accepted on 3 May 1945 and the orthography on 7 June 1945, and the first primer in the new language appeared by 1946, in which year a Macedonian Department in the Faculty of Philosophy at the University of Skopje was also founded.

1 Barker, *op. cit.*
2 The most comprehensive refutation is *Edinstvoto na Bâlgarskiya Ezik b Minaloto i Dnes*, Bulgarian Academy of Sciences, Sofia, 1978.

A grammar of the Macedonian literary language appeared in 1952 and the Institute for the Macedonian Language "Krste P. Misirkov" was founded the following year. Since the Second World War the new republic has used the full weight of the education system and the bureaucracy to make the new language common parlance, and indeed it is noticeable that old people still tend to speak a mixture of dialects which include obvious Serbianisms and Bulgarianisms, while those young enough to have gone through the education system in its entirety speak a 'purer' Macedonian.

In addition to the new language, the new republic needed a history and this was quickly reflected in the new school textbooks. Here again bitter resentment was caused in Bulgaria since the Macedonian historical figures are also claimed by Bulgaria as Bulgarian heroes, e.g. the medieval emperor Samuil whose empire. was centred around lake Ohrid and Gotse Delchev, one of the leaders of the abortive rising of 1903 in Macedonia—Macedonian textbooks even hint at Bulgarian complicity in his death at the hands of the Ottomans.[3]

Such a policy needed careful massaging and concealment. As Bulgarians pointed out, in the museum of the SR Macedonia it was not possible to see original works by the likes of the Miladinov brothers, who had been in the forefront of Slav consciousness in the mid-nineteenth century, and were now claimed to be Macedonian as opposed to Bulgarian: in some of their works they clearly stated that they were Bulgarians. Suitably edited versions in the new language were promoted to boost the new line, and similar methods were used for a host of other leaders in the nineteenth century Bulgarian revival process who came from Macedonia. Similar editing was done on the history of VMRO with, so Bulgarians claimed, unnatural emphasis on the thought and activity of the so-called 'left' autonomist wing, despite its actually being a small minority within VMRO, and its views were now claimed to support a Macedonian nationality separate from the Bulgarians.[4]

3 E.g. *Istorija za VII Oddelenie* (IV Isdanie), Skopje, 1980.
4 The Peshtera committee of VMRO-SMD, the pro-Bulgarian Macedonian organisation in Bulgaria (see Chapter 7), claims that the original documents of the VMRO 'left' show that they supported the unity of the Bulgarian people in Macedonia—letter of Peshtera VMRO-SMD city committee '3rd March', 2 November 1991, signed by Kostadinov (president) and Tashev (secretary).

Religion. Religion was another important tool for the new authorities, and the freeing of the Orthodox Church in Yugoslav Macedonia from Serbian control, with the establishment of the autocephalous Macedonian Orthodox Church and the revival of the ancient archdiocese of Ohrid in 1958, was an important step along the path to nationhood—a rare incidence of co-operation between an atheist state and organised religion. The Serbian Orthodox Church resisted this move, as it did the final declaration of the autocephalous status of the Macedonian Church on 18 July 1967, and in common with the other Orthodox Churches, remains firm in its refusal to recognise it. There have been reports of a faction within the Macedonian Church that wishes the Church to give up its claim to independence and rejoin the Serbian Orthodox Church. This faction, apparently centred around Bishop Petar of Prespa and Bitola, was believed by some to be the true reason for the ultimatum issued by 200 Macedonian Orthodox priests in 1990 for the bishop's resignation ostensibly on grounds of neglect and embezzlement[5] although others denied this. On the other hand, relations between the Macedonian Orthodox Church and the authorities in Yugoslav Macedonia have remained cordial, encouraged by a common front against the threat of Albanian nationalism and the attendant growth of Islam.

Thus the new authorities overcame much of the residual pro-Bulgarian feeling among the population, and survived the split between Yugoslavia and Bulgaria in 1948. They were apparently successful in building a distinct national consciousness based on such differences as existed between Macedonia and Bulgaria proper. However, there were those who retained their pro-Bulgarian sympathies and suffered severe repression as a result. Bulgarian sources assert that thousands lost their lives due to this cause after 1944, and that more than 100,000 people were imprisoned under 'the law for the protection of Macedonian national honour' for opposing the new ethnogenesis. In January 1945 1,260 leading Bulgarians were allegedly killed in Skopje, Veles, Kumanovo, Prilep, Bitola and Štip under the supervision—so the Bulgarians claim—of Vukmanović-Tempo and Ranković.[6] In 1946 Dimitar Guzelev and Yordan and Dimitar Chatrov were sentenced to death, and seventy-four

5 *Keston News Service*, no. 349, 3 May 1990, Keston, England.
6 *Memorandum*, Union des Associations Macédoniennes en Bulgarie VMRO-SDS to the Copenhagen Conference 1990.

people led by Angel Dimov were imprisoned for trying to detach Vardar Macedonia and join it to Bulgaria. Another organisation called the 'Ilinden Democratic Front' was uncovered in 1947 and similarly accused, and there were successive trials throughout the new republic in 1947 and 1948 of which the most celebrated was that of Metodi Antonov Chento.[7] Sporadic trials of those who denied the existence of the Macedonian nation continued, for example as reported in *Politika* of Belgrade—Petar Zaharov was tried for asserting that Macedonians were Bulgarians, and in April 1977 two Skopje citizens, Lazar Krajnichanec and Angel Miterev (Gerojski), were each sentenced to five years' imprisonment for similar offences under Article 118 of the then criminal code dealing with 'hostile propaganda'.[8]

Such punishment was used in S.R. Macedonia not only against recalcitrant Yugoslav citizens. In January 1984 Ivan Zografski, a seventy-year-old retired doctor living in Sarejevo who was a Bulgarian citizen, was tried under Article 136 (which had replaced the analogous Article 118) having been accused of 'denying the existence of the brotherhood and unity of Yugoslavia's peoples and in particular denying the existence of the Macedonian nation', as well as making disparaging remarks about Tito and the situation in Yugoslavia. For this he was sentenced to six and a half years' imprisonment, reduced on appeal to five years, with confiscation of his property and permanent expulsion form Yugoslavia on completion of his sentence by the Sarejevo district court.[9] While the punishments for such actions had been reduced by the time Yugoslavia came to an end, the attitudes behind them remained and, as late as 21 January 1991, a Bulgarian citizen, Nedka Doneva Ivanova, was arrested and fined for stating that all Macedonians were Bulgarians.[10]

The change from the pre-war situation of unrecognised minority status and attempted assimilation by Serbia to that in which the Macedonians were the majority people in their own republic

7   *Ibid.* See Blaga Bozhinova, *Izpoved to Titoviya "Ray"*, Sofia, 1992, for a first-hand account of imprisonment and repression.
8   VMRO-SMD letter from Peshtera city committee of VMRO-SMD, 2 November 1991.
9   *Yugoslavia: Prisoners of Conscience*, Amnesty International, EUR 48/20/85, pp. 25-6.
10 VMRO-SMD letter, *op. cit.* Interestingly one of the two witnesses against her was an ethnic Albanian—Ali Rahman.

with considerable autonomy within the Yugoslav federation had obvious attractions. The authorities were also aided by the comparative lack of attraction for its population of Bulgaria, which remained within the Soviet bloc, in comparison to the new Yugoslavia. However the increasingly desperate economic, political and social situation in Yugoslavia which developed throughout the 1980s, and the national question of the Albanians within Yugoslavia which threatened the new republic probably more than any of the other republics including Serbia, as well as Bulgaria's continuing ambitions, made the future of the Macedonian republic seem full of uncertainties.

Emigrés. Such a process of ethnogenesis, or 'mutation' as the Greek observer Evangelos Kofos named it,[11] required careful treatment of the large Macedonian émigré communities, especially in Canada and Australia. Because such groups have often become émigrés to escape repression in the first place, they often exhibit a fiercer nationalism than their compatriots who did not leave. In the Macedonian case this is particularly evident among those who have remained in Greece in contrast to those who left. The authorities of SR Macedonia turned to the émigré question in particular in the 1960s when the lax policies of the Tito regime on freedom of movement led to large numbers of Yugoslav citizens travelling abroad. These new waves of arrivals in Canada and Australia came up against pre-war immigrants with a more pro-Bulgarian consciousness. To cope with this and help to spread the new consciousness, a well-financed central agency for emigrants named *Matica* was set up in Skopje to coordinate relevant activities. Again the Church was the key institution: priests as well as teachers were sent to administer classes and help teach the new language. In cities with a sizeable Macedonian population, the Yugoslav consuls were usually nominees of the Skopje government.[12]

This policy in its way was very successful. However, along with those who rejected the new ethnogenesis, there were also those the intensity of whose Macedonian nationalism disturbed the authorities in Skopje. The unease of those authorities, manifested in the never-ending polemics against Bulgaria and the treatment

11 Evangelos Kofos, *The Macedonian Question: The Politics of Mutation,* Institute for Balkan Studies, Salonika, 1987.
12 Kofos, *ibid.,* p. 7.

of Albanian nationalism, also resulted in a harsh attitude towards émigre groups deemed hostile to the republic. An example of this was the thirteen-year prison sentence imposed by the Skopje district court in 1979 on Dragan Bogdanovski, then a Macedonian émigré and later mentor of VMRO-DPMNE, for leading an organisation calling for a united independent Macedonian state that would incorporate not only the Yugoslav republic of Macedonia but also the Macedonian territories in Greece and Bulgaria—ironically a similar aim to that of Gotse Delchev, who is lionised by the authorities.[13]

A further development in the diaspora, especially in Australia, was the formation of a different concept of the Macedonian nation which, instead of claiming descent from Slav tribes in the sixth and seventh centuries AD who were distinct from tribes that coalesced into Bulgarians, as the Communist Skopje authorities did, rather claimed descent from the subjects of Philip of Macedon whom they regarded as non-Greek.[14] Such a view was perhaps bound to lead to a collision with competing Greek claims over the inhabitants at that time. However, these groups had considerable influence later as can be seen in the current use by the Former Yugoslav Republic of Macedonia of symbols of that era for official purposes—notably incorporation of the Star of Vergina on its flag. Also, by joining in the nationalist pastime of ransacking history and backdating modern concepts (which the authorities in Skopje were themselves already doing), they further complicate the already problematic mix of ethnic and civic components of the Macedonian nation.

Relations with other ethnic groups

In the census of 1981 the population of the SR Macedonia was stated to be 1,912,257 of which 1,281,195 were Macedonians, 377,726 Albanians, 44,613 Serbs, 39,555 Muslims, 47,223 Roma, 86,691 Turks and 7,190 Vlachs; the remainder consisted of a variety of other ethnic groups. There were also 1,984 Bulgarians

13 Amnesty International, *Yugoslavia: Prisoners of Conscience*, EUR/48/20/85.
14 See many different articles in *Glas na Makedoncite*, Kogarah, NSW, Australia. Some of these articles backdate the nation even further to '124 years after the cataclysm' and extend the boundaries of the supposed nation to Thrace and even Anatolia including Istanbul! (noted in Kofos, *op. cit.*, p. 16, *ff 30*).

(as opposed to Macedonians) recorded. All the ethnic minorities with the exception of the Serbs had a smaller proportion of membership in the League of Communists (LC) than their proportion in the population. For example, these proportions in the Skopje League of Communists in 1981 were as follows:[15]

	% of population	% of membership	% of group in LC
Macedonians	67.00	82.95	20.95
Albanians	14.36	5.43	6.39
Serbs	4.88	5.59	19.39
Roma	3.59	0.63	2.95
Turks	3.42	1.13	5.57
Muslims (Torbeshi)	3.42	0.90	4.44

Thus the Macedonians had a considerably higher representation in the LC membership than in the population, while the opposite was the case with the ethnic minorities, excepting the Serbs. This was typical of the situation in the republic as a whole. The minorities of Macedonia were not keen to join the ruling LC and it appears that the Socialist Republic of Macedonia was a state effectively run by Macedonians to a greater extent than their demographic position merited. In the upper ranks of the Yugoslav army (JNA), perhaps the only all-Yugoslav institution but one in which the Serb/Montenegrin elements were over-represented, the Macedonians were also well represented.[16]

The Torbeshi. This apparent confusion over identity of the different Muslim groups shows again that in the Balkans religion has often been of paramount importance in ethnic differentiation. This is again illustrated by the Muslim Macedonians, known as Torbeshi, Pomaks, or Poturs. In former 'Yugoslavia', the term 'Muslim' was used to describe descendants of Slavs who converted to Islam during the Ottoman period, and *not* the mostly Muslim Albanians or wholly Muslim Turkish minorities. The Muslims were recognised

15 Figures from Boris Vušković 'Nationalities in the LCY: Ethnic composition of the membership of the League of Communists in Major Cities and Republics and Provinces' in *Naše Teme*, nos 3-4, March/April 1986, Zagreb.
16 In terms of their percentage of total population, the Slav Macedonians had 33% too many generals, 26% too few full colonels, 8% too many lieutenant-colonels and 30% too many majors in 1981. See Vlatko Cvrtila, 'Who is What in the Armed Forces', *Danas*, Zagreb, 5 February 1991, in JPRS-EER-91-0270.

as a 'nationality' of Yugoslavia in 1961 and as a separate 'nation' in 1971.[17] Although a large majority of them spoke Serbo-Croat and lived mainly in Bosnia–Hercegovina or the Sandžak area on the Serbian/Montenegrin border, there were some 40,000 in Yugoslav Macedonia most of whom spoke Macedonian. These are descendants of the Slav population of Macedonia who converted during the Ottoman period and thus should perhaps have been differentiated from the Serbo-Croat-speaking Muslim Slavs. To complicate the issue further, Muslim sources in Sandžak claim that many of the Torbeshi are recent arrivals who have taken advantage of emigration agreements made in the 1950s with Turkey and left Sandžak for Turkey but settled in Macedonia on the way there.[18]

Like the Pomaks in Bulgaria, these Muslims in the past often showed greater identification with fellow-Muslims, especially Turks, than with fellow-Bulgarians, although as noted below the authorities have been worried by the penetration of Albanian

17 In former Yugoslavia the nationality policy of the Communist authorities, while always officially espousing the slogan 'brotherhood and unity', evolved from a Serb-oriented polity when Aleksander Ranković headed the all-powerful security apparatus, to a three-tier system of national rights which was enshrined in the 1974 Constitution. This system divided the population in descending order of recognised 'rights' into: (*a*) the six 'Nations of Yugoslavia'—Croats, Macedonians, Montenegrins, Muslims, Serbs and Slovenes—each with a national home based in one of the republics; (*b*) the 'Nationalities of Yugoslavia'—the largest being the Albanians (more numerous than some of the 'nations' but, having a 'national home' outside the country, not eligible for the status of a 'nation'), Bulgarians, Czechs, Hungarians, Italians, Roma, Romanians, Ruthenians, Slovaks and Turks—which were legally allowed a variety of language and cultural rights; and (*c*) 'Other nationalities and Ethnic Groups'—Austrians, Germans, Greeks, Jews, Poles, Russians, Ukrainians, Vlachs and others including those who classified themselves as 'Yugoslavs'. For the genesis and development of official recognition of the Muslims as a separate 'Nation', see Poulton *op. cit.*, Chapter 4.

18 The emigration agreement in the 1950s which lasted till the fall of Ranković in 1966 referred in theory only to Turks but, due to the *millet* system and the strength of Islam as a binding creed of identification cutting across national boundaries, many non-Turkish Muslims took advantage of the agreement and went to Turkey where they have become peacefully assimilated into the Turkish majority. The Sandžak Muslims claim that some twenty-nine villages in Macedonia are completely settled by Muslims from Sandžak—see *State Terror Against the Muslims in Sanjak*, paper presented to the Vienna Conference on Human Rights, June 1993, p. 6. They are Muslims who were caught in transit and unable to leave the country due to the end of the emigration agreement.

nationalism into this community by way of, among other things, Albanian-speaking *hodzhas*. The numbers of these Slav Muslims has fluctuated greatly in past censuses—1,591 in 1953; 3,002 in 1961; 1,248 in 1971; and a dramatically increased figure of 39,555 in 1981. This last figure presumably includes many who previously declared themselves as Turks.

The Muslims of Macedonia formed themselves into an association and held their first historico-cultural meeting in 1970 at the monastery of St Jovan Bigorski in Western Macedonia. This association claims that more than 70,000 of their numbers have been assimilated by other Muslim groups since the war, especially the Albanians.[19] If this is true, then the rise in their numbers as reflected in the 1981 census shows that the association has achieved its aims. But despite this apparent success there were contrary signs that the Slav Muslim Macedonians continue to be susceptible to assimilation into the Muslim (Albanian) majority in the republic—once again showing that in the Balkans Islam is more often a unifying factor than ethnicity. On 13 August 1990, Dr Riza Memedovski, chairman of the republican community for cultural and scientific events of Macedonian Muslims, sent an open letter to the Chairman of the Party for Democratic Prosperity of Macedonia (PDP)—the predominately ethnic Albanian party based in Tetovo—on the subject of this 'quiet assimilation', accusing the PDP of abusing religion for political ends by attempted 'Kosovoisation and Albanianisation of western Macedonia'.[20] The same concern was voiced by the council of elders of the Islamic community of Macedonia on 6 November.[21] This tendency for Macedonian Muslims to lean towards the ethnic Albanians was underlined by the apparent support of Slav Muslims for the PDP. In the second round of elections in Macedonia on 25 November 1990, the PDP complained that inhabitants of Slav Muslim villages in western Macedonia were prevented from voting for the PDP by members of the nationalist parties in the Front for Macedonian National Unity, the militia organs, and even by members of the electoral commissions.[22]

19 *Duga*, Belgrade, 8 May 1982.
20 Tanjug, 13 August 1990, in BBC SWB EE/0843/ B/10, 15 August 1990.
21 Tanjug, 6 November 1990, in BBC SWB EE/0916 B/7, 8 November 1990.
22 Tanjug, 27 November 1990, in BBC SWB EE/0934 B/15, 29 November 1990.

The Albanians of Macedonia. The ethnic Albanians, by far the largest minority in the area of former Yugoslav Macedonia, lived and continue to live in compact settlements in the west of the republic bordering on Albania, the north-west bordering on the predominantly Albanian province of Kosovo, and in Skopje where they make up over 14 per cent of the population. They are a majority of the population in many western areas, notably the districts of Tetovo (about 113,000 Albanians to 38,000 Macedonians), Gostivar (63,000 to 18,000), Kičevo (23,000 to 21,000), and Debar (10,000 to 2,500). In the towns the difference is less marked: for example, there are some 22,000 Albanians, 18,000 Macedonians and 2,000 Turks in Tetovo itself.[23] In addition, due to recent migration from the country to the city, in 1988 nearly half of Skopje's population of 560,000 were estimated by the republican Ministry of Internal Affairs to be Albanians. As well as the high birth rate observers say that as many as 150,000 Kosovo Albanians entered Macedonia illegally resulting in VMRO-DPMNE calls for preventive measures.[24]

The census of 1981 showed 377,726 Albanians, comprising 19.8 per cent of the population—an increase of 36 per cent over the figures in the previous census of 1971, when Albanians numbered 279,871 or 17 per cent of the population. Thus the Albanians had a much higher birthrate than the Macedonians, and a delegate from Tetovo, an area of high Albanian concentration, reported to the Macedonian League of Communists on 26 April 1988 that the birthrate there was three times the national average.

Education and culture. The Yugoslavian authorities pledged after the Second World War to solve the country's seemingly intractable national problems under the slogan of 'Brotherhood and Unity', and the Macedonians were recognised for the first time as a separate nation. The Albanians were recognised as a nationality of Yugoslavia but not as a nation—the Albanian national 'home' being outside Yugoslavia—and as such had a number of educational and cultural rights. By 1951 there were over 200 Albanian schools in SR

---

23 Figures for the numbers of ethnic Albanians in Macedonia are highly contentious. These are taken from 'Much Discomfort in Macedonia' by Viktor Meier in *Frankfurter Allgemeine Zeitung*, 23 June 1983, p. 10.
24 Milan Andrejevich, 'Resurgent Nationalism in Macedonia: A Challenge to Pluralism' in *RFE/Report on Eastern Europe*, 17 May 1991.

Macedonia employing at least 600 teachers and catering for more than 26,000 pupils—by 1973 this had been expanded to 248 schools employing 2,150 teachers and with over 60,000 pupils.[25] On 9 July 1981 Tanjug, the official Yugoslav news agency, reported that there were 287 Albanian-language elementary schools employing about 3,000 teachers with over 74,000 pupils in SR Macedonia, with a further 8,200 secondary school pupils attending classes in the Albanian language—figures which had changed little by 1989.[26] There were also in 1980 2,365 students of Albanian nationality enrolled at university-level institutions. Additionally there was an Albanian newspaper *Flaka e Vëllazërimit*, Albanian television and radio programmes were broadcast, and many Albanian cultural associations, theatre groups, sports clubs and the like. In reality, however, the picture was less harmonious than this would suggest.

The growth of Albanian nationalism and the authorities' reaction. The fall of Ranković in 1966 allowed Albanian dissatisfaction in Kosovo to come into the open, and there were large-scale demonstrations there in November 1968 calling for the granting to Kosovo of republican status,[27] followed by similar demonstrations in Tetovo demanding that the Albanian areas of Macedonia join Kosovo in a seventh republic. To have granted such a republic was seen, probably correctly, by many in Yugoslavia as being merely the first stage in an Albanian plot aimed at eventually separating these areas and joining them with neighbouring Albania. The events in Kosovo in 1981 and beyond were mirrored by similar if smaller-scale nationalist manifestations by Albanians in SR Macedonia, and the authorities in their increasing anxiety reacted by imposing even harder prison sentences than the authorities in Kosovo had done. The proposed seventh republic comprising the Albanian-dominated areas of Western Macedonia would have severely truncated SR Macedonia and almost certainly have revived Bulgarian (and even Serbian and Greek) claims to the rump. Thus the growth of Albanian nationalism in SR Macedonia was seen as

25 Risto Kantardzhiev and Lazo Lazaroski, 'Schools and Education' in Mihailo Apostoloski and Haralampie Plenkovich (eds), *The Socialist Republic of Macedonia*, Skopje, p. 110.
26 According to *Oslobodjenje*, Sarajevo, 6 January 1989.

possibly fatal, not only to the territorial integrity of the republic but even to the very existence of the Macedonian nation.

In July 1981, in an attempt to stem the rising nationalist tide among Albanians, the Macedonian Assembly's Commission for Intra-National Relations backed the demand by its Socio-Political Chamber for a revision of syllabuses and textbooks. The Commission called for the number of hours devoted to teaching Macedonian in Albanian-language schools to be increased and measures taken to prevent schools from not teaching Macedonian at all. In August 1981 the Macedonian Republican Pedagogical Council in Skopje noted 'weaknesses in the teaching syllabuses, programmes, textbooks and reference works used by the Albanian nationality in Macedonia' and it was stated that 'publishers had been insufficiently vigilant in preventing the penetration of Albanian nationalistic, irredentist and counter-revolutionary tendencies through printed textbooks and other literature'.[28] On 7 May 1984 the Macedonian Secretary for Internal Affairs reported that 'activity by the internal enemy from positions of Albanian nationalism and irredentism' had become more pronounced and that 'in 1983 alone, three illegal groups with eleven members, six organisers of leaflet circulation and fifteen authors of leaflets with contents from positions of Albanian nationalism and irredentism', had been detected in the republic. A further 'total of 160 persons had been detected making hostile verbal statements'.[29]

On 10 December 1986 *Borba*, the LCY organ published in Belgrade, reported on the increasingly frequent party punishments for 'unvigilant' participation in weddings and other celebrations in the Tetovo area by Albanian officials; this followed a wedding in Strimnica village attended by senior officials at which supposed 'expressions of nationalist euphoria' had occurred. The same article reported that Muamer Vishko, editor-in chief of the Albanian-language service broadcast by Radio Skopje, had listened to the entire record library of Albanian popular tunes and folksongs and from just over 1,000 records had found 260 with 'nationalistic or national-romantic' content—many from the People's' Socialist Republic of Albania and some even recorded by 'Balkanton' in Sofia. The article went on to point to the dangers of unregistered Albanian artistic societies using unapproved repertoires of nationalist

28 Tanjug, 28 August 1981.
29 Tanjug, 7 May 1984, in BBC SWB EE/7639 B/9, 10 May 1984.

content, especially on local radio stations broadcasting in the Albanian language in Kumanovo, Tetovo, Kičevo, Gostivar, Struga and Resen. The Macedonian authorities also turned their attention to Albanian names. On 17 December 1986 Tanjug reported that a registrar in Tetovo commune was expelled from his post for registering names 'which stimulated nationalist sentiment and adherence to the People's Socialist Republic of Albania' to Albanian infants of 'nationalist-inspired parents'. The offending names quoted were Alban, Albana, Shqipë, Fljamur (Albanian flag), Kustrim (call), Ljiriduam (we want freedom), and one meaning 'Red Eagle'. Additionally it was reported that for the names of cities and towns the Macedonian forms, not the Albanian ones, were to be used. The banning of Albanian names and folksongs prompted protests from Albanian writers in Kosovo.

The high birthrate of the Albanian population also worried (and continues to worry) the Macedonian authorities, and the spectre of expanding 'ethnically pure' Albanian areas akin to the situation developing in Kosovo apparently prompted them to contemplate punitive administrative measures against those with large families. On 28 January 1988 ATA, the official news agency of PSR Albania, using extracts from the Yugoslav newspapers *Rilindja* of Pristina in Kosovo and *Večerne Novosti* of Belgrade, accused the Macedonian authorities of 'neo-Malthusian' policies after it was reported that in Tetovo commune a 'package of administrative measures' would be introduced at the beginning of 1988 aimed at restraining the birthrate. Among the measures were that families should pay for medical services for any children above the ideal number of two and that there would be no child allowance and possibly even a financial penalty for such extra children. ATA reported that these measures were also to be introduced in the communes of Gostivar, Debar, Kičevo and Struga.

The campaign against Albanian nationalism, called 'differentiation', escalated. On 25 October 1987 *Flaka e Vëllazërimit* reported the decision by the President of the Tetovo LC Municipal Committee to dismiss a further 100 Albanian officials from the state administration and subject them to 'ideological differentiation', and on 30 October the same paper reported measures taken by the Republican Secretariat for People's Defence against thirty-four Albanian officers in Tetovo commune, most of whom were apparently discharged for attending Albanian weddings at which 'nationalist' songs were sung. Many cultural clubs were also disbanded.

These and other measures, which went even further than the corresponding anti-Albanian nationalism policies of 'differentiation' taking place at the same time in Kosovo, provoked opposition within the League of Communists especially among the Albanian members in Kosovo, and this in turn angered the Macedonian members. The delegates at the Macedonian Assembly session in February 1988 reacted sharply to criticism of Macedonian policies by Azem Vllazi, then President of the Kosovo LC Provincial Committee. The Assembly agreed that the legal measures—'above all, the provisions concerning personal names, the ban on the sale of property in the western part of the republic [to prevent Albanians buying out Macedonians and creating 'ethnically pure territories'], the amendment to the law on religious teaching [to prohibit the attendance of organised religious instruction by young people up to the age of 15], and the resolution on population policy, whose purpose is to stop aggressive demographic expansion'—were 'to prevent the activities of Albanian nationalists and separatists'.[30]

For the Albanian population in SR Macedonia it was perhaps events concerning education and language rights which caused the most opposition. In 1983 teachers in Tetovo were disciplined and some dismissed from the LC for not observing regulations on the use of Macedonian in official matters, and Tanjug on 5 October 1983 reported that 'a large number of pupils of Albanian nationality also followed their teachers' example by boycotting and belittling the Macedonian language'. A law of 1985 on secondary school education in SR Macedonia stipulated that classes with Albanian as the language of instruction could only be created if more than thirty Albanian pupils enrolled for the class and there were enough qualified teachers. This law was progressively more strictly enforced, resulting in the closure of classes with an insufficient intake of Albanian pupils, and compelling Albanians to attend mixed classes with the instruction in Macedonian. The consequence was that whereas in 1981 there had been 8,200 pupils attending classes in secondary schools in Albanian, it was

30 *Belgrade home service*, 23 February 1988, in BBC SWB EE/0084 B/5, 25 February 1988.

reported in the Sarajevo newspaper *Oslobodjenje* on 6 January 1989 that the figure had fallen to 4,221.

Some of the 'missing' pupils can be accounted for by the failure of growing numbers of Albanian children to attend primary school and the impact of this on secondary schools—on 8 October 1987 Tanjug reported that in 1986, 3,802 criminal prosecutions had been initiated in the municipalities of Gostivar, Tetovo, Skopje, Struga, Kičevo, Titov Veles and Kumanovo, almost always against Albanians. The compulsory instruction of some Albanian pupils in Macedonian caused great resentment and boycotts resulted, e.g. that staged by sixty Albanian pupils in September 1987 at the Nace Budjoni centre for vocational training in Kumanovo. According to a Tanjug report of 10 September 1987, some of the pupils did not even know Macedonian and were therefore unable to follow mixed classes. Albanian teachers also protested against the measures, and at the Nace Budjoni and Pero Nakov centres in Kumanovo nine teachers and twenty-six pupils were expelled. Similar events took place in Gostivar.

The situation boiled over in 1988 with demonstrations by young Albanians, in Kumanovo in August and Gostivar in October, holding banners and shouting slogans against the measures and claiming their rights as guaranteed in the 1974 Constitution. In Kumanovo at least 128 Albanians were detained for up to sixty days and the authorities responded in both instances by arresting the organisers, twenty of whom were subsequently imprisoned. For example at the district court of Skopje in January, three men aged 32, 29 and 19 were sentenced to between six and eleven years' imprisonment and two boys and two girls aged sixteen and seventeen, all of them pupils at the Panche Popovski school in Gostivar, received between four and six years' imprisonment for their part in the Gostivar demonstration.

Religion. The Albanians of Macedonia are overwhelmingly Muslim, with only a few Orthodox villages around Lake Ohrid and Gostivar. There are also a small number of Roman Catholics in Skopje of whom Mother Theresa is the best known. Some observers have maintained that Islam is not held in high esteem among the Albanians of former Yugoslavia and that most *hodzhas* opposed the growth of Albanian nationalism. However in SR Macedonia the authorities saw Islam as a tool of Albanian nationalism and as a way for the Albanians to assimilate other smaller Islamic minority groups like the Turks, Torbeshi and Muslim Roma. This was detailed in a 23-page supplement published by the Skopje daily, *Vecher*, between 25 September and 21 October 1980 entitled 'Islamism in Macedonia'. An article in *Nova Makedonija* published in Skopje on 19 June 1981 while reporting on the rejection by the Macedonian Islamic community of Albanian nationalism noted that in some villages where Muslim Macedonians live, *hodzhas* who preach in Albanian had been appointed.

On 21 December 1986 an article in *NIN*, a magazine published in Belgrade, commented on the large number of Albanians from Macedonia who were undergoing religious instruction in Arab countries and stated that in the preceding ten years 210 mosques had been renovated or built in western Macedonia. Many ethnic Albanians were educating their children in Islamic precepts and using Arabic rather than Macedonian as the language of instruction in these classes. The Communist authorities tried unsuccessfully to restrict this.[31] There were a number of subsequent articles and reports about 'too extensive' Islamic religious instruction in SR Macedonia and on how the Islamic community in Macedonia was overstepping the legal regulations especially on the instruction of under-age girls. This last point was highlighted by the problem of the Teteks clothing factory in Pirok, just outside Tetovo, in recruiting women employees although there were some 20,000 unemployed Albanian women in and around Tetovo; thus over 200 workers had to commute daily from Skopje.[32] Local Albanians however saw, and continue to see, such 'bussing-in' of non-Albanian labour as another example of the authorities' anti-Albanian policies. The latter for their part blamed Islamic indoctrination of women and traditional Albanian attitudes to women, and were loath to co-operate in allowing new mosques to be opened. For example in 1983 authorisation was sought for the erection of a minaret, privately financed by the Albanian inhabitants, in the village of Donja Arnakija but was refused. The villagers went ahead and built the minaret but in December 1986 it was dynamited

---

31 See Janice Broun, 'Islam in the Balkans: The Rebirth of a Dormant Faith Could Threaten National Security', *News Network International*, 12 February 1991, pp. 23-8.
32 Djordje Janković in *Vjesnik*, Zagreb, 12 October 1986, p. 7.

by the authorities.[33] As noted above the authorities also amended the law on religious teaching to prohibit attendance at organised religious instruction by young people up to the age of fifteen specifically to counter the growing influence of Islam. Conversely the Communist authorities, as noted above, had good relations with the Macedonian Orthodox Church which was and is seen as a standard-bearer of the Macedonian nation in the ethnically mixed areas of Western Macedonia.

Communities apart. The reality of the situation in SR Macedonia was that there was very little mixing between ethnic groups—a sad situation which has continued to the present. A study published in 1974 by the sociologist Dr Ilija Josifovski[34] on the Macedonian, Albanian and Turkish populations in the villages of Polog, which includes the areas around Tetovo and Gostivar, showed that 95 per cent of Albanian and Macedonian and 84 per cent of Turkish heads of individual households would not let their sons marry a girl of different nationality, while for daughters the percentages were even higher. Many Albanian students attended Priština University in Kosovo, which in the 1980s was almost entirely Albanian in intake. Mixed marriages between Macedonians on one hand and Albanians and Turks on the other were found by the study not to exist. Religion was again seen as being of paramount importance: "A religious isolation stands behind the deceptive impression of national, ethnic cleavages". The drift from village to town among the Macedonian population was shown by a 42 per cent decline in the agricultural population over the period 1963-1971, while for the same period the Albanian agricultural population declined by only 11 per cent so that many Macedonian villages came to be populated almost entirely by the old despite the authorities offering financial inducements for young Macedonians either to stay in the villages or to return to them. These declining communities and the new villages of '*weekendicas*'— holiday homes for the Macedonian well-to-do which are empty during the week—contrasted greatly with the Albanian and Roma

---

33 *IRNA* (Iranian report), 13 December 1986, in BBC SWB EE/8444 B/19, 17 December 1986.

34 Ilija Josifovski, *Opshtestvenite Promeni na Selo: Makedonskoto Albanskoto i Turskoto Naselenie na Selo vo Polog: Socioloshka Studija*, published by the Institute of Sociological, Political and Juridical Research, Skopje, 1974.

(and Muslim Macedonian) villages with their large numbers of youths and children visible on the streets.

Thus despite the aim of 'Brotherhood and Unity' espoused by the Communist authorities, the picture was one of mistrust and increasing alienation between the Macedonians and the rapidly expanding Albanian population of SR Macedonia, mirrored in everyday relations by chauvinist attitudes on both sides. This view is at odds with that held currently by some that relations between Slav Macedonians and ethnic Albanians have only recently deteriorated; they point to the fact that the former president of the League of Communists of Yugoslavia, Milan Panchevski, spoke fluent Albanian[35] and that many Albanians likewise speak fluent Macedonian. However such a rosy view of the past is unfounded and the legacy of mistrust and hostility, unfortunately, has a longer history.

In 1989 the Macedonian authorities amended the republic's constitution so that SR Macedonia was defined as a 'nation-state of Macedonian people' instead of the previous formulation which defined it as 'a state of the Macedonian people and the Albanian and Turkish minorities'. This change reflected the growing unease of the Macedonian authorities in the face of Albanian nationalism and the possible break-up of Yugoslavia which manifested itself in a more aggressive Macedonian nationalism, from both the authorities and outright nationalists in new groups like VMRO-DPMNE.

Events in 1990 and 1991. During 1990 the situation in Kosovo, always closely watched by all Albanians in Macedonia and often an important pointer to future action in the republic, deteriorated. On 1 February some 2,000 ethnic Albanians, demanding that the Albanian-dominated areas of western Macedonia be granted independence, and chanting 'We want a Greater Albania' attempted to block the centre of Tetovo, but were quickly dispersed by police.[36] However the situation in Macedonia remained relatively quiet throughout most of 1990 as Kosovo took centre stage.

The language issue in and out of the schools remained. On 19 June over 11,000 ethnic Albanians from Struga signed a petition

---

35 See Milan Andrejvich, 'Resurgent Nationalism in Macedonia: A Challenge to Pluralism' in *RFE, Report on Eastern Europe,* 17 May 1991, footnote 2.
36 *RFE Weekly Record of Events,* 1 February 1990.

to the SFRJ Assembly, the Macedonian Assembly and the Struga Municipal Assembly, calling for 'pure' parallel tuition in Albanian to be opened in the Niko Nestor secondary school centre in Struga,[37] but the authorities remained unmoved. On 28 August the Macedonian government rejected a petition from several Albanian alternative groups and civic leaders calling for the use of Albanian in teaching and school administration, the revision of the curriculum, and the reinstatement of ethnic Albanian teachers who had been suspended on political pretexts. The government justified its rejection by reference to the newly-worded Constitution by saying that the demands 'deviated from existing legal regulations and the constitution, which states that Macedonia is a state of the Macedonian nation'.[38] On 16 August a Tetovo Albanian, Remzi Redzhepi, was sentenced to a month's imprisonment and a fine for 'causing anxiety and a feeling of insecurity among the citizens' after he 'warned' the speaker of the Tetovo municipal assembly, Trpko Nikolovski (a Slav Macedonian), that he wanted documents in Albanian not Macedonian.[39]

One reason for the lack of major inter-ethnic incidents was that the political relaxation allowed the ethnic Albanians to organise openly. The main ethnic Albanian party, founded by Nevzat Halili, a teacher of English from Tetovo, who was elected chairman on 25 August 1990, quickly became the Party for Democratic Prosperity of Macedonia (PDP). Despite its non-ethnic name, the PDP was accused of being essentially an ethnic Albanian party, and this was underlined at the August session when the majority of participants reportedly boycotted Macedonian and Turkish.[40] Other reports however indicated that the PDP was not an ethnocentric party and that Muslims from other national groups had gravitated towards it.[41] It was frequently accused by the authorities and by rival Macedonian political parties of being merely an appendage of the mainly ethnic Albanian Democratic League of Kosovo (DSK) led by Ibrahim Rugova and of aiming for the break up of Macedonia and ultimately Yugoslavia. Halili expressly denied this and acknowledged the territorial integrity and sovereignty

37 Tanjug, 19 June 1990, in BBC SWB EE/0796 B/15, 21 June 1990.
38 *RFE Weekly Record of Events*, 28 August 1990.
39 Tanjug, 16 August 1990, in BBC SWB EE/0846 B/5, 18 August 1990.
40 Tanjug, 25 August 1990, in BBC SWB EE/0853 B/19, 27 August 1990.
41 See *East European Newsletter*, EEN vol. 4, no 23, London, 19 November 1990.

of Macedonia and Yugoslavia and the inviolability of Yugoslavia's borders, and confirmed commitment to its federal arrangement.[42] Such statements, however, had to be seen in the light of the then situation of the ethnic Albanians in Macedonia, an oppressed minority able for the first time to operate openly and faced by authorities dominated by a hostile majority nationality which itself viewed the future with some alarm. Jovan Trpenoski, the secretary of internal affairs for SR Macedonia, stated that the PDP was formed by Halili probably 'under the influence of separatists from Kosovo' and that while the PDP did not have a separatist programme, its members frequently voiced irredentist demands at meetings.[43] This last claim has been often repeated and 'hostile Albanian émigrés' are also seen as financial support to the PDP.[44] Less convincingly, Trpenovski also claimed that the *Sigurimi* —the secret police of PSR Albania—had been active in Macedonia, especially in Tetovo, and that if ethnic Albanian parties took power in Kosovo and western Macedonia through the ballot-box then this would facilitate the establishment of a Greater Albania. Trpenovski saw irredentism in almost every ethnic Albanian action including the campaign organised by Albanians in Tetovo, Gostivar, Kumanovo and Struga to end the traditional blood feuds between ethnic Albanian families, as had already happened in Kosovo.[45]

The first round of elections in Macedonia was held on 11 November, and there were decisive results in only eleven out of the total of 120 seats. In these the PDP in alliance with the small People's Democratic Party, another predominantly ethnic Albanian party from Tetovo led by Jusuf Redzhepi, won six seats—the remainder went to the Communist and socialist parties with Ante Marković's all-Yugoslav party gaining one, but with the Macedonian nationalist parties apparently nowhere in sight. In a number of predominately Albanian constituencies including Gostivar, Debar, Kumanovo, Struga, Tetovo and four in Skopje, there were apparent irregularities[46] with Macedonians claiming that some ethnic Albanians had voted in more than one constituency and that newly-arrived migrants had not been adequately screened to see who was eligible to vote and who was not. The second

42 Tanjug, 1 September 1990, in BBC SWB EE/0861 B/18, 5 September 1990.
43 *Intervju*, Belgrade, 31 August 1990.
44 Tanjug, 19 September 1990, in BBC SWB EE/0876 B/6, 22 September 1990.
45 *Intervju*, Belgrade, 31 August 1990.
46 Tanjug, 17 November 1990, in BBC SWB EE/0928 B/19, 22 November 1990.

round of voting took place on 25 November and the PDP claimed that it had been blatantly hindered. After the third and final round of voting the PDP and People's Democratic Party alliance finished with 25 seats to 37 for the Macedonian nationalist party, VMRO-DPMNE, and 31 for the Communists. No real winner had emerged. When a referendum on autonomy for the Albanians in Macedonia was held in January 1992, more than 90 per cent voted, and the vote in favour exceeded 99 per cent.[47] Tensions rose in November 1991 over the wording of the new Constitution, with the Macedonian nationalist VMRO-DPMNE wanting a more nationalistic wording while the PDP, the main Albanian party, wanted the Albanian language to have equal status with Macedonian and a formulation which would specifically include the Albanians as an integral component.[48] More serious perhaps was the declaration of an autonomous republic of 'Ilirid' centred on Tetovo.[49] This, however, proved something of a hoax and seemed to be based on supposed statements, subsequently denied, by an Albanian deputy.[50] Hoax or not, the ramifications from it continued.

The Vlachs. There is little information on the situation of the Vlachs, traditionally a pastoral people and speaking a form of Romanian. They live primarily in Greece but also in Albania and areas of former Yugoslavia. Assessing their numbers is difficult, and is compounded by the lack of any separatist current among them, which has resulted in their apparent peaceful assimilation into majority ethnic groups. In this a shared religious faith, Orthodoxy, has been an important factor. The Vlachs of former Yugoslavia—where they were also known as Koutsovlachs, Aromani and Cincari—lived in Serbia and especially in Macedonia.

The Vlachs in SR Macedonia live especially in and around Bitola, Resen and Kruševo. In the Communist period there were Vlach societies in Bitola and Skopje which highlighted the lack

---

47 Tanjug and Radio Belgrade, 15 January 1992, BBC SWB EE/1280 C1/9, 17 January 1992.
48 Radio Belgrade, 15 and 16 November 1991, BBC SWB EE/1233 i, 19 November 1991.
49 ATA, 4 April 1992, BBC SWB EE/1349 C1/6, 7 April 1992.
50 Yves Heller, 'Skopje Anxious for Recognition', from *Le Monde*, Paris, 15 April 1992.

of language rights for Vlachs in schools and over religious matters—e.g. in an appeal in February 1988 by the Pitu Guli cultural association in Skopje to the Foreign Ministers of Yugoslavia, Albania, Bulgaria, Greece, Romania and Turkey who were meeting in Belgrade. However, this had little apparent effect. Successive censuses showed a gradual decline in their declared numbers in SR Macedonia from 8,669 in 1953 to 6,392 in 1981, and it appeared that they were becoming assimilated by the majority Macedonian population.

The assimilatory trend already under way in the first Yugoslav state was amplified after the Second World War when, after 1948, ownership of big flocks of sheep or herds of horses was not permitted under the new economic system. Most Vlachs abandoned their nomadic way of life and settled in existing villages, having already become well acquainted with the areas through dwelling in them the previous winter. Others from Ovče Polje settled in surrounding areas—Štip, Kočani, Titov Veles—but mostly moved back to Ovče Polje after 1948 when land became available there due to the complete emigration of Turks in the area. A result of this was contact between the Vlach culture and the indigenous Macedonian/Slavic culture. Studies by Josif Trifonoski in 1971 showed that the Vlachs of eastern Macedonia living among the mass of the Slavic population were fading away as a separate group, and that the growth of industry in Titov Veles, Štip and Skopje, causing mass emigration of the young from the villages, had further escalated this process.[51] However, this process was not complete and many Vlachs retained a secret consciousness of their seperate ethnicity.

The Turks. According to the census of 1981, there were 101,292 Turks in Yugoslavia, remnants of the long Ottoman occupation. Of them, 86,691 lived in Macedonia where they made up 4 per cent of the population. Assessing the true numbers of minority populations like the Turks in Macedonia was and is problematic. From 95,940 Turks, in the census of 1948, the figure had risen to 203,938 in 1953, yet by the next census seven years later it had fallen again to 131,481. Such big fluctuations were due

51 For a Summary of Dr Trifonoski's findings in Ovče Polje and other references to the Vlachs, see A. Dragoslav Antonijević, 'Tzintzari in Ovče Polje in SR Macedonia', *Balkanica*, V, Belgrade, 1975.

to external events. In the immediate post-war period, the Turks were seen as suspect due to the alliance between Turkey and the West, and in January 1948, seventeen Macedonian Turks were tried as members of '*Judzel*'—ostensibly a terrorist/espionage organisation. The trial was given great publicity within Macedonia to intimidate the Turkish minority, and as a result many of them declared themselves to be Albanians in the 1948 census. However, by 1953, after the break with Albania and the Tito-Stalin split, the Albanians were seen as suspect and many Albanians therefore declared themselves to be Turks—of the 203,938 in the 1953 census, 32,392 gave Macedonian as their native language and 27,086 gave Albanian, and the number of declared Albanians fell from 179,389 in 1948 to 165,524 in 1953.

Between 1953 and 1966 there was also extensive emigration of Yugoslav Turks to Turkey—some 80,000 according to Yugoslavia's statistical yearbooks, or more than 150,000 according to some Turkish sources. However, some of these emigrants had no knowledge of Turkish and were either Muslim Albanians or Slavs who were claiming to be Turks to escape from Communist Yugoslavia.[52]

Between the Yugoslav censuses of 1971 and 1981, the number of declared Turks dropped from 108,552 to 86,690. Such a decline was the more surprising given the high birthrate of ethnic Turks in Macedonia, from which an increase of some 20,000 in the period might have been expected rather than a decrease of that number. It appeared that many who had previously claimed to be Turks were now calling themselves Muslims and others Albanians or Roma. In the April 1991 census the figure for 'Turks' had risen slightly to 97,416 or 4.79 per cent of the population.[53] A further complicating factor in assessing the numbers of small minority groups in Yugoslav Macedonia was the rise from 3,652 to 14,240 between 1971 and 1981 of those declaring themselves to be 'Yugoslavs' rather than as belonging to a particular ethnic group (although the percentage of such people was still low in comparison to other republics in former Yugoslavia).

The Communist authorities, worried at the rise of Albanian

52 Paul Shoup, *Communism and the Yugoslav National Question*, New York, 1968, pp. 181-2; and Stephen Pazlmer and Robert King, *Yugoslav Communism and the Macedonian Question*, Hamden, Conn., Archon Books, 1971, p 178.

53 Tanjug, 2 December 1991, in BBC SWB EE/1246 C1/10, 4 December 1991.

nationalism, asserted that many Turks in Macedonia had been Albanianised under pressure. According to the director of the Macedonian Republic Bureau of Statistics in Skopje,[54] this was especially pronounced in Tetovo, Gostivar, Struga and Kičevo regions, and in September 1987 the Macedonian League of Communists Central Committee Presidium cited the expansion of Albanian nationalism as one of the main reasons for the emigration of Turkish families from the Gostivar municipality.[55] The Albanians apparently claimed that these were not Turks but actually 'Illyrians [who they claim to be the forerunners of the Albanians] turned into Turks' who were 'returning to their flock'—i.e. rejoining the Albanian mother-nation.[56] (In a similar fashion, PDP leader Halili called on Torbeshi and Roma to declare themselves as Albanians.[57])

Like the Albanians, the Turks were a recognised 'nationality' of former Yugoslavia, who were allowed educational and cultural rights from the outset—in 1944/5, the first academic year under the new Yugoslav republic of Macedonia, there were sixty primary schools with 3,334 pupils using Turkish as the language of instruction. In 1950/1 there were over 100 such schools with over 12,000 pupils and 267 teachers, but by 1958/9 after the emigration to Turkey, the number had dropped to one secondary and twenty-six primary schools with just over 6,000 pupils and 219 teachers. By the end of 1988, the number of primary schools had risen to fifty-three, but with the number of pupils remaining more or less the same.[58] As with the Albanians of Macedonia, there were television and radio programmes and a newspaper, *Birlik*, together with various cultural organisations. Their main political movement was the Democratic Alliance of Turks in Macedonia.

The Roma and assimilation. Yugoslavia had one of the largest Rom populations in Europe, and this had important links with emigrant Rom groups in France, Germany, the United States, Australia and elsewhere. From 1981, the estimated 850,000 Roma in Yugoslavia

54 *Duga*, Belgrade, 8 May 1982.
55 Tanjug, 21 September 1987, in BBC SWB EE/8683 B/7, 26 September 1987.
56 *Duga*, Belgrade, 8 May 1982.
57 Andrejevich, *op. cit.* Unofficially 98% of Albanians in Macedonia are Muslim—in the April 1991 census, households were asked to declare their religion as well as national affiliation.
58 From Kantardzhiev and Lazaroski, *op. cit.*

had—in theory—nationality status equal to that of other national minorities like the Albanians, Turks or Hungarians, but in practice this was not uniformly applied by the republics which, with the exception of Bosnia-Hercegovina and Montenegro, placed Roma in the lower category of an 'ethnic group'.

Beginning in 1983, Romani was used in some state schools as the teaching medium for the first four grades, and regular radio programmes were broadcast in it. In May 1980 the Naša Kniga publishing house of Skopje brought out the first Romani grammar written entirely in the Romani script and orthography, but it used a modified version of the 32-letter Romani alphabet to make it as widely understood as possible. On 21 March 1990 it was reported that Dobra Vjest, the publishing house of the Association of Baptist Churches of Yugoslavia, would publish the first Romani translation of the Bible,[59] and this was subsequently done.

The bigger communities in Belgrade, Niš, Šuto Orizari (Skopje) and other towns have had their own cultural and social associations for many years. The Belgrade Društva Rom was founded in 1930 and Skopje's Phralipe (Brotherhood) in 1948. In former Yugoslavia perhaps the most significant feature was in Macedonia. This was the setting up, after the devastating earthquake in the early 1960s, of the Romani town of Šuto Orizari outside Skopje, with some 35,000 inhabitants and its own elected council and member of parliament. This town enjoyed a higher standard of living than many Macedonian villages.

Despite these advances, the majority of Roma continued to live at well below the average economic level and there was discrimination in the labour market, with many of the men unemployed and women employed only in the most menial occupations. Few Roma benefited from university education and entered the professions. In former Yugoslavia, half the Roma in employment were industrial workers and 20 per cent were farmers, many of these owning their land. The rest were self-employed artisans and small traders.

Despite the recognition they had won, there remained an unwillingness among Roma to identify themselves as such because of the continuing stigma attached to being a Rom, encapsulated in the pejorative term '*cigane*' by which they were and are widely

59 Poulton, *op. cit.*

known. In Macedonia their number in the censuses remained more or less static until that of 1981 when it rose dramatically from 24,505 to 43,223 reflecting their greater official status and the lessening importance of the stigma. The last census of April 1991 recorded 55,575 Roma in Macedonia—some 2.73 per cent of the total population of just over 2 million. However, the real figure is certainly much higher and Roma leaders claim some 200,000 in Macedonia

While many Roma have declared themselves to be Macedonians or Turks, the former Communist authorities in Macedonia alleged over a long period that the Roma, especially the Muslims who comprise the vast majority, were being subjected to Albanianisation—the Albanians being seen by many Macedonians as the main internal threat. This claim was made again on 1 August 1990 by the presidium of the republican committee for nurturing the ethnic and cultural traditions of Roma in SR Macedonia, which accused the PDP of persistently manipulating Roma on a religious Muslim basis. On 1 September 1990 the Macedonian Romani community called on all Roma to stop declaring themselves to be Albanians simply on the basis of shared religion, and decided to mark 11 October—already a Macedonian public day—with the first republican festival of the cultural achievements of Roma in Macedonia.[60]

'Egyptians'. Given the problems faced by Roma and the ethnic uncertainty of many Muslim citizens (a survival from Ottoman times when religion rather than ethnicity was the main factor of differentiation) especially in areas dominated by highly organised and nationalistic Muslim Albanians, it is perhaps not surprising that unusual national claims appear from time to time. In Macedonia in 1990 the 'Egipcani' Association of Citizens in Ohrid was set up by approximately 4,000 inhabitants of Ohrid and neighbouring Struga, under the leadership of Nazim Arifi, who renounced being Roma in favour of being Egyptian.[61] A sister association was soon set up in Kosovo, and by September 1990 the two associations claimed 100,000 'descendants of the Pharaohs' in Kosovo and 20-30,000 in Macedonia. They petitioned the Federal Assembly and the Serbian and Macedonian national assemblies to include

60 Tanjug, 1 September 1990, in BBC SWB EE/0681 B/17, 5 September 1990.
61 Tanjug, 6 August 1990, in BBC SWB EE/0837 B/10, 8 August 1990.

the separate category of 'Egyptian' in the 1991 population census.[62] It was included in the 1991 Macedonian census, but this phenomenon of Roma claiming to be Egyptians (to avoid the stigma associated with being Gypsies) has not become widespread and is unlikely to develop despite recent discovery of documents in the Vatican Library purporting to show that Egyptians came to Macedonia between 306 and 337 AD in the form of 150,000 infantry and 150,000 horsemen.[63]

Despite these advances, the situation of Roma in former Yugoslavia remained difficult, and Roma leaders felt that there was not a genuine will by the Communist authorities to include Roma in the political and social process. For example, the Roma Deputy Abdi Faik had his passport removed for five years after his initial term as a representative of local government had expired, illustrating that the Communist regime did not practise the 'brotherhood and unity' that it preached.[64]

Bulgarians. Just as there are those in Bulgaria who see themselves as Macedonians rather than Bulgarians, there were and continue to be those in Vardar Macedonia who see themselves as Bulgarians rather than Macedonians; in the 1991 census there were 1,762 such people.[65]

Thus in the post-war Communist period and beyond, the new state-sponsored majority Macedonian nationalism took hold in Yugoslav Macedonia. The Communist authorities espoused an ideology of 'Brotherhood and Unity', and in many ways this was a genuine attempt to include all ethnic groups in the political and social life of the state—albeit firmly within Yugoslavia's somewhat idiosyncratic Communist set-up. Yet beneath the rosy exterior there remained acute inter-ethnic conflict. In Macedonia this was especially pronounced between the new power majority—the Macedonians—and the Albanians. This conflict has continued.

---

62 Tanjug, 24 September 1990, in BBC SWB EE/0879 B/10, 26 September 1990.
63 Tanjug, April 1991 in BBC SWB EE/1043 B/17 11 April 1991.
64 Interview with author, April 1993, Skopje.
65 *Nova Makedonija*, Skopje, 28 February 1992, in JPRS-FER-92-040, 1 April 1992.

Despite safeguards for minority rights, SR Macedonia was effectively a state run by the Macedonians for the Macedonians.

8

MACEDONIANS AS MINORITIES

Albania

Communist-isolationism. The triumphant National Liberation Front, led by the Communists under Enver Hoxha, which took power in Albania in November 1944 was at this time a junior partner in Tito's grand plans for the Balkans. As such the new authorities implemented the Tito line of a Macedonian nation distinct from its neighbours whether they were Serbs or, more pertinently, Bulgarians. Thus in 1945 at the end of the war, thirteen Macedonian schools were opened in villages with predominately Slav populations, and in November 1945 a Yugoslav-Albanian agreement between the new Communist authorities allowed a number of Macedonian teachers into Albania to facilitate the running of these schools which only taught Albanian for two hours a week in the fourth grade. However, after the Tito-Stalin break in 1948 and the corresponding Yugoslav-Albanian break, these schools apparently closed and Albanian became the main language of instruction. While there were textbooks in the newly codified Macedonian language for first- and second-grade pupils published in Tirana, all contact with neighbouring Yugoslavia and Greece was ended and Albania under Hoxha exhibited an almost complete fortress-like isolation.

This greatly hindered estimates of the numbers of Slav Macedonians in Albania, whether Christian or Muslim. Estimates range from '3,000 to 4,000 distributed in nine villages of Prespa', quoted by Hoxha to the 7th Congress of the Albanian Labour Party (the Communist Party) in 1975, to over 100,000 according to a book published in Skopje in 1983.[1] Equally exaggerated would appear to be the figure of 100,000 Muslim Macedonians (Torbeshi) claimed by the former Yugoslav institution the Macedonian Association of Cultural and Scientific Manifestations of Macedonian Muslims.[2] While it is likely that, as in the west of FYROM, there are many Torbeshi in the area, such a large figure seems improbable at any time—especially when one considers the natural assimilatory tendency of Balkan Muslims towards the majority Muslim group in a particular area (compounded here by that group being the majority in the country) which is noticeable in Balkan countries where the Muslims are not the majority population.[3]

The official Albanian statistics based on successive censuses give 4,235 in 1960; 4,097 in 1979; and 4,697 in 1989—the 1960 figure included other 'Yugoslav' peoples like Serbs and Montenegrins which in later censuses were separated from Macedonians and only numbered 66 and 100 in 1979 and 1989[4]—but these are certainly under-estimates. Given Albania's nationalistic self-assertion under Hoxha, it seems likely that many would feel under pressure to identify themselves as part of the majority ethnic Albanians, declared to account for 95 per cent of the population. Indeed in July 1991 the head of the Yugoslav CSCE delegation, Vladislav Jovanović stated that about 2,000 Serbs and Montenegrins had recently crossed into Yugoslavia from Albania in a single wave, indicating that the figures for the Slav minorities were higher than in the official statistics.[5] Conversely the former Yugoslav figures are certainly exaggerated—at the Moscow Conference on Human Rights in September 1991 the Macedonian member of the Yugoslav delegation, Ljupco Naumovski, claimed '140,000 ethnic Macedonians in Albania'[6]—a dramatic increase from 'between 55,000 and 60,000' as claimed by the Yugoslav news agency, Tanjug, in April 1991.[7] Most observers outside Albania and the

1 D.K. Budimovski, *Makedontsite vo Albanija NIP*, 'Studenski Zbor', Skopje, 1993.
2 Tanjug, 31 January 1990, in BBC SWB EE/0680, A2/2, 5 February 1990.
3 For more on this tendency of Muslim groups in the Balkans to coalesce with the larger ones in the area, whether Slavs as in Bosnia, Albanians in and around the periphery of Albania, and Turks in Bulgaria and Western Thrace, see Poulton *op. cit.*
4 *Vjetari Statistikor 1. RPS Të Shqipërise* 1990, Tirana.
5 Tanjug, 9 July 1991, in BBC SWB EE/1122 A2/3, 12 July 1991.
6 Tanjug, 24 September 1991, in BBC SWB EE/1188 A2/3, 27 September 1991.

Former Yugoslav Republic of Macedonia (FYROM) put the figure at between 10,000 and 20,000.

In October 1980, Blagoj Popov from the Socialist Republic of Macedonia in Yugoslavia visited Albania and reported that at Pustets in Mala Prespa there was a Macedonian school in operation, although in the local libraries there was reportedly not a single book the language.[8]

While the abolition of organised religion in 1967, when Albania was officially proclaimed 'the first atheist state in the world' and all forms of organised religious activity were banned, affected the entire population whether Albanian, Slav Macedonian, Greek, or Muslim or Christian, the effect can be seen to have been greatest among the Orthodox minorities.[9] This is because their identity, due again to the Ottoman legacy, is closely entwined with religious practices as well as with language use.

Furthermore, in 1975 the government ordered name-changes for 'citizens who have inappropriate names and offensive surnames from a political, ideological, and moral standpoint'.[10] In practice this meant that all names that were not Albanian had to be replaced, and, combined with Hoxha's ferocious Albanian nationalism, it aided the gradual Albanianisation of young Slavs. For example, in Pustets which was entirely Slav, the whole population was renamed Licenas.[11] However, the Albanian Communist authorities, while pursuing social policies at least as restrictive as any in the region (and almost certainly more so), did not attempt the policies of negation or outright assimilation practised in both Greece and Bulgaria at this time. As such the small Slav Macedonian minority was in a position to take advantage of the changes afforded by the collapse of the previous Communist system in Albania and to make contact with other Macedonian communities outside the country.

Post-Communism. One of the first signs of change was the new-found freedom of movement which enabled Macedonians to

7   Tanjug, 5 April 1991, in BBC SWB EE/1041 B/4, 9 April 1991.
8   Tosho Popovski, *op. cit.*, pp. 247-8.
9   For more on this see Peter Prifti, *Socialist Albania since 1994: Domestic and Foreign Developments*, MIT Press, Cambridge, Mass., 1978, and Poulton, *op. cit.*
10 Administrative Decree 5339, cited in Prifti, *op. cit.*, p. 164.
11 Popovski, *op. cit.*, p. 251.

leave Albania. In March 1991 some forty fled to neighbouring Yugoslav Macedonia from villages in the region of Mala Prespa, and they claimed that, contrary to some Yugoslav assertions, they had not been forced out but had come on their own initiative as 'there [in Albania] Albanians live better than ethnic Macedonians'. They also asserted that Slav Macedonians were attempting to flee to the border areas of Greece populated by their own kind but that the Greek authorities were sending them back to Albania.[12]

More promising has been the agreement in June 1991 on co-operation between the state archives of FYROM and Albania,[13] the visit by the then FYROM Prime Minister Nikola Kljushev to the village of Liqenas in Korçë district to meet members of the Macedonian minority,[14] and especially the emergence of legal political associations. In April 1991 a Slav Macedonian organisation called 'Prespa' was set up, and in September the Justice Minister approved the application to create the 'Bratska Political Association of Macedonians in Albania'.[15] In August 1991 Korçë local radio station broadcast a programme in Macedonian to celebrate the 2 August Ilinden national holiday, thus celebrated in Albania for the first time, and a concert and exhibition were held in Pogradec.[16]

Finally, new connections were established between Albanians living in the FYROM and in Albanian Macedonia. The Albanian daily *Zeri i Popullit* in April 1992 stated that the 'wall separating the "Two Dibers" [referring to the border town of Debar in FYROM and neighbouring Diber in Albania] has been cracked' and—quoting Macedonian Radio and TV—that more than 30,000 Albanians had crossed the border for a joint celebration of Ramadan.[17] While the article was essentially about Albanian national unity, it was clear that the post-war isolation of the Albanian portion of Macedonia from the others was over. The proposed Durrës-Skopje-Sofia-Istanbul highway—the new *Via Egnatia*—will greatly assist this new process of east-west communication.

12 Tanjug, 11 March 1991, in BBC SWB EE/1021 B/4, 15 March 1991.
13 Tanjug, 8 June 1991, in BBC SWB EE/1095 A2/3, 11 June 1991.
14 ATA, 28 July 1991, in BBC SWB EE/1140 A2/1, 2 August 1991.
15 Tanjug, 5 April 1991, in BBC SWB EE/1041 B/4 9 April 1991, and Albanian Radio, Tirana, 8 September 1991, in BBC SWB EE/1175 B/2 12 September 1991.
16 Tanjug, 3 August 1991, in BBC SWB EE/1144 B/2, 7 August 1991.
17 *Zeri i Popullit*, 10 April 1992, in JPRS-EER-92-053, 30 April 1992.

Bulgaria

Oppression and the rise of the 'one-nation' state. In Bulgaria successive censuses have given conflicting figures for the numbers of Macedonians. The Bulgarian authorities did not publish the results of the 1946 census concerning the Macedonian population. Yugoslav sources claim that 252,908 people declared themselves to be Macedonians in that census,[18] but in 1991 the Bulgarian embassy in London stated that 169,544 people registered themselves as Macedonians in 1946.[19] The census of 1956 recorded 187,789 Macedonians, with more than 95 per cent of them living in the Pirin region where they made up 63.8 per cent of the population. However, in the 1965 census the number of self-declared Macedonians had dropped to 8,750, and in the district of Blagoevgrad, which previously had the highest percentage of Macedonians, it was less than 1 per cent.[20]

We saw in Chapter 5 how immediately after the Second World War when Georgi Dimitrov, both of whose parents were from Macedonia, was leader, the Bulgarian Communist Party gave full recognition to a separate Macedonian nationality and allowed extensive contact between Pirin Macedonia and the newly-formed Macedonian Republic in post-war Yugoslavia. After his death and the break between Yugoslavia and the Soviet Union, the unease of the Bulgarians at this recognition became more apparent and the Bulgarians would admit no more than that the process of creating a nationality for the Macedonians had begun in 1918. Later the date was changed to 1944, and at the BCP plenum in April 1956, when Todor Zhivkov cemented his power, it was apparently decided no longer to recognise a separate Macedonian nationality.[21] Throughout the early 1960s the Bulgarian authorities, when renewing compulsory personal identity cards, issued ones stating that the holder was ethnically Bulgarian, to those whose cards had previously stated that they were Macedonian. It appears that repression began soon after the Stalin-Tito rupture.

18 Pedrag Vukovic, 'U Sluzbi Starog', *Politika*, Belgrade, 7 December 1975.
19 Letter to author, 28 July 1991.
20 *Bulgaria: Imprisonment of Ethnic Turks*, Amnesty International, EUR/15/03/86, p. 26.
21 Robert King, *Minorities under Communism, Nationalities as a source of Tension among Balkan Communist States*, Cambridge, Mass., Harvard University Press, 1973, pp. 188-9.

At Blagoevgrad in 1949 and 1950 twelve people were put on trial, including BCP members accused of being agents of 'foreign intelligence services'. It is claimed by UMO Ilinden (see below) that the real reason for their prosecution—five were sentenced to death and the others received long sentences—was their Macedonian orientation.[22] Hints of continuing similar trials have occasionally surfaced, and from the late 1950s reports of political trials of people accused of activity based on Macedonian nationalism continued. In 1958 three youths from the villages of Nikudin and Sandanski were sentenced for having 'established an organisation whose aim was to overthrow the People's democratic government in the District of Blagoevgrad of PR Bulgaria, by riots, disturbances, terroristic activities and crimes of mass danger'.[23]

A group of inhabitants of Blagoevgrad was tried in 1962 by the local District Court on charges of creating a group with the aim of bringing about the secession of Pirin Macedonia from the People's Republic of Bulgaria and in 1964 four people from there were reportedly tried for writing 'We are Macedonians' and 'Long live the Macedonian nation' on the wall of a restaurant. Since the introduction of the Criminal Code in 1968, most of those accused of propagating such 'anti-democratic and nationalist ideology' in the Communist period were charged under Articles 108 and 109 which deal respectively with 'anti-state agitation and propaganda' and with forming, leading or membership of an illegal group. Article 39(1) of the People's Militia Law of 1976 (amended on 12 August 1983) also allowed administrative punishment (i.e. without trial), which has reportedly been used to resettle members of the Macedonian ethnic minority forcibly in other areas of the country.[24] According to Yugoslav sources, the Bulgarian authorities forced whole families to move from the Pirin region to other regions in the north because of their affirmation of a distinct Macedonian ethnicity.[25] At the same time, the authorities concentrated resources in the Pirin region, notably in the health resort of Sandanski, apparently to lessen any possible attraction from neighbouring Yugoslavia.[26]

22 '*Testimonies*' submitted to the CSCE by UMO Ilinden in 1992.
23 *Ibid.*
24 Amnesty International, *op. cit.*, p. 26.
25 *NIN* Belgrade, 5 January 1975
26 *RFE Research Bulgaria* SR/2, 12 March 1985, p 5.

In 1973 another group of Macedonian nationalists—all from Petrich except for one, Ivan Tipchev from Pârvomay, 6 km. to the west—were arrested and tried reportedly for propagating Macedonian nationalism. The leader, Sokrat Markilov, and the others, including Stoyan Georgiev who had spent sixty days in detention in 1956 when aged nineteen and then been given a four-year sentence for Macedonian activism under Article 108 in 1957, were sentenced to up to five years' imprisonment. Sokrat Markilov, a long-time Macedonian activist, spent a total of nine years in prison and several in external exile for his activity, and his children were reportedly sent to live in other parts of Bulgaria.

Under Zhivkov, Bulgaria progressively moved towards expounding the ideology that the population of the country was a 'unified Bulgarian socialist nation', as it was commonly referred to in official statements in the 1970s. In this nation there were officially no minorities, with the exception of the small Jewish and Armenian minorities which were recognised for reasons of political propaganda. As Stanko Todorov—then member of the BCP Central committee and the Politburo, and Chairman of the National Assembly—stated in a speech on 28 March 1985, Bulgaria was a 'one-nation state' and in the Bulgarian nation 'there are no parts of any other peoples and nations'.[27]

The collapse of the Zhivkov regime brought about a dramatic improvement in the position of some of Bulgaria's minority groups, notably the ethnic Turks who had also suffered from the attempted ethnic homogenisation. For the Macedonians, however, the situation remained difficult. While there remained no problem with espousing a Macedonian consciousness if it formed a part of the wider Bulgarian one, any form of separate Macedonian self-identification continued to be prohibited, although the penalties for

---

27 Tanjug, 28 March 1985, in BBC SWB EE/7914 B/1, April 1985. Bulgaria is proud of its treatment of its Jewish minority in the Second World War and the Armenians were probably recognised both because there were few of them and also because of the massacres by Turkey in 1915—Turkey being the traditional enemy and a leading member of NATO's anti-Warsaw Pact alliance. Bulgaria's denial of minorities, similar to that in Greece, led to great friction with other groups in addition to those espousing a Macedonian consciousness—most notably the ethnic Turkish minority, numbering at least 1 million and comprising some 10 per cent of the total population. In 1984 the state summarily denied their existence as a separate ethnic group. For this and the attempted assimilation of the groups in Bulgaria see Poulton, *op. cit.*

breaking this ban were greatly reduced. Essentially, the state in post-totalitarian Bulgaria has banned, or at least actively discouraged, those who see themselves as Macedonian and not Bulgarian from public manifestations or any political activity related to this self-perception. Given the history of the area and Bulgaria's repeated defeats at the hands of Serbia/Yugoslavia and Greece in its attempt to acquire Macedonia, it is not surprising that many Bulgarians see such manifestations, and attemptes to make a connection between Pirin Macedonia and FYROM, as yet another ploy by Serbia/Yugoslavia to deprive Bulgaria of what rightfully belongs to it. There is a widespread sense that Serbia/Yugoslavia, which in the past 'stole' Vardar Macedonia from Bulgaria, is now also trying to take Pirin Macedonia.

This was stressed in February 1990 at the start of the new post-totalitarian period when the leaders of the main Bulgarian political parties—Aleksandar Lilov, chairman of the BCP Supreme Council; Angel Dimitrov, secretary of the Bulgarian National Agrarian Union (BZNS); Zhelyu Zhelev, then chairman of the Union of Democratic Forces (SDS) and subsequently Bulgarian President; and Petâr Dertliev, leader of the Bulgarian Social Democratic Party—all stressed that there was no 'Macedonian Question' and that Macedonians were Bulgarians.[28]

UMO Ilinden. On the other hand, within the country there were contradictory signals. In March 1990 a communiqué from an organisation calling itself the 'Solidarity and Struggle Committee of Pirin Macedonia' claiming to speak for 'the 250,000 Pirin Macedonians', stated that Pirin Macedonians 'have decided to fight on the side of the Macedonian Liberation Army' and called for an independent Macedonia 'uniting our Macedonian brethren struggling in Greece'. While this can be dismissed as fantasy, the Independent Macedonian Organisation, Ilinden, formed by Georgi Angelov Solunski in November 1989 immediately after Zhivkov's downfall, was more serious. On 11 March 1990 it organised a rally in Sofia with some 100 participants which demanded cultural and national autonomy for Macedonians in Bulgaria. It displayed slogans such as 'We are Macedonians and nothing else' and 'United Macedonia: a guarantee for peace'.[29]

28 BTA, 22 February 1990, in BBC SWB EE/0697, 24 February 1990.
29 BTA, 11 March 1990, in BBC SWB EE/0711 B/2, 13 March 1990.

This organisation was to some extent superseded on 14 April 1990 when out of it the United Macedonian Organisation (UMO) Ilinden was formed, and a variety of political clubs emerged in Petrich, Blagoevgrad and Sandanski. Along with Solunski's organisation, these were the Committee for the Defence and Rights of Macedonians in the Pirin part of Macedonia; the cultural-enlightenment Society 'Jane Sandanski' from Mikrevo village; and the Committee on the Repression of Macedonians in the Pirin part of Macedonia.[30] Solunski's Sofia organisation, while maintaining links with UMO Ilinden, retained its autonomy as a separate organisation with 2-300 members in Sofia (the authorities tended to see it as merely a part of UMO Ilinden). On 22 April 1990 UMO Ilinden held another rally at the Rozhen monastery where Yane Sandanski is buried. BTA claimed that Yugoslav citizens took part in this rally and the reaction of mainstream Bulgarian public opinion was to see it as a Yugoslav plot to dismember Bulgaria. UMO Ilinden also sent a declaration calling for an autonomous Macedonia to the UN, the Bulgarian National Assembly, the UDF, Bulgarian television, the European Parliament and the International Court of Justice in the Hague.[31]

The authorities were quick to respond and on 15 May 1990 the Sofia official prosecutor served a written communication on Georgi Solunski with the warning that his organisation should either register as a political party or disband within a month,[32] and on 23 May further specified that the 15 May communication meant that UMO Ilinden was to 'terminate its activities immediately'.[33] On 27 May BTA further reported that the organisation intended to go underground under 'the direct guidance of organisations in the Yugoslav constituent Socialist Republic of Macedonia'. It was clear that the Bulgarian authorities saw UMO Ilinden as a Yugoslav Trojan horse. On 6 June, its members taking part in a hunger strike outside Blagoevgrad district court in protest at the official measures against them were forcibly removed and deposited some 20 km. from town.

In July 1990, UMO Ilinden applied for registration at the

---

30 Stoyan Georgiev (Tomovichin), *Makedonija Nad Se*, Bitola, 1990 pp. 13-14, and BTA, 14 May 1990, in BBC SWB EE/0765 B/3, 16 May 1990.
31 BTA, 22 April 1990, in BBC SWB EE/0747 B/1, 25 April 1990.
32 BTA, 15 May 1990, in SWB EE/0757 B/1, 18 May 1990.
33 BTA, 23 May 1990, in BBC SWB EE/0774 B/2, 26 May 1990.

district court of Blagoevgrad but was turned down because its aims and the means for their attainment were contrary to Bulgarian unity, and would act as a spur to 'national and ethnic hostility'.[34] The Blagoevgrad prosecutor warned that the leaders faced prosecution under Article 162 of the penal code, which allowed for up to six years' imprisonment. Atanas Kiryakov, chief coordinator of UMO Ilinden, refused to accept the notification of warning.[35] The organisation attempted to hold its first constituent congress in Oshtava village, Sofia region, but the authorities prevented it and the leaders were fined.[36] The organisation claimed that 103 members had been prevented from taking part in this congress, with the leaders being subjected to short-term arrest. August saw the anniversary of the Ilinden-Preobrazhenie uprising against the Ottomans in 1903, and the major political parties including the new President of Bulgaria, Zhelyu Zhelev, again stressed that Macedonians were Bulgarians—a point which the Bulgarians tried to reinforce by publishing a letter from those claiming to be such living in Yugoslav Macedonia.[37]

Throughout 1990 the leaders of UMO Ilinden suffered harassment and short-term arrest. In October 1990 the authorities removed the passports of its then leader Stoyan Georgiev and of Sokrat Markilov. This sanction was also applied to others including a student studying in Skopje, Damyan Milenov Rizakov; his passport was removed on 16 October. In late 1990 and early 1991, police broke up an attempt to collect signatures in favour of Macedonian rights. UMO Ilinden again organised a demonstration in April 1991 at Sandanski's grave at the Rozhen monastery and protested that soldiers and police prevented many from Petrich from attending despite previous assurances that they were free to do so. Even so, the crowd gathered there numbered several thousands. However, a similar demonstration in April 1992 was less well attended, but this may have been partly due to bad weather—it was pouring with rain at the time.

The census in December 1992 provoked further complaints.

34 BTA, 18 July 1990.
35 BTA, 31 July 1990, in BBC SWB EE/0832 B/2, 2 August 1990.
36 Sofia Home Service, 2 August 1990, in BBC SWB EE/0836 B/5, 7 August 1990.
37 Sofia Home Service, 4 August 1990, in BBC SWB EE/0837 A2/3, 8 August 1990.

UMO Ilinden objected that while it was technically allowed to register as 'Macedonian' for ethnicity, there was no allowance for this on the forms. Yet the forms specifically mentioned, along with ethnic Bulgarians, most other groups no matter how small: Turks, Pomaks (Slav Muslims), Roma, Gagauz (Christian Turkish-speakers), Vlachs, Armenians, Jews and Sarakatsani (Greek-speaking transhumants). Thus to register as a 'Macedonian' it was necessary actually to deface the form. The UMO Ilinden activist Georgi Suhanov was arrested on 4 December 1992 in Petrich for putting up posters calling on Macedonians to register as such in the census. While passports of Ilinden activists have ceased to be withdrawn, the low-level repression continued in 1993. Police once again prevented UMO Ilinden supporters from meeting to commemorate the death of Yane Sandanski at the Rozhen monastery on 24 April; those who tried were reportedly beaten. The organisation was warned that such rallies would not be tolerated,[38] and in April the authorities confiscated copies of its paper *Skornuvane*. In mid-June 1993, Georgi Solunski was accused of firing shots at Luchezar Stoyanov, the leader of the ultra-nationalist Bulgarian National Democratic Party, in Sofia[39] in an incident which at the time of writing is still unclear.

UMO Ilinden claims more than 1,000 active members with organisations in all towns and most villages in Pirin Macedonia. It also claims organisations in Sofia, Plovdiv, Burgas and other major Bulgarian cities outside Macedonia. The membership fee is 5 leva a month which is used to arrange meetings etc. Its central organisational structure is a 25-member coordinating body which meets twice a month and is voted in each year, together with officers, from five regions of Pirin Macedonia: Blagoevgrad, (site of its headquarters), Petrich, Sandanski, Razlog and Gotse Delchev.[40] For two years its president was Stoyan Georgiev but he was replaced by Yordan Kostadinov. Relations between the two are not cordial and Georgiev left the coordinating committee in protest at what he saw as Kostadinov's extremist programme.

At its founding meeting in April 1990 UMO Ilinden adopted a constitution and an eleven-point programme. The constitution

38 BTA, 24 April 1993, in BBC SWB EE/1673 B/5, 27/4/93.
39 Bulgarian Radio Sofia, 21 June 1993 in BBC SWB EE/1722 B/3 23 June 1993, and BTA, 23 June 1993 in BBC SWB EE/1729 B/3, 1 July 1993.
40 Interview with Stoyan Georgiev, 7 April 1993, Petrich.

declared the aim to unite all Macedonian citizens of Bulgaria culturally (Article 1), and to strive for rights in accordance with Article 19 of the Helsinki Declaration on Human Rights and Article 52 of the Bulgarian Constitution (Article 2). Article 8 stated that the organisation would not attempt to violate Bulgaria's integrity, and Article 9 expressly eschewed violence and illegal activity. Article 10 stated that the organisation was against all forms of separatism, nationalism, chauvinism, assimilation and genocide, while Article 11 underlined religious freedom for all faiths. The party programme aimed at popularising and defending Macedonian history and culture (points 1 and 2), creating free tribunes for alternative thinking on the social and political development of Macedonia (point 3), and establishing connections with Macedonian organisations elsewhere (point 4).[41] Thus at the outset the organisation was moderate and legalistic in its aims and proposed methods. However tensions soon developed between moderates and radicals.

Georgiev, a builder by profession from Petrich who was sacked from his job as an inspector of schools in 1990 because of his activities in UMO Ilinden, represents the 'soft' wing of UMO Ilinden which is based more in Petrich and Gotse Delchev. This wing's programme foresaw a gradual policy of attempting to bring about a more tolerant political atmosphere, and totally rejected violence and any pressure on people. It asserted the right for everyone to express ethnic and religious identity freely without pressure from any side, and for closer connections with FYROM.[42]

Kostadinov is more radical and represents the 'hard-liners' associated with the Sandanski region. Born in 1932 in Vrapcha village in that region and a teacher by profession, he has spent five years in prison for his Macedonian activities—suffering eleven months in solitary confinement. He has even been threatened with being declared insane, and has repeatedly been dismissed from employment. In an interview of September 1992, he accused Georgiev and others including Yordan Berbatov of being 'pro-Bulgarian elements' and of reneging on signed agreements relating to issues of autonomy, the church, schools, radio and TV, and

---

41 Georgiev, *op.cit.*, pp. 87–90.
42 Ilona Tomova, 'Pirinska Makedonija—dve izsledvaniya', in *Aspekti na Etnokulturnata Situatsia b Bâlgariya*, Sofia, 1992.

language in Macedonia.[43] On this occasion he made his position clear:

'We are not a minority in Pirin Macedonia. It is inhabited exclusively by Macedonians, a few Muslim Macedonians who are under the influence of Turkish propaganda, and a few Bulgarophiles. However their percentage is small. We demand an autonomous status; an autonomous *oblast*, with the Macedonian language taught in the schools and spoken by the administration; a Macedonian Orthodox Church, independent of the Bulgarian Church; and radio and television in Blagoevgrad in the Macedonian language and in all other institutions. We shall demand the withdrawal of the Bulgarian occupation forces from Pirin Macedonia and keep only a militia to fight crime. Within this framework, we demand that we be supported by the Republic of Macedonia, the CSCE, the United Nations, and all other international institutions. Only in that way can we put a halt to the assimilation of the Macedonians in Pirin Macedonia.'

On irredentism and possible border changes he was ambivalent. On the one hand, 'We are not engaged in a fight. We do not favour territorial secession by force of arms. We are demanding our rights within the framework of Bulgaria.' He qualified this as follows: 'The separation of Pirin Macedonia and Aegean Macedonia and the unification of Macedonia are the concern of the Macedonian state, the United Nations, and the CSCE. However that is a separate phase. That is our right.'

The church question, as so often in the Balkans, was crucial. While Kostadinov called for a separate Macedonian Church, the real aim, according to Bulgarian observers, is not just separation but unification with the Ohrid Patriarchate—i.e. with the church in the former Yugoslav Republic of Macedonia.[44] Just how seriously the Bulgarians take the church issue is shown by the ban demanded by Nikolay Slatinski, chairman of the Parliament's National Security Committee, on all religious groups not in existence at 'the time of the liberation of Bulgaria from the Turkish domination' so that only the Bulgarian Orthodox Church, Islam, the Roman Catholic Church, the Armenian Apostolic Church and Judaism

---

43 Interview published in *Puls*, Skopje, 3 September 1992, in JPRS-EER-92-145, 14 October 1992.
44 Tomova, *op. cit.*, p. 298.

would be officially recognised. While this was aimed primarily at the mushrooming Protestant sects, the clear inference was that the Bulgarian Orthodox Church should be seen as an essential component in defining Bulgarian nationality and not allowed to be diluted by 'foreign' influences.[45] The inclusion of the Armenian church and Judaism alongside Islam and Roman Catholicism recalls Zhivkov's policy of recognising only those two small minorities.[46]

The relationship between those espousing a Macedonian consciousness and other non-mainstream Bulgarian groups is complex. The Slav Muslims in Pirin—the Pomaks—in the Mesta valley are under competing pressures as they are elsewhere in southern Bulgaria, especially the central Rhodope region where many live. Previously they lived traditional rural lives, but the opening up of the country, the new severe economic pressures on them, and the pressures of the Zhivkov regime's ludicrous assimilation campaign against them and the ethnic Turks[47] changed this. They are under pressure to identify either with the ethnic Bulgarian population or with the ethnic Turkish one and there have been reports of their forcible Turkicisation by ethnic Turkish activists. These charges are hard to assess. However there was a definite problem in ethnic identification registered by many Pomaks in the Mesta valley, and recent indications are that this ethnic group is being polarised between those espousing a Bulgarian and a Turkish consciousness, and the minority looks likely to lose its ethnic distinctiveness in the near future.[48] It does not seem at the time of writing that the Pomaks of Pirin are especially attracted by 'Macedonianism'.

Georgiev criticised Kostadinov specifically over his policy towards other peoples in Pirin Macedonia and accused him of inconsistency: he said in 1991 on Skopje TV that all nations in Macedonia were brothers—Macedonians, Roma, Jews and so on—and that the Balkans was 'a mosaic of nations'. However, Georgiev asserted that Kostadinov really wanted the expulsion

45 Randy Tift, 'Bulgarian Protestants unite to resist attacks on "sects"' in *News Network International—News Service*, 30 June 1993, p. 2.
46 See note 27 above, p. 150.
47 See Poulton, *op. cit.*
48 See studies by Aleksey Kalyonski, e.g. 'Pogled vârhy etnoreligioznoto sâzhitelstvo b Srednite Rodopi—Dospatcko, Devisko i Chepelarsko, in *Aspekti na Etnokulturnata*, Sofia, 1992.

of all Turks and those who consider themselves to be Bulgarians.[49] In his 1992 interview Kostadinov stated: 'In Pirin Macedonia, we have not cooperated with the Turks. Naturally we would like to establish relations with all parties. I believe that we shall have good relations with the Turks. However, it will be difficult to find a common language with the Bulgarians.'

There have been allegations by the security forces that there is an agreement between UMO Ilinden and the ethnic Turkish Movement for Rights and Freedom (DPS). At a news conference on 3 September 1991 it was stated that a treaty 'signed in blood' existed between the DPS and UMO Ilinden on the territorial partition of Bulgaria.[50] This however seems fanciful.

The Roma community in Pirin Macedonia remains firmly at the bottom of the social scale as it does elsewhere in Bulgaria, and subject to everyday racism. In Petrich they number up to 4,000 and are mostly Muslim, but in April 1993, according to community leaders, only some 100 had proper employment.[51] They do not seem to be involved in the 'Macedonian question'.

Exactly how many members UMO Ilinden has and how popular it is in Pirin Macedonia is hard to ascertain. The organisation's strength appears to reside mainly in the villages, especially in the Petrich, Sandanski and Strumyanski districts, notably Musomishte, Eleshnitsa, Mikrevo, Krupnik and Kolarovo. Tomova estimates that it has about 1,500 members in all.[52] The mainstream Bulgarian media repeatedly suggest that it is not popular in Pirin Macedonia[53] but this is perhaps to be expected. Bulgarian commentators invariably state that UMO Ilinden receives material aid from outside, notably from the former Yugoslav Republic of Macedonia but also from émigré circles in Canada and Australia.[54] Georgiev stated that he personally had good contacts with VMRO-DPMNE in Skopje, while Kostadinov expressed disappointment in what he saw as the lack of support from that quarter.[55]

Bulgarian commentators repeatedly (and irrelevantly) stress that

49 Georgiev interview.
50 BTA, 3 September 1991, in BBC SWB EE/1169 ii, 5 September 1991.
51 Interview with author, 7 April 1993, Petrich.
52 Tomova, *op. cit.,* pp. 294-5.
53 e.g. BTA 18 April 1991, in BBC SWB EE/1054 B/2, 24 April 1991.
54 See *Duma,* Sofia, 16 February 1991, in JPRS-EER-91-033, and Tomova, *op. cit.,* pp. 292-3.
55 *Puls* interview, *op. cit.*

UMO Ilinden members, as well as being agents of foreign powers, are people of inferior education and culture, especially in the cities—alcoholics, 'rabble' and 'criminal types'.[56] The very nature of these attacks on UMO Ilinden members illustrates the unease felt over the position of Pirin Macedonia by mainstream Bulgarian opinion, which points with some justification to the influence of an adverse economic situation there in the appearance and growth of UMO Ilinden.

The socio-economic situation. The total population of Blagoevgrad district, which is effectively co-terminous with Pirin Macedonia, was 356,512 on 31 December 1989, and the region was not noticeably affected by the mass exodus of ethnic Turks in that year—an indication of the small number of ethnic Turks in the Muslim population there as opposed to Pomaks and Roma.[57] In 1992 the district had the second highest number of officially registered unemployed among Bulgaria's twenty-nine districts. Official figures on 30 August 1991 gave the number as 20,527, i.e. about 6.5 per cent of the national total and almost 10 per cent of the working population in the district. The majority of these were young people under the age of thirty and more than half were women. The high unemployment level among Roma in Pirin Macedonia has already been noted. Some 55 per cent of the population of the district live in cities and of these about 80 per cent need social help due to their poverty.[58] Moreover, according to an aside in the Sofia daily *Demokratsiya* in May 1991, Blagoevgrad was the city with the highest food prices in the country, Razlog had the worst unemployment, because of their poor transport system and lack of fuel the regions of Bansko and Gotse Delchev were 'practically cut off from the world', and Petrich and Sandanski were 'on the threshold of misery'. The article blamed the incompetence of the Bulgarian Communist Party for this state of affairs which it said accounted for the support there for UMO Ilinden.[59]

In the election to the Grand National Assembly, the regional

56 E.g. see Tomova *op. cit,* p. 290.
57 *Demokratsiya,* Sofia, 3 September 1991.
58 Tomova, *op. cit.,* pp. 287 and 295.
59 Lyudmill Georgiev, 'Makedonskiyat vâpros kato politicheska propaganda 2', *Demokratsiya,* Sofia, 24 May 1991.

alliance of the SDS convincingly came out on top in the district. It won ten seats while the Bulgarian Socialist (former Communist) Party won three, the ethnic Turkish DPS two (no doubt aided by Muslim Pomak support), and the Bulgarian National Agrarian Union one. *Demokratsiya*, which supported the SDS, pointed out that in Blagoevgrad and Petrich that party had been the first socio-political organisation to react 'sharply and categorically to the new anti-Bulgarian wave of the Skopje and Serbian Communist propaganda of the end of 1989'. It referred also to the killing in Pirin of 'Bulgarian patriots' and their burial in 'mass graves near Dobrinishte and Blagoevgrad' immediately after the Communist take-over of 9 September 1944 when the Tito-Dimitrov agreement on the Macedonian issue was in operation. The article ended with a ringing attack on current views in Western Europe concerning the 'non-existent "Macedonian minority"', pointing again to the Bulgarian Communist Party's culpability immediately after the Second World War in helping to propagate such views.[60]

Other Bulgarian-Macedonian organisations. The prominence we have given to UMO Ilinden is due to its espousal of a Macedonian nation distinct from the Bulgarian. There are however many legal organisations of Macedonians, apparently with a greater membership, identifying themselves as part of the ethnic Bulgarian nation. As noted above, all mainstream Bulgarian political parties—not just the ultra-nationalist fringe represented by Dr Ivan Georgiev of the National Democratic Party, who saw in the Western attack on Iraq after its invasion of Kuwait justification for similar actions over Bulgaria's 'lost' Macedonian territories[61]— contest any notion of a Macedonian national consciousness in Pirin Bulgaria. President Zhelev again stressed this in an interview on Hungarian television in April 1991: 'Regarding the Macedonian minority it is an invented concept and the problem does not exist. It is only an excuse to find failures not in the neighbours but in us.'[62]

The main pro-Bulgarian Macedonian organisation is the Internal Macedonian Revolutionary Organisation-Union of Macedonian

60 Lyudmil Georgiev, 'Makedonskiyat vâpros kato politicheska propaganda', *Demokratsiya*, Sofia, 23 May 1991.
61 See *Borba*, Belgrade, 21 January 1991.
62 Hungarian Television, Budapest, 14 April 1991.

Societies (VMRO-SMD) led by Docent Dimitâr Gotsev. It has fifty-six branches throughout the country, and its supporters consist mainly of descendants of migrants from parts of Macedonia outside Bulgaria who fled to Bulgaria in the past, as well as from Pirin. The associated Macedonian Scientific Institute aims to propagate the Bulgarian side of the great historical arguments over Macedonia.[63] Article 1 of VMRO-SMD's statute states: 'It shall struggle against the denationalisation and assimilation of the Bulgarian population in Vardar and Aegean Macedonia.'[64] The perception of Serbia as the main enemy was underlined by VMRO-SMD's announcement in July 1991 that it had set up a committee to recruit volunteers to fight for Slovenia and Croatia against Serbia.[65]

At a pro-Bulgarian Macedonian Fair in Blagoevgrad in May 1991, Gotsev stated that VMRO-SMD's prime objective was to counter 'Pan-Serbian and Pan-Greek ambitions at the expense of the Macedonian Bulgarians', and he urged the Greek government—with which, so BTA stated, there were good relations—'to recognise the Bulgarian nationality in Aegean Macedonia and to set up Bulgarian schools there.' He added: 'We are against the lies of the Comintern and of Tito that we are Macedonians and not Bulgarians.'[66] The list of enemies was extended in 1993 when the VMRO-SMD leader Evgeni Ekov, referring to UMO Ilinden, said: 'Macedonianism and Pan-Turkism are two threats to Bulgaria', and accusing the government of 'criminal inaction' over Macedonia, he directly accused the United States of being the world power that inspired and supported these forces in Bulgaria.[67]

The Bulgarian state, in contrast to its hostility to UMO Ilinden, is supportive of VMRO-SMD. However, some think that it did not do enough to 'rebuff the pseudo-historians from neighbouring countries', and a more radical organisation—the All-Bulgarian Macedonia Union, headed by Hristov Tzavela—was set up in 1990 as an alternative to VMRO-SMD. This new organisation

63 Prof. Dobrin Michev, 'Macedonian separatism threatens national unity', *Duma*, Sofia, 15 February 1991.
64 Vladimir Tulevski, 'European Exterior but Balkan Interior!', *Nova Makedonija*, Skopje, 16 March 1992, in JPRS-EER-92- 044.
65 BTA, 4 July 1991, in JPRS-EER-91-100.
66 BTA, 25 May 1991, in BBC SWB EE/1086 B/5, 31 May 1991.
67 BTA, 8 April 1993, in BBC SWB EE/1660 B/4, 12 April 1993.

reportedly wanted to create a militarised structure with loyalty oaths, local managements and even a mail and courier service of its own.[68] This suggested worrying similarities with the VMRO 'state within a state' which was so destructive of Bulgarian political life in the 1920s.

Either way, both these organisations are unremittingly hostile to UMO Ilinden, and there have been clashes between rival bands of supporters with UMO Ilinden supporters being met with such shouts as 'Traitors' and 'Serbomens'.[69] VMRO-SMD also called on the National Assembly not to allow the proposed new 'Slavonic University' in Bulgaria to introduce the Macedonian language as a separate subject, and asked it to investigate allegations that the project was financed by a 'foreign intelligence agency'.[70] In June 1993 a new monthly publication called *Makedoniya* came out in Blagoevgrad, claiming to be the successor to one of the same title published by Nikola Kolarov in Skopje in 1943, when Bulgaria controlled Vardar Macedonia. The monthly aimed to highlight 'the contribution of the Macedonian region to Bulgarian history'.[71]

Greece

Continued denial. In the period after the civil war, the Macedonians were not surprisingly seen as potentially disloyal to the Greek state and steps were taken to try and remove such 'undesirable aliens' from the sensitive border regions with Yugoslavia. The census of 1951 recorded only some 47,000 'Slavophones', although the nature of the official attitude should cause this figure to be treated with scepticism. In 1953, decree no. 2536 was enacted to settle the northern territories 'with new colonists possessing a healthy national consciousness.'[72] The anti-Macedonian character of this law was evident in the exclusion of the Turks in Western

68 *Ibid.*
69 E.g. on 4 May in Blagoevgrad when UMO Ilinden members were prevented from laying wreaths in homage to Gotse Delchev, BTA, 5 May 1991, in BBC SWB EE/1066 B/2, 8 May 1991.
70 BTA, 14 June 1993, in BBC SWB EE/1716 B/4, 16 June 1993.
71 BTA, 6 June 1993, in BBC SWB EE/1710 B/3, 9 June 1993.
72 Lazo Mojsov, *Okoly Prashenjeto na Makedonskoto Natsionalno Maltsinstvo vo Grtsija*, published by the Institute for National History, Skopje, 1954, p. 17.

Thrace from such measures.[73] It was forbidden in this period for Macedonians to use the Slavonic forms for their names; only Greek forms could be used for official purposes—a measure with obvious parallels to recent Bulgarian measures against its minorities. It the beginning of 1954 the Papagos government resolved to remove all Macedonians from official posts in Greek Macedonia. In the regions bordering Yugoslavia peasants were not allowed to move from their villages and, in 1959 around Florina (Lerin) and Kastoria (Kostur) villages, were asked to confirm publicly in front of officials that they did not speak Macedonian. As the result many emigrated to Australia or Canada.[74]

However, in 1959 the Greek and Yugoslav authorities came to an agreement on the freedom of movement of people living in border areas around Florina in Greece and Bitola in Yugoslavia. Several thousands were allowed to move freely in this designated area—10km. either side of the border—and within it to cross the official frontier without passports. This step can be seen as a humanitarian gesture since many families were divided by the borders. It can also perhaps be seen as a tacit recognition by the Greek authorities of the Slav nature of the population in this area. The agreement was ended in 1967 by the Greek military rulers.

Since the civil war, the official denial of a Macedonian minority in Greece has remained constant regardless of the government in power, whether democratic or the military dictatorship of 1967-74. The return to democracy in Greece saw an improvement with the abandonment of the official terror which had held sway over the whole population. However, the education system and the lack of job opportunities in any branch of the state bureaucracy for those declaring themselves to be Macedonian have greatly aided assimilation into the Greek majority, and the Greek authorities have apparently come a long way towards achieving this aim. It is notable that Macedonian nationalism appears much stronger in émigrés from Greek Macedonia, not only in former Yugoslavia but also in Australia and Canada, than in the area itself.

Given the situation in Greece, this is not surprising. In a letter in May 1992 to Greek president Karamanlis, Tilman Zileich, president of the Society of Threatened Peoples in the World

73 Tosho Popovski, *op. cit.*, p. 223.
74 *Ibid.* p. 196.

(based in Göttingen, Germany), accused successive Greek governments of active repression against Slav Macedonians. The Skopje newspaper *Nova Makedonija* gleefully reported on this letter and went on to enumerate a detailed list of repressive actions allegedly taken by the Greek authorities against all aspects of Slav Macedonian national self-identification. These included the restriction of employment in Greek Macedonia to only Greek citizens whose mother-tongue was Greek, while mother-tongue Slav speakers could only work in the south of the country; rigorous steps to prohibit use of the Macedonian language and customs by party and youth organisations in rural areas of Greek Macedonia; Slav Macedonian women being forced to deny their ethnic identity when marrying ethnic Greeks; prohibition of the use of the Macedonian language on pain of a variety of punishments including 'threats, and imprisonment, not only in [prisons]...but also in the very homes of the Macedonians.'[75]

Zileich's letter was apparently prompted by the alleged discovery of a secret document, 'Measures Against Macedonia', dated 16 February 1981and signed by Lieutenant-General Dimitris Katelaris. This was reprinted in the article in *Nova Makedonija*:

> The efforts of the people of Skopje to gain Macedonian independence must be blocked by all possible means. The best ways are :

> —To prohibit the use of the Macedonian language and for Macedonians to move to other parts of Greece and be replaced by Greeks, thus eliminating the 'Macedonia question'.

> —To prohibit the return of Macedonians who have escaped and lived elsewhere, so that not a single Macedonian will remain in the northern part of Greece, and to block any type of cultural and linguistic propaganda coming from Skopje to that part of Greece.

> —To set up special organisations under the supervision of the Ministry of Internal Affairs and thus block the spread of Macedonianism in northern Greece.

> —To employ individuals who do not speak Macedonian.

75 *Nova Makedonija*, Skopje, 15 May 1992, in JPRS-EER-92- 069, 2 June 1992.

—To encourage those who are employed with free housing, recreation and other state benefits.

—To promote Greek cultural societies and expand them; to publish books and pamphlets to promote the concept that, abroad, Aegean Macedonia will be considered Greek, thus deleting the word "Macedonia".

—To cause various difficulties for students from Greece studying in Skopje to prevent them from pursuing their studies (deferment [of compulsory military service] denied and so forth).

—To encourage young people everywhere to promote the Greek idea and, if necessary, to persuade the people, also with the help of money, that neither the Macedonian language nor Macedonians exist.

—To move immediately to the southern part of Greece all employed individuals in Lerin [Florina] who speak Macedonian.

—To give service benefits and promotions to soldiers who marry Macedonian women and make them adopt Greek customs.

—To industrialise the land with a view to full employment for the Greeks and the development of high standards, thus blocking the spread of propaganda coming from Skopje and neutralising the Macedonians.

If this document is authentic—even if it is not, many of its recommendations have been carried out by successive Greek administrations—it sets forth in great detail an official policy of repression against Slav Macedonians.

Despite this repression and the successful Hellenising of Greek Macedonia, there have nevertheless been some recent internal manifestations of Macedonian nationalism there. In 1989 an organisation appeared, calling itself the Central Committee for Macedonian Human Rights and claiming to be based in Salonika. Five of its members from Greece joined a delegation of Macedonians which visited the UN Centre for Human Rights in Geneva, the Council of Europe, and the European Parliament in May 1989, claiming that by doing so they risked 'severe reprisals for both themselves and their families' from the Greek authorities.[76]

76 *The Way Ahead for Macedonian Human Rights—Report of the Europe 89 Delegation,*

On 20 July 1990 the local authorities were reported to have forcibly disrupted a Macedonian 'national day' in the village of Meliti in Florina district, and émigrés allege that similar incidents took place in other Macedonian areas during that week, and some Macedonians in government employment have been forced to transfer to distant regions of the country on pain of dismissal. The Macedonian activist and president of the above-named committee, Christos Sideropoulos, a forestry worker, reportedly received an ultimatum from his employer, the regional government of Florina, to transfer to the island of Kefalonia within twenty-four hours or face dismissal.[77] He complied with the order but later, as we see below, returned to face stiffer repression.

Another organisation, the Macedonian Movement for Balkan Prosperity (MAKIVE), appeared in January 1993,[78] It has occasionally published a newspaper called at first *Moglena* and later *Zora*. How much local popular backing these organisations have is hard to gauge, but it appears that much of their support comes from elements who are resentful at the lack of opportunity in this underdeveloped area of north-western Greece; many of the activists, who face a variety of harassments, are from families who suffered persecution after the civil war. In the local elections of early 1993, Pavlos Voskopoulos from MAKIVE received 14 per cent of the vote.

However, the massive dilution of the Macedonian population both by emigration and by the influx of Greeks, combined with natural assimilation into the majority aided through their shared religion, and the experience of the civil war has made the aim of some kind of Macedonian state incorporating Greek Macedonia a notion predominantly held by those outside Greece.

Refugees and relations between Greece, Yugoslavia and Bulgaria. A continuing legacy of the Greek civil war has been the refugees who fled from the country when the war ended. According to Association of Refugee Children from Yugoslav Macedonia and Red Cross

---

prepared by Michael Radin and Dr Christopher Popov, Central Organizational Committee for Macedonian Human Rights, Salonika (no date).

77 The minority Turks in western Thrace claim that similar methods are used against them by the Greek authorities. See Poulton, *op. cit.*

78 I am indebted to Anastasia Karakasidou for much of the information on MAKIVE.

estimates, they included some 25-30,000 children aged between two and fourteen. The Greek government alleged that many of these children had been virtually kidnapped by Communists, but relatively few parents requested Red Cross help for their return.[79] Many of the refugees were Slav Macedonians who went to Yugoslavia or other East European Communist countries, and from 1955 onwards Yugoslavia made efforts to attract the refugees from other countries to Yugoslav Macedonia. *Borba*, published in Belgrade on 6 June 1988, stated that there were 150,000 such people who were full citizens of Yugoslavia; however, other Yugoslav sources put the numbers of Macedonians who emigrated in the period 1945-9 from Yugoslav Macedonia as only some 40–50,000 out of a total of 60-70,000. As often occurs with Yugoslav sources, there appears to be confusion about the numbers as there is about the numbers of Macedonians in Greek Macedonia at present: some Yugoslav sources put the latter figure at 350,000 but more sober estimates put it at 150-200,000.

The Greek government confiscated the property of these refugees by Decree 2536/53, which also deprived them of their Greek citizenship.[80] It later enacted a law enabling the property to be returned to refugees who were 'Greek by birth'—by which was meant those who renounced their Macedonian nationality and adopted Greek names.[81] Greece has also consistently denied entry visas to these refugees except in a few cases, e.g. to attend funerals, but even then with difficulty. In July 1988, following a reunion in Skopje, more than 100 of these former refugees attempted to visit northern Greece but were turned back at the border after Greek officials refused some of them entry. Lefter Lajovski, a participant at the reunion, who was by then a Canadian citizen, claimed that the authorities had asked him to change his name to a Greek one if he wanted to enter Greece, even though no visa is required for Canadian citizens.[82]

Such actions by the Greek government against Macedonians and the Yugoslav Socialist Republic of Macedonia escalated after Andreas Papandreou and his socialist party, PASOK, come to

79 Richard Clogg, *A Short History of Modern Greece*, Cambridge University Press, 1979, p. 164.
80 Popovski, *op. cit.,* p. 196.
81 Tanjug, 6 June 1988, in BBC SWB EE/0712 A1/3, 8 June 1988.
82 Reuter 201651 GMT of 30 June 1988.

power in Greece. Skopje's Kiril i Metodija University was removed from the list of foreign academic institutions whose degrees were recognised by Greece because the language of instruction at the university, Macedonian, was 'not internationally recognised'.[83] Greece repeatedly refused Yugoslavia's bilateral initiatives to abolish visas, and while Serbs, Croats and other Yugoslav nationals had few problems, Tanjug on 12 July 1984 reported that the Greek consulate in Skopje was asking for special proof from Macedonian applicants for entry visas that they were not natives of Greek Macedonia. Papandreou himself explicitly denied the existence of a Macedonian minority in Greece, and said that he would not accept any dialogue on this matter.[84] An example of the lengths to which this was taken was the last-minute cancellation in September 1987, when the players were already on court and 5,000 spectators were present, of a friendly basketball match between Aris of Salonika and Metalno Zavod Tito of Skopje due to take place in Salonika. According to the Skopje paper *Vecher* of 1 October 1987, this was because the letter 'M' in the name of the Skopje team was seen by the Minister for Northern Greece as standing for Macedonia.

The Greek conservative party, *Nea Democratia*, also continued its hostility to the Socialist Republic of Macedonia and in early 1986 set up a monitoring centre in Florina to monitor broadcasts from Skopje for anti-Yugoslav commentaries. Papandreou himself was attacked by some Greek newspapers for travelling to Yugoslavia in January 1986 'at a time of an allegedly stepped-up Yugoslav propaganda drive concerning the so-called Macedonian question', and the small-circulation Greek newspaper *Stohos*, which takes an extreme nationalistic line on minority matters, has alleged that Greek students in Skopje have been pressured to declare themselves as Macedonians, and urged Greeks to fight with all available means against those who speak Slav Macedonian.[85]

Relations between the Papandreou government and Bulgaria, on the other hand, were good. It appears that the Bulgarians have acquiesced in the loss of Aegean Macedonia to Greece, and have united with Greece in denying the existence of a Macedonian nation as espoused by the Yugoslavs—even going

83 Tanjug, 15 May 1986, in BBC SWB EE/8262 Al/6, 19 March 1986.
84 *Ibid.*
85 Tanjug, 19 April 1986, in BBC SWB EE/8328 Al/1, 21 April 1986.

as far as to exclude from Bulgarian television the Yugoslav entry (a Macedonian song) in the 1988 Eurovision Song Contest along with the Turkish and Israeli entries.[86] The shared problem of enmity to Turkey and Turkish minorities was another factor in this Greek–Bulgarian friendship, as was well illustrated by the visit of the Greek Foreign Minister to Sofia and subsequent public thanks to Bulgaria, then a Warsaw Pact member, for its support in 1988 during a confrontation with Turkey, ostensibly Greece's NATO ally, over territorial problems in the Aegean. The Greeks apparently did not react with the same outrage as the Yugoslavs to the perennial Bulgarian statements about the 'unjust' annulment of the 'Greater Bulgaria' of the San Stefano treaty of 1878, which included part of present-day Greece as well as Yugoslav Macedonia; also, the Greeks do not claim any part in historical events like the Ilinden uprising of 1903 as both the Bulgarians and Macedonians do. Also the Bulgarians do not antagonise the Greeks by making films like 'The Rescue' which won the highest Bulgarian honour, the Dimitrov prize, in 1986 and which claimed that the population of Ohrid in 1944 was Bulgarian.

Worsening relations and the rise of Greek nationalism. After Papandreou's fall from power in 1990, relations between Greece and Yugoslavia over the Macedonian question continued to deteriorate. One factor in this was the rise of a more assertive Macedonian nationalism in Yugoslavia as the Yugoslav state began to disintegrate. A mass demonstration in Skopje protesting at the lack of minority rights for Macedonians in Greece and Bulgaria was organised on 20 February 1990 to coincide with a visit to Belgrade by the Greek Premier, Constantin Mitsotakis. In protest at Greece continuing to obstruct the granting of visas to some of their fellow-citizens, Yugoslav Macedonians organised a series of rallies on the Yugoslav border with the support of the Presidency of the Macedonian Republic of Yugoslavia. These began in May and after a ten-hour blockade of the Yugoslav–Greek border by Yugoslav protestors on 16 June, Greece responded by obliging all Yugoslav travellers to Greece to show proof of possession of 1,000 US dollars.[87] Additionally, on 3 June 1990 a new organisation bearing the English name 'Dignity' was founded in Skopje dedicated to protecting

86 *Večernje Novosti*, Zagreb, 10 June 1988, in BBC SWB EE/0177 i, 14 June 1988.
87 Tanjug in BBC SWB EE/0795 i, 20 June 1990.

the rights and freedoms of Macedonians living in Greece.[88] A similar organisation with a branch in Skopje was *Dostoinstvo*, which met FYROM President Gligorov on 17 June 1991.[89]

The continuing unravelling of Yugoslavia aroused strong reactions in Greece. In March 1991 the Yugoslav Embassy in Athens was daubed with graffiti saying 'Macedonia is Greek', 'Gypsies of Skopje get out of Greece' and 'Down with the Skopje Traitors'.[90] Polemics escalated sharply with the break-up of Yugoslavia and the independence of FYROM which followed. The use by the new country of symbols (like the star of Vergina on the new flag) from Philip of Macedon incensed Greek opinion and helped to fuel an extraordinary rise in nationalism with Greece resolutely vetoing any attempt to recognise the new country with the name Macedonia.

The issue of the name, along with the rise in Greek nationalism, have led to a situation where even discussion of it or of the minority situation can be dangerous even for ethnic Greeks. An illustration of Greek sensitivity over the issue was a series of arrests and trials of left-wing Greeks for attempting to criticise the government's refusal to move on the recognition issue. Six members of a group called the 'Organisation for the Reconstruction of the KKE' were tried on 27 January 1992 and sentenced to six and a half months' imprisonment for putting up posters saying 'Recognise Independent Slav Macedonia', and four students, members of a 'Coalition against Nationalism and War', were sentenced to nineteen months' imprisonment for distributing a leaflet entitled 'The neighbouring peoples are not our enemies'. In both cases the accused were released pending appeal. Five other left-wing Greeks were tried on a variety of charges due to the publication and distribution of a pamphlet on Macedonia. The trial was due to begin in Athens in September 1992 but has been repeatedly postponed due to a lawyers' strike. The defendants were eventually acquitted after international concern had been expressed.

Less fortunate were the two leading Macedonian activists, Christos Sideropoulos and Tasos Boulis, who were sentenced on 1 April 1993 to five months' imprisonment for spreading false information and instigating conflict among Greeks due to comments

88 Tanjug, 3 June 1990, in BBC SWB EE/0784 B/10, 7 June 1990.
89 Tanjug, 17 June 1991, in BBC SWB EE/1107 Al/3, 25 June 1991.
90 Tanjug, 8 March 1991, in BBC SWB EE/1024 Al/4, 19 March 1991.

they had made in an interview with the Greek weekly magazine *ENA* on 11 March 1992, in which they accused Greece of violating the rights of Slav Macedonians.[91] Both claim that half of Greek Macedonia's 2-million-strong community are Slav, but deny any autonomist aspirations: they insist that they are citizens of Greece but nonetheless want the right to express themselves freely.[92] On the other hand they would not oppose border changes 'if this were legal'.[93] At the time of writing they remained free pending appeal. In another case the Greek Orthodox hierarchy reportedly relieved Archimandrite Nikodimos Tsarknias of his duties in his parish outside Salonika due to his self-identification as a Macedonian and then expelled him from the church.[94]

91 Macedonian Information Centre, Balga (Western Australia), 26 October 1992.
92 *The Guardian*, London, 2 April 1993.
93 Quoted in Paulina Lampsa, 'Macedonians in Greece: A Trial and its Implications', *Helsinki Citizens Assembly*, no. 7, Summer 1993, p. 6.
94 *The West Australian*, 8 March 1993, and issue no. 14 (no date) from the Macedonian Information Centre, Balga.

9

INDEPENDENT MACEDONIA

Political relaxation and nationalist expression in 1989 and 1990

In mid-1989, in line with developments elsewhere in Yugoslavia and the momentous changes taking place in Eastern Europe, the ruling League of Communists of Macedonia committed itself to the introduction of a multi-party system in SR Macedonia.[1] However as noted above, the Macedonians had probably as much if not more to lose if Yugoslavia broke up: perhaps their very existence. One reaction to this was to assert Macedonian nationalism more aggressively to hide potential weakness. In 1989 the constitution was reworded so that SR Macedonia was redefined as 'a nation-state of Macedonian people' in place of the previous 'a state of the Macedonian people and the Albanian and Turkish minorities'. In September 1990, the Assembly adopted a constitutional amendment stating: 'The SR of Macedonia takes care of the status and rights of parts of the Macedonian nation living in neighbouring countries, takes care of Macedonians living in other countries, Macedonian emigrants and guest workers from Macedonia; it encourages and aids forging and developing ties with all them.'[2]

In October 1989 the slogans 'Solun [Salonika] is ours', 'Prohor Pčinjski [a monastery near the border with SR Macedonia which since 1953 has been part of Serbia] is Macedonian', 'Chento'

1 Tanjug, 31 August 1990.
2 Tanjug, 6 September 1990 in BBC SWB EE/0864 B/8, 8 September 1990. This became the basis of Article 49 of the new 1991 Constitution which despite passing the Badinter commission's appraisal has upset both Greece and Bulgaria.

(a Macedonian nationalist leader tried by the Communists after the war), and 'We fight for a united Macedonia' began to be chanted by supporters of Vardar, the main Skopje football team.[3] Similar slogans soon appeared on the walls of Skopje, with the authorities apparently not hunting down such activity once viewed as 'hostile'.[4]

More serious manifestations soon emerged. On 4 February the founding assembly of the Movement for All-Macedonian Action (MAAK) was set up mainly by the Macedonian intelligentsia initially with the head of the Writers Union, the poet Ante Popovski, as its leader.[5] MAAK stated that it had no territorial ambitions on Macedonia's neighbours, but it has criticised Bulgaria and Greece, and in July 1990 local MAAK leaders from Strumica met delegates from the UMO Ilinden movement in Bulgaria to discuss co-operation.[6] On 20 February a large demonstration of Macedonians—estimates of the number present varied from 30,000 to 120,000—took place in Skopje as an assertion of their identity and to protest at perceived oppression of Macedonians in Bulgaria, Greece and Albania. The rally was apparently timed to coincide with the visit to Belgrade of the Greek Prime Minister, Constantin Mitsotakis.[7] A more radical nationalist party than MAAK emerged in June 1990 with the founding congress in Skopje on 17 June of the Internal Macedonian Revolutionary Organisation Democratic Party of Macedonian National Unity (VMRO-DPMNE)—a significant choice of name—with delegates from the Macedonian diaspora. Led by Ljupco Georgijevski, it pledged to carry on the principles of the Ilinden uprising of 1903 and work for 'the ideal of all free Macedonians united' in a Macedonian state.[8] It also expressed the desire for improvements in relations with Slovenia and Croatia and for the return of some territories currently in Serbia, and on 2 August, to mark the Ilinden uprising, it held a demonstration of over 100 members at Prohor Pčinjski monastery which Serbian police forcibly dispersed.[9]

3 *Politika*, Belgrade, 27 October 1989.
4 *Borba*, Belgrade, 4/5 November 1989.
5 Tanjug, 4 February 1990, in BBC SWB EE/0682 B/11, 7 February 1990.
6 *RFE Weekly Record of Events*, 16 July 1990.
7 *RFE Weekly Record of Events*, 20 February 1990.
8 *Oslobodjenje*, Sarajevo, 23 June 1990.
9 *RFE Weekly Record of Events*, 2 August 1990.

Meanwhile an organisation for Bulgarians in SR Macedonia had begun to be active, and on 4 August the Society of Bulgarians in Vardar Macedonia published an appeal 'to the Bulgarian people' denying the whole concept of a Macedonian nation and stressing the Bulgarian nature of all Macedonians in Yugoslavia and Greece as well as Bulgaria. The letter appealed to the 'new democratic Bulgaria to intercede on their [Bulgarians outside Bulgaria] behalf.... millions of Bulgarians live outside their native land but part of them for decades have been denied by all possible means their rights to self-determination as a nation and people.'[10] Such actions prompted the Communist authorities in SR Macedonia to suspect VMRO-DPMNE of provoking national intolerance towards the Serbian people and favouring 'the Bulgarian nation'.[11] This latter charge of being pro-Bulgarian seems unfounded but as with VMRO at the turn of the century there have apparently been splits in VMRO-DPMNE, even with a case of a member being sentenced to death by a kangaroo court of fellow members.[12] Further pro-Bulgarian manifestations were evident with the Human Rights Party led by Ilija Ilijevski, although this appeared to have little support outside Bulgaria,[13] and was banned by the Macedonian Supreme Court in January 1994.

The growing Serbian nationalism of the 1980s, triggered off by perceived repression of Serbs in Kosovo and used by Milošević for his own ends,[14] also worked to revive fears of Serbian claims on Macedonia. Laws passed by Milošević's government on 'returns', whereby Serb emigrants who had allegedly been forced out of Kosovo and received compensation, could in theory be applied to Serbs forced out of SR Macedonia after the war when the territory changed from being 'South Serbia'. On 2 June 1990 Petar Goshev, president of the Macedonian Communist party now called the League of Communists of Macedonia-Party for Democratic Renewal (SKM-PDP),[15] while indulging in the routine

10 Sofia Home Service, 4 August 1990, in BBC SWB EE/0837 A2/3, 8 August 1990.
11 Tanjug, 2 September 1990, in BBC SWB EE/0861 B/17, 5 September 1990.
12 *Oslobodjenje*, Sarajevo, 5 September 1990.
13 See BTA, 2 September 1991 in BBC SWB EE/1170 B/9, 6 September 1991, and *Demokratsiya*, 20 March 1991.
14 For this see Poulton, *op. cit.*
15 At its congress in 21 April 1991, the SKM-PDP changed its name again to the Social Democratic Alliance of Macedonia and elected the then twenty-eight-

castigation of Bulgaria and Greece for failing to recognise Macedonian rights in their countries, also criticised Serbian nationalism and said that Serbia too, like Bulgaria and Greece, had designs on Macedonia.[16] Such designs were explicitly formulated on 3 November by Vuk Drašković, leader of Serbia's main opposition party and Milošević's main rival, when he told a Bulgarian newspaper that a new alliance of Orthodox Balkan countries including Serbia, Bulgaria and Greece was needed to resist the advance of Islam, and that Macedonia would cease to be a republic and be reabsorbed by Serbia if Yugoslavia became a confederation.[17] At about the same time Drašković also called for the partition of SR Macedonia between Serbia and Bulgaria.[18]

In November MAAK and VMRO-DPMNE formed an alliance, the Front of Macedonian National Unity, for the forthcoming elections, specifically to combat the SKM-PDP Communists who were expected to perform well. After apparent failure in the first round, when it won no seats, the Front complained of many irregularities and announced that it would boycott the second round due to be held on 25 November.[19] However they rescinded this decision, and VMRO-DPMNE in particular achieved great success so that after the third and final round they were the leading party with 37 seats out of 120 in the assembly with the SKM-PDP coming second with 31 seats and the mainly ethnic Albanian PDP third with 25.

Peaceful JNA withdrawal and gaining independence

In the final death throes of united Yugoslavia, the Macedonian leadership was led by Kiro Gligorov, a leading member of the old Communist élite and the Macedonian member on Yugoslavia's collective leadership. He was in the forefront with Alija Izetbegović of Bosnia in trying to preserve the old state in some form of

---

year-old engineer Branko Crvenkovski—the current Prime Minister—as its president and adopted party statutes abondoning democratic socialism and espousing West European social democracy instead. See *Večernje Novosti* and *Vjesnik*, 21 April 1991.

16 *RFE Weekly Record of Events*, 2 June 1990.
17 *RFE Weekly Record of Events*, 3 November 1990.
18 Tanjug, 5 November 1990, in BBC SWB EE/0916 B/7, 8 November 1990.
19 Tanjug, 19 November 1990, in BBC SWB EE/0928 B/19, 22 November 1990.

confederation and he repeatedly played down any aims at outright independence, apparently viewing the break-up of the state as potentially fatal to Macedonian consciousness which was still a relatively new phenomenon. The ensuing tragic events in Bosnia-Hercegovina have shown that such concerns for that area were well founded. In Macedonia also there was, and to some extent remains, a serious fear that with the presence of large ethnic Albanian regions in the north-west bordering Albania and Kosovo, Vardar Macedonia might be truncated with the ensuing rump falling prey to predatory neighbours who view the very concept of a Macedonian nation as historically false. Thus Gligorov was justifiably cautious, but he was swept along by events.

By contrast VMRO-DPMNE from the outset was not affected by such doubts. While the Gligorov group pushed for Macedonia's independence within a new Yugoslav framework which would include a common army, currency and foreign policy, VMRO-DPMNE rejected this even before the elections and called for complete separation from Yugoslavia together with the establishment of an independent army. The hostilities in Croatia provided support for this view within the military itself. In April 1991 within the Bitola garrison of the JNA (the Yugoslav National Army) the Secret Macedonian-Revolutionary Organisation (TMRO-Officers) was founded with the main object of preventing Macedonian soldiers from being sent to fight in Croatia; the cause received massive popular backing even to the extent of busloads of soldiers' parents setting off from Skopje to Titograd in September 1991, with financial backing from the Macedonian government, in an attempt to locate their sons who were recruits and bring them back.[20] This organisation in early 1992 further protested at the JNA stripping barracks of all equipment during the JNA's agreed peaceful pull-out from Macedonia.[21] This protest was repeated by other Macedonian observers who complained that the JNA was violating the 16-point agreement between Gligorov and JNA General Adzić.[22]

Despite these problems, the peaceful withdrawal of the JNA

---

20 Tanjug, 17 September 1991, in BBC SWB EE/1181 B/14, 19 September 1991.
21 *Nova Makedonija*, Skopje, 29 February 1992, in JPRS- EER-92-031, 13 March 1992.
22 E.g. see *Nova Makedonija*, Skopje, 29 February 1992, in JPRS-EER-92-031, 13 March 1992.

from Macedonia and the country's peaceful attainment of independence, the only such non-violent withdrawal in former
Yugoslavia, must be counted a triumph for Gligorov's diplomacy.
On 8 September 1991 a referendum on independence was held
and obtained endorsment by the overwhelming majority of those
voting—to be valid it needed a turn-out of above 50 per cent
of registered voters and in the event more than 65% voted.[23]
However, the ethnic Albanians boycotted the referendum in protest
at what they saw as the government's non-compliance with their
demands—e.g. for the reopening of Albanian secondary schools
which had recently been closed. There was a backlash against
this non-participation of the ethnic Albanians, with *Vecher*, the
Skopje daily newspaper, stating that this showed that the
Macedonian state could not rely on their loyalty and that 'pos-
sibilities should not be ruled out for the state to set up repressive
measures towards the Albanian minority in Macedonia if the PDP
[the main Albanian political party] seek the answers to its dilemmas
in aggression and if a scenario of an all-Albanian referendum
becomes reality'.[24] As we see below, this scenario did become
a reality.

The name issue

On 8 April 1993 Macedonia was finally admitted into the United
Nations under the temporary name of the Former Yugoslav
Republic of Macedonia. This compromise arose out of intransigence in Greece over the name 'Macedonia' which the authorities
there, spurred on by the overwhelming mass of public opinion,
insist is part of Greek heritage and cannot be 'usurped' by others.
The celebrations that evening in the main square in Skopje were
muted. While there was satisfaction at finally gaining UN recognition anger was widespread at the acceptance of the temporary
name. There were protest rallies in Skopje, Kočani and Resen,
and 600 Macedonian intellectuals protested in front of the National

23 The referendum endorsed 'an independent and sovereign Macedonia, with the
   right to join the future alliance of sovereign states of Yugoslavia'—Tanjug, 8
   September 1991, in BBC SWB EE/1173 i, 10 September 1991.
24 *Vecher*, 10 September 1991, quoted by Tanjug, 10 September 1991, in BBC
   SWB EE/1175 B/14, 12 September 1991.

Assembly building.[25] Acceptance of the temporary name was close with 30 voting for, 28 against and 13 abstentions in the 120-seat parliament.[26] Most of those who were present at the celebrations felt that the reference to Yugoslavia in the compromise name left open the possibility of Macedonia rejoining, or being forced to rejoin, the rump Yugoslavia dominated by Serbia. On 13 April the government survived with 62 deputies voting in its favour during a vote of no-confidence called by the nationalist opposition party, the VMRO-DPMNE, over the name issue and the economy.

The compromise name resulted from an initiative by Britain, France and Spain to break the deadlock between Greece and Macedonia. Even then there were Greek wrangles and accusations that the Skopje authorities were attempting to use the formula of 'former Yugoslav Republic' rather than 'Former [with a capital letter] Yugoslav Republic,' although in view of the widespread fears in Macedonia of reincorporation into the rump Yugoslavia this accusation appeared groundless.[27] Attempts to find a long-term compromise have so far failed. In May 1993 Greece rejected the suggestions by the international negotiators Cyrus Vance and David Owen of 'Nova Macedonia' and 'Upper Macedonia'—the Greek refusal to yield over the use of 'Macedonia' remains firm.[28] More acceptable to the Greek side appeared to be the name 'Slavomacedonia' but this was strongly objected to by the Albanians both inside and outside Macedonia.[29] In July, UN Secretary-General Boutros-Ghali announced that he would personally take over the name negotiations and he subsequently requested Cyrus Vance to preside over the mediation.[30]

25 Tanjug, 7 May 1993, BBC SWB EE/1659 C1/13, 9 May 1993.

26 Tanjug, 7 May 1993, BBC SWB EE/1659 C1/11, 9 May 1993.

27 Greek Radio, Athens, 27 March 1993, BBC SWB EE/1629 C1/14, 5 March 1993.

28 Greek Radio, Athens, 19 May 1993, in BBC SWB EE/1694 C1/15, 21 May 1993.

29 President Berisha of Albania made it clear to Owen and Stoltenberg (who had replaced Vance) that this was unacceptable for the Albanians—Albanian Radio, Tirane, 10 June 1993 in BBC SWB EE/1713 C1/6, 12 June 1993. Similarly Ibrahim Rugova, the Kosovo Albanian leader said the Greek proposal of 'Slav Macedonia' was unacceptable to the Albanians—Tanjug, 4 June 1993, in BBC SWB EE/1710 C1/13, 9 June 1993. For Albanian objections from within Macedonia see below.

30 Greek Radio, Athens, 7 and 8 July 1993 in BBC SWB EE/1736 i, 9 July 1993, and EE/1737 i, 10 July 1993.

The threat from the north?

Just how serious the threat is from Serbia and the north is an unanswered question, and one which goes beyond mere political and defence considerations. Macedonia's economy was closely linked with Serbia's in the old Yugoslav federation—so much so that some saw no future for Macedonia without Serbia. Nearly all of Macedonia's communication links, whether by rail or telephone, tended to go through Serbia and Belgrade. Additionally there was some initial support from the Skopje governing élite to the rise of Milošević in Serbia due to his avowed stance against the Kosovo Albanians which reflected their own hostility to Macedonia's large Albanian community. Some sections, notably the Vlachs, remain somewhat pro-Serbian.

However the war and the brutalities in Bosnia have changed much of this. One argument in favour of the introduction of the Macedonian *denar* as a separate currency was precisely that this would free the Macedonian economy from helping to finance the Serbian war effort and thus being dragged into the hyperinflation which has so devastated the Yugoslav *dinar*. Along with this sound economic motive there were also obvious political implications. The UN peacekeeping forces have been concentrated on the northern border, and one reason for Gligorov relieving Lieutenant-Colonel-General Mitre Arsovski of his post as Chief of General Staff of the Macedonian army was his stating in Canada that Macedonia was not threatened from the north.[31] The 'threat from the north' was restated by Defence Minister Vlado Popovski in April when he affirmed that Serbia posed the greatest military threat to the republic.[32]

To complicate matters, the Serbian minority (some 44,159 or 2.2 per cent in March 1991, although they claim up to 300,000 people) held marches and protested at their lack of recognition as a minority. Under the old Yugoslav set-up, the Serbs were of course one of the 'nations of Yugoslavia' and thus not a minority, and it is surprising that the Macedonian authorities were so lax in addressing the question of their new status in the republic —especially given Serbia's position and the activity of the Serbian extremist Vojislav Šešelj's radicals in attempting to create a Serbian

31 Tanjug, 4 March 1993, BBC SWB EE/1631 C1/11, 8 March 1993.
32 Tanjug, 7 April 1993, BBC SWB EE/1659 C1/13, 9 April 1993.

Autonomous Region of the Kumanovo Valley and the Skopska Crna Gora.[33] The Association of Serbs and Montenegrins in Macedonia, which elected Nebojsa Tomovich as chairman at its second annual assembly in June 1993,[34] pointed to the problems of education in the Serbian language, and that there was not a single radio or TV programme for Serbs although Turks, Roma and even Vlachs (who speak a form of Romanian) had both educational facilities and media outlets.[35] They also complained that they had received no replies from the relevant authorities to these complaints.[36] The 1993 New Year incident in Kučevište village when police clashed with Serbian youths highlighted the problems.

The CSCE Mission to Macedonia had trilateral talks with the government and with representatives of the Serbian minority to try and solve the problems peculiar to the latter. The authorities claimed that resistance by Macedonian nationalist groups in parliament was making progress impossible; however, in late June the government finally agreed to initiate procedures to change the constitution in order to include recognition of the Serbs. In the mean time the minority would have the same guaranteed rights as other recognised minorities. For primary and secondary education in Serbian to be provided, at least fifteen pupils would need to express interest. After a public debate the Serbs requested two classes in Skopje and Kumanovo grammar schools and one in either Negotino or Kavadarci.[37]

The church issue

A further complication has been the church issue. The former Communist authorities, despite their avowed atheism, had entered into an uneasy alliance with the Macedonian Autocephalous Orthodox Church, declared in 1967 as an integral part of the creation of a Macedonian nation. However the Communist state never gave a free hand to the church and many of Macedonia's church buildings remained in the hands of the state as national monuments.

33 Radio Bosnia-Hercegovina, Sarajevo, 10 September 1992, BBC SWB EE/1487 C1/8, 16 September 1992.
34 Tanjug, 27 June 1993, in BBC SWB EE/1730 C1/12, 2 July 1993.
35 Tanjug, 19 November 1992, BBC SWB EE/1544 C1/11, 21 November 1992.
36 Tanjug, 10 January 1993, BBC SWB EE/1584 C1/14, 12 January 1993.
37 Tanjug, 29 June 1993, in BBC SWB EE/1730 C1/11, 2 July 1993.

At the end of 1992 this changed when many of these churches were returned to ecclesiastical control. The debate about church-state connections continues with one faction pointing to the benefits of state support for religious education—for example, at Skopje University—while opponents point to the past experiences with the Communist authorities.

However, the Macedonian Autocephalous Orthodox Church has never been recognised by the Serbian Orthodox hierarchy (or other Orthodox hierarchies for that matter). While continuing in its efforts to bring the Macedonian Church back within its jurisdiction, the Serbian Church has grudgingly accepted that buildings put up since 1967 belong to the Macedonian Church. However, it views churches and monasteries dating from before that date as its property and wants them back.[38] In late 1992, Serbian bishops came to Macedonia to discuss the issue and there seemed to be some progress, but this was followed in December by the setting up of a quasi-Patriarchate in Niš by the Holy Council of the Hierarchy of the Serbian Orthodox Church. This body under Irenej, Bishop of Niš, was to administer all former 'Serbian' dioceses until the appointment of a new (Serbian) Metropolitan of Skopje.[39] It appears that the attempt at compromise by pro-dialogue circles within the Macedonian Church associated with Bishop Petar of Prespa and Bitola has failed. The Macedonian government entered the fray with the Ministry of Information calling Serbian measures a 'provocation' and interference,[40] illustrating once more the importance of the church issue in the Balkans.

There are even rumours that if the Orthodox Churches continue in their opposition to the Macedonian Church, the latter may turn to Rome and seek to become a Uniate Church. It claims however that relations with the Bulgarian Orthodox Church are good, and the chief secretary of the Holy Synod of the Bulgarian Orthodox Church, Bishop Neofit, immediately denied the claim made by Metropolitan Irinej on 17 March 1993 that the Bulgarian

---

38 For polemics and attempts to bring the Macedonian Church back under the control of the Serbian Church see statements by Metropolitan Jovan of Zagreb and Ljubljana etc. in Tanjug, 17 December 1992, BBC SWB EE/1570 C1/7, 22 December 1992.

39 *East European Newsletter*, vol. 7, no. 4, 16 February 1993.

40 Croatian Radio, Zagreb, 31 May 1993, in BBC SWB EE/1704 C1/5, 2 June 1993.

Church supported its Serbian brethren in the conflict.[41] In June 1993 the head of the Macedonian Church, Gavrilo, resigned 'for health reasons' and on 5 December was succeeded by the leader of the Macedonian nationalist wing, Metropolitan Mihail, Bishop of Skopje-Gevgalia.

It is hard to assess accurately the strength of Orthodox religious belief in Macedonia but it appears that many see the church as the key to nationhood; indeed the nationalist party VMRO-DPMNE proposed Metropolitan Mihail as president of the country. This role of the church as an essential component of the Macedonian nation and its position in the constitution inevitably alienates the predominantly Muslim Albanians.

The Albanian question

Relations between the majority Macedonians and the largest other group in the country, the Albanians, has historically been problematic, and under the old Communist system all forms of Albanian nationalism were heavily penalised. Tensions have continued and have been mirrored within the PDP, the main ethnic Albanian party, which is divided between those who favour autonomy along the lines of the controversial 'Ilirid' declaration, those supporting closer links with Albania, and a third bloc opposed to any notion of autonomy but seeking a civic state of Macedonia,[42] rather than an ethnic state.

The PDP leader Halili, who was replaced in an internal coup in February 1994, maintained fairly good relations with President Gligorov, and in mid-1992, sixteen months after elections, the authorities finally allowed the Tetovo municipal government to take office.[43] However, there was a worrying development in January 1993 when the Macedonian members abandoned the Albanian-dominated Tetovo assembly and formed their own parallel Macedonian one.[44] Halili has been ambivalent over the whole nature of Macedonia. The Macedonian Albanians have always looked to Kosovo, and during the Communist period all Albanian

41 BTA, 18 March 1993, BBC SWB EE/1646 A2/6, 25 March 1993.
42 Yves Heller, 'Skopje Anxious for Recognition', *Le Monde*, Paris, 15 April 1992.
43 *The East European Newsletter*, vol. 6. no. 11, 25 May 1992, London.
44 ATA, 27 January 1993, BBC SWB EE/1598 C1/14, 29 January 1993.

university students from Macedonia went to Priština University. In 1989-90, of 71,505 pupils continuing into higher education in Macedonia only 2,794 were Albanians, and at university level the situation was worse: of 22,994 registered students in 1991-2, only 386 were Albanians, 172 were Turks and fourteen were Roma. Instruction is in Macedonian only.[45] The Albanians are also unhappy about secondary education and point out that under the Communist authorities schooling was in Albanian in ten secondary schools, yet by mid-1993 there only remained one such school.[46]

The Albanians also boycotted the census, the Macedonian independence referendum and the vote on the constitution, this last by a majority of 13-10 in the PDP leadership. The census question is especially difficult. The Albanians claim to constitute 35-48 per cent of the population, while the government says that the figure should be no more than 21 per cent. Similarly the Serbs claim a far higher figure than the official one.

Many Albanians from Kosovo are believed to have come to settle in Macedonia, thus swelling the numbers, and the authorities viewed such new arrivals as ineligible for Macedonian citizenship, which required one's own or both parents' birth in the republic, continuous residence there for the past fifteen years, or marriage to a Macedonian citizen. To this the Albanians answer that while this has happened, many Albanian intellectuals from Macedonia moved to Kosovo in the past due to official pressure against them in Macedonia. In addition there has been a return of thousands of Albanians who used to work in other parts of former Yugoslavia—e.g. some 130,000 used to be in Croatia—and many of these came from Macedonia. Thus the Albanians see this charge as unfair and instead accuse the authorities of refusing to recognise the true ethnic breakdown in the republic, which they claim would negate the constitutional position of ethnic Macedonians. The Albanians called for a census under international supervision, and one was scheduled to take place in April 1994 with the international community bearing the estimated cost of US$1.5

45 Aleksander Soljakovski, 'An Education in Ethnic Complexity' in *Balkan War Report*, no. 15, October 1992, London.
46 Qemal Hajdini in *Flaka e Vëllazërimit*, Skopje, quoted by ATA, 14 May 1993, in BBC SWB EE/1690 C1/22, 17 May 1993.

million,[47] but was delayed till June/July with the Albanians still reluctant to take part.

The Albanians point to the confusion between ethnic and civic nationalism present in the constitution—which, despite the modifications made to it to comply with the Badinter Commission's recommendations, still has explicit references to the Macedonian Orthodox Church in Article 19 as well as stating in the preamble that 'Macedonia is constituted as the national state of the Macedonian people [in the ethnic sense since Albanians and others are mentioned separately].' The PDP petitioned the UN to delay recognition until this issue had been solved.[48] The former PDP vice-chairman Sami Ibrahimi has emphasised that the best solution would be to make the constitution one based purely on the citizens of Macedonia without any leading place for any group or groups, but in view of the Macedonian insistence on their own role, the Albanians should be accorded equal status.[49] This is the current PDP line with petitions to the UN, the CSCE and the EC for Macedonia's Albanians to be accorded 'state-building status'.[50] The PDP is seeking an institutionalised form of proportional representation in all levels of decision-making in society based on the results of an 'impartial' census.[51]

Despite the positions of the two sides, the CSCE reported agreement on revising the constitution so that it would become a 'citizen's constitution' rather than one based on a dominant nation with minorities, or on two nations (i.e. including the Albanians as an integral part) and minorities, or a federation etc.[52] This proposed constitution would also include no mention of the Macedonian Orthodox Church. However, it can only be accepted with a two-thirds majority in parliament. Thus support from VMRO-DPMNE is needed, and this is not forthcoming. In addition, the nationalist Bishop Mihail, who became Metropolitan on 5 December 1993, explicitly stated that while

47 Tanjug, 27 March 1993, SWB EE/1650 C1/8, 30 March 1993.
48 ATA, 13 February 1993, BBC SWB EE/1617 C1/9, 19 February 1993.
49 Interview with the author, 15 April 1993, Skopje.
50 Croatian Radio, Zagreb, 3 April 1993, BBC SWB EE/1659 C1/12, 9 April 1993.
51 Ibrahimi interview.
52 Ambassador Geert Ahrens, 4 February 1993.

he supported the separation of church and state, his church did not countenance the removal of references to it in the constitution.[53]

As for the vexed issue of the name, the Albanians do not see it as a major problem. They view the name 'Republic of Macedonia' as being territorial without any special ethnic Slav connotations, and they do not object to the references to antiquity by the authorities which so infuriate the Greeks.[54] However, as noted above, they do object to the use of Slav symbols, pointing out that Macedonia has always been ethnically mixed, and have specifically objected to pictures of Orthodox churches being including in the design of the new banknotes.[55] Their position is that if there has to be a new name, then an ethnically neutral one, such as 'the Central Balkan Republic' or 'the Vardar Republic' would be best. However, they insist on being consulted first.[56]

In the media the Albanians complain of the lack of reporting in their language. Skopje television has only fifty-five minutes in Albanian per day while of the total of sixty-four hours of broadcasting by different stations each day, only six are in Albanian.[57] (To compensate for this, Albanian Radio in Tirane broadcasts for five hours a day for the Albanians outside the country in Kosovo and Macedonia.[58]) However, an agreement was reached to extend Albanian programmes to nine hours a day beginning on 1 June 1994. The Albanian newspaper *Flaka e Vëllazërimit* was published only three times a week but from 27 May 1994 became a daily. Newspapers from Albania are not available, but hitherto the main Albanian paper in Kosovo, *Bujku*, was distributed—even if somewhat unreliably due to problems in Kosovo— up till the full embargo on Serbia.

On the language issue and the transcription of identity cards there has been some progress, with agreement that Albanian names can be in the original, but the application forms are not bilingual. For school documents, the previous regulations specified that all

53 Interview with author, 13 April 1993, Skopje.
54 Ibrahimi interview.
55 Tanjug, 7 April 1993, BBC SWB EE/1659 C1/14, 9 April 1993.
56 Ibrahimi interview. In *East European Newsletter*, vol. 6 no. 19, 21 September 1992, it was reported that the Albanians of Macedonia had also proposed the, Classical name 'Dardania'.
57 Albanian Radio, Tirana, 12 June 1993, in BBC SWB EE/1714 C1/22, 14 June 1993.
58 ATA, 12 June 1993, in BBC SWB EE/1716 B/1, 16 June 1993.

documents however insignificant had to be in Macedonian as well as Albanian in Albanian schools, and some Albanians have refused to comply and have consequently been fined. Again a compromise was reached that this regulation should apply only to important documents. However, fines continued to be imposed but were not paid, leading to cases of short-term detention. Consideration of the creation of an Albanian faculty in Skopje is under way, as is the creation of between forty and fifty new secondary classes with Albanian teachers. There is also agreement on textbooks and measures to get more Albanians into higher education.

One area that needs addressing is the lack of representation of Albanians at all levels. In an open letter published in *Nova Makedonija* in June 1993, the then PDP leader Halili pointed out that there were no courts presided over by Albanians, no ethnic Albanians in the Macedonian Army General Staff or in the Interior or Foreign Affairs Ministries, and there was no region where Albanians are in the majority which had place- or street-names in Albanian. He also said that the PDP has collected 150,000 signatures calling for amendments to the constitution to upgrade the constitutional status of Albanians.[59] Some measures are promised, but there has been little progress due in part to the enormous economic difficulties, which recognition could help to alleviate. Another problem is the need for local autonomy to combat the move towards centralisation—a common Balkan tendency. Municipalities, including the Albanian-dominated ones of Tetovo and Gostivar, have provisions for local self-government (the problems which such measures produced in practice in Tetovo have already been noted). Agreement was also reached over the display of national symbols so that it is permitted to fly the Albanian flag provided that the Macedonian national flag is flown too—this is common to other countries including Germany.

On the matter of representation, the coalition government that is in office at the time of writing has five Albanian ministers but the Albanians feel cynical about the amount of genuine power they have. Ibrahimi maintained that the coalition is unreal and exists only to avert a government crisis caused by persistent attacks by VMRO-DPMNE on Gligorov and the government. To avert

59 Reported by *Borba*, Belgrade, 22 June 1993, in BBC SWB EE/1726 C1/11, 28 June 1993.

a crisis, the PDP joined the government but, Ibrahimi claimed, they would prefer to have five of their members as directors of big firms like the Teteks factory outside Tetovo than as ministers, since only 4 per cent of state sector employees are ethnic Albanians and most of them are teachers and physical labourers without any in the higher ranks of management.[60]

Such views are held with greater vehemence in Tetovo where the PDP has its headquarters, and where the legacy of the former system and its measures against Albanians in Macedonia after the events in Kosovo in 1981 are bitterly remembered. The 'differentiation' measures against ethnic Albanian teachers, the closing of the their training college and of Albanian middle schools, the enforcement of teaching in Macedonian, the forbidding of some 'nationalist' names, and the destruction in 1988-9 of the traditional walls built around Albanian houses are vividly recalled. Many see the Albanian ministers as mere tokens with no real power and they point to the centralised system whereby, even though the PDP controls local government in Tetovo, this in reality means little more than the power to clean the streets while real power resides in Skopje. For example there are few Albanian policemen. Conversely Slav Macedonians in Tetovo complain that the Albanian local government is such that 'Ilirida is practically being realised' in Tetovo.[61] Armed groups of VMRO-DPMNE supporters—the so-called 'Defence Committees'—have appeared in areas of mixed population around Ohrid and Struga and there are reports of similar groups of armed Albanians despite denials by the PDP.[62] Many Albanian radicals view the Albanian government members as little less than traitors to their cause.

Between the two main communities of Slav Macedonians and Albanians, distrust and suspicion are widespread and they have little communication with each other. According to Albanian reports, 80 per cent of prisoners in the main gaols are ethnic Albanians—the inference is that Albanians are the object of dis-

60 Ibrahimi interview.
61 President of the Democratic Party of Macedonia, Tomislav Stojanovski, who claims that streets and institutions, especially schools, are being given Albanian names: Tanjug, 25 May 1993, in BBC SWB EE/1701 C1/15, 29 May 1993.
62 For reports of the smuggling of weapons in Western Macedonia and the arrest of ethnic Albanians see *Nova Makedonija*, Skopje, 3 May and 22 September 1992, in JPRS-EER-92-071 and JPRS-EER-92-147. For VMRO-DPMNE 'Defence Committees' see below.

crimination.[63] There is an underlying wish among Albanians for Albanian unification but at the same time a realisation that, after the horrors of Bosnia, this can never happen. The Albanians of Macedonia do have a stake in the system despite their non-representation in the state sector. The private sector has many successful Albanians and many have also gained wealth through working abroad in western Europe. The Albanian villages between Tetovo and Skopje with their many new buildings and general air of well-being bear witness to this relative prosperity. Civil war would be a disaster for all concerned.

The Albanians of former Yugoslavia have shown an impressive solidarity of which the underground quasi-state structures in Kosovo are the best example. The PDP claims the loyalty of the majority of Albanians in Macedonia, and there is careful coordination of action between Albania, the Democratic League of Kosovo (DSK), and the PDP in Macedonia. (The DSK, the main political grouping of Kosovo Albanians, is led by Ibrahim Rugova—the would-be president of the Republic of Kosovo, which the Serbs refuse to allow, and head of the underground Albanian government there.) Many see the PDP as the junior partner in this triad. Either way there are good communications up to the time of writing with the DSK but at the same time a fear of the Serb government imminently trying to seal Kosovo off. There is irony in the change from the situation that existed for almost fifty years whereby contact with Albania was totally impossible while that with all Albanians in former Yugoslavia was easy, to the present situation where the reverse is true. The Macedonian Defence Ministry announced that whereas in 1992 there had been 2,568 Albanians caught trying to cross the border illegally, in the first six months of 1993 the figure had risen to 3,200 with sixty-nine border incidents,[64] some involving gunfire. Additionally there have been a number of Albanian complaints that Macedonian border-guards have arbitrarily confiscated large sums of foreign currency from ethnic Albanians at the border with Kosovo.[65] However all sides seemed to agree that Macedonia has to remain intact,

63 *Kosova Communication*—The Bulletin of the Ministry of Information of the Republic of Kosova, no. 118, 1 July 1993.
64 Tanjug, 30 June 1993, in BBC SWB EE/1730, 2 July 1993.
65 E.g. Albanian Radio, Tirana, 22 May 1993, in BBC SWB EE/1697 C1/10, 25 May 1993.

and the calls for 'Iliridia' (Ilirid) seem to have receded along with those for a Greater Albania to include Western Macedonia. However the events which began in November 1993 may portend a different outcome.

What is certain is that if there is no appreciable improvement in the position of Albanians in Macedonia, radicalisation—which has already begun—will grow. PDP delegates claimed that the Macedonians prevented them from meeting the then Turkish President Turgut Özal on 18 February 1993,[66] and the Albanian parties have petitioned international bodies demanding safeguards for ethnic Albanian rights before recognition is accorded to the republic.[67] In June 1993 *Nova Makedonija* reported that the PDP secretary Mithat Emin, the chairman of the Tetovo PDP municipal organisation Genc Kuriu, and others also considered 'soft' had been purged and replaced by PDP hard-liners.[68] At the PDP annual congress in August 1993 members from Tetovo called for the resignation of the entire party leadership.[69] In December an extraordinary PDP Congress of radicals at Gostivar declared a new leadership.[70]

The final split came in February 1994 in Tetovo when the old PDP leadership including the Albanian coalition government ministers walked out of the final congress and formed a separate party named 'the Party of Continuity' with Xelladin Murati, Deputy Speaker of the Macedonian Parliament, as chairman and Halili as honorary chairman. The new PDP, which retained the support of most of the delegates, chose as leader Arben Xhaferri, who besides being an Albanian from Macedonia was a former journalist in Priština in Kosovo.[71] The new leadership, among whom the Tetovo PDP chairman Menduh Thaci is prominent, appears to have close links with the factions within the ruling Democratic Party in Albania around Eduard Selami, which may presage a new harder-line policy of Albanian unity. They also have many links with Kosovo. In this it appears that the

66 ATA, 21 February 1993.
67 ATA, 13 February 1993, and Tanjug, 11 February 1993.
68 *Nova Makedonija*, Skopje, 24 June 1993, quoted by Tanjug, 24 June 1993, in BBC SWB EE/1725 C1/12, 26 June 1993.
69 Tanjug, 30 August 1993, quoting the Albanian daily *Bujku* of Priština, and Croatian Radio, Zagreb, 31 August 1993.
70 ATA, 9 December 1993.
71 Tanjug, 14 February 1994, in SWB EE/1923, 16 February 1994.

current Kosovo Albanian leadership of Rugova may well find themselves subject to similar pressures from younger radicals impatient at the lack of apparent progress. It was noticeable at the final congress that visiting delegates from Albania sided with the new radicals while those from Kosovo walked out with the old guard.[72]

One factor in the split may have been the weapons scandal. In November 1993 nine ethnic Albanians including Hisen Haskaj, Assistant Deputy Minister in the coalition government, were arrested while another, the Deputy Health Minister Imer Imeri, sought refuge in the German consulate. Skopje television, alleging co-operation between the group and Kosovo and Albania, reported that the accused were in possession of 300 machine-guns and were planning an armed uprising of 20,000 Albanians to create the republic of 'Iliridia' and join Albania.[73] Both Albania, which alleged that the whole plot was a Belgrade-inspired fabrication similar to the earlier one concerning the call for Ilirid,[74] and Rugova in Kosovo denied the charges. However the initial PDP response was remarkably muted and merely pointed out that arms-smuggling was the result of a general insecurity felt by many citizens and was to some extent to be expected after the JNA (the Yugoslav army) withdrawal. However, now that there was a Macedonian army, those circumstances had passed.[75] In June 1994 the defendants were sentenced to between five and eight years' imprisonment, which resulted in more resolute PDP protests.

The two communities are as far apart as ever, and mutual misunderstanding and distrust are widespread. The potential for conflict remains high and is demonstrated by the Bit Pazar riot in Skopje in November 1992, caused by police shooting at an Albanian street-vendor, which resulted in the deaths of three Albanians and one Macedonian.[76] The legacy of distrust and antagonism may yet lead to inter-ethnic conflict and even civil war, and there have been reports of Albanian gangs terrorising

---

72 ATA Tirana, 26 February, 1994, quoting *Koha Jone*, Lezhe, Albania, of 22 February 1994, in BBC SWB EE/1934, 1 March 1994.

73 Tanjug, 9 November 1993, in SWB EE/1843 C/8, 11 November 1993.

74 ATA, 12 November 1993, in SWB EE/1846, B/2, 15 November 1993.

75 Tanjug, 12 November 1993, in SWB EE/1846, C/18, 15 November 1993.

76 This incident appears to have been used by the Interior Ministry, still staffed by anti-Albanian ex-Communist hardliners, to stop recruitment of Albanians into the security forces.

Slav Macedonian villages in Western Macedonia.[77] On the other hand, the Macedonian police, which has few if any ethnic Albanian members, reportedly opened fire on Albanian youths in Velešta village near Struga in October 1993, resulting in demands for ethnic Albanians to constitute half of the force.[78] The economy, as elsewhere in former Yugoslavia with the partial exception of Slovenia, is in extreme difficulties, amplified by Greek hostility to the south and the official embargo against Serbia to the north. On top of everything remains the possibility of an explosion in Kosovo with attendant refugee flows on a massive scale which could drastically destabilise the whole region.

The Roma and 'Romanistan'

In Macedonia the Roma have some outlets in the media and in education, and indeed enjoy the best situation of any Roma group in the Balkans. It appears that they do not suffer from the same everyday racism as they do elsewhere in the region. This has come about with the ending of the Communist monopoly on power. President Gligorov has shown sympathy towards the situation of Roma, and has repeatedly and explicitly included them as equal citizens of the state along with Macedonians, Albanians and Turks. Unlike the situation in many other Balkan states, the overt majority-nationalists—in Macedonia the VMRO-DPMNE party—are not in government, a factor which has aided inter-ethnic relations among all groups.

At the time of writing the Roma see educational matters as paramount for them. Since the fall of the Communist authorities, there have been good contacts and communication between the Roma community and the Ministry of Education. A Romani primer has been prepared for publication, and the Ministry and leading Roma educational experts are expected to agree a programme for Romani education. Beginning in September 1993, two hours of Romani teaching a week for Roma was introduced in Grades 1 to 8 in primary schools . A 40,000-word Macedonian-Romani dictionary is also being prepared.

A problem throughout Eastern Europe in Roma educational

77 Tanjug, 8 and 12 December 1993.
78 ATA, 22 October 1993, in SWB EE/1829, C/11, 26 October 1993.

matters is the lack of standardisation of the Romani language: many different dialects are spoken. In Macedonia the estimated 200,000-strong Roma community is spread throughout the republic with some 40,000 estimated to live in Skopje. There are three main Romani dialects in Macedonia: Arlija, Dzambazi and Burgudzi. The most widely spoken is Arlija—spoken mainly in Skopje, Štip, Kočani and Kumanovo—and it has been used as the basis for the new textbooks. Burgudzi and Dzambazi predominate in the north of the republic. An estimated 80 per cent of Macedonian Roma speak Romani as their mother-tongue—which for the rest is either Macedonian, Albanian or Turkish.

At the same time as Romani primary education begins in the 1993/4 academic year, a faculty will be opened at Skopje University for the language. This is the product of a three-month seminar organised by the Ministry of Education at the University between March and June 1992, convened especially to prepare the syllabus and materials for the opening of the faculty in October 1993. One hundred Roma teachers in middle and higher education were convened along with some 150 Roma students to work on subjects like the history, grammar, syntax, phonetics and dialects of the Romani language, and children's literature. At present there are perhaps some fifty Roma students at the University in all faculties, and it is expected that with the opening of this new faculty many more will be trained. Classes in middle schools are not immediately planned, but may be introduced in the future.

Romani television and radio are each broadcast for half an hour a week and the programmes cover teaching, news, music and information. It is hoped to expand this minimal amount to include children's and other programmes. While there are not yet any Romani newspapers, the authorities are supportive of the idea of having them in the future. Meanwhile education is seen as the priority.

The internationally known Roma theatre group *Phralipe* was forced to vacate its buildings in Skopje and move to Mülheim in Germany in 1990 before the final collapse of the old regime,[79] and there is now no professional Roma theatre group in the country. However, an amateur theatre group gives regular per-

---

79 Frankfurter Rundschau, 23 November 1990, noted in 'Democratic Changes Bring Mixed Blessings for Gypsies' by Zoltan D. Barany, RFE/RL, vol 1. no. 20, 15 May 1992.

formances in Šuto Orizari, where there is also a cinema that sometimes shows Indian films which, because of the Roma's remote Indian origins, are very popular. Additionally television and video ownership is becoming more widespread and there is a flourishing trade in Indian film videos.

The main political party for the Roma in Macedonia is the Party for the Complete Emancipation of Romanies in Macedonia (PSER) which, despite the recent formation of a small rival Roma party, continues to be the main political vehicle for Roma aspirations. Claiming 36,000 members and branches all over the republic, it has as president Abdi Faik who is also member of parliament for Šuto Orizari. He points to the progress made with the recognition of Roma, along with Albanians, Turks and Vlachs, as nationalities of the republic, and contrasts the new situation with that in former Yugoslavia. The PSER has campaigned for the introduction of three to four lessons of Romani for Roma in elementary schools, the opening of a Romani faculty at the University of Skopje, and daily TV and radio news and current affairs programmes in Romani—demands which as noted above, are beginning to be met.

Abdi Faik acknowledges that many of his constituents are suffering from the bad economic situation and that poverty, often caused by the wage-earner being unemployed, affects many Roma families. However, he recognises that this problem affects other ethnic groups also: according to his figures, by far the largest number of those without work declare themselves to be Slav Macedonians, while unemployed persons who admit to being Roma do not figure significantly higher than their percentage of the population. The Roma are reluctant to identify themselves, and Faik is aware that in real percentage terms the Roma may be most disadvantaged because of their overall poor level of education. However, he does not view the high unemployment among the Roma as evidence of racism against them in Macedonia.

In late March, the PSER wrote a letter to the UN calling 'for the setting up of the Romani nation and state called Romanistan'.[80] Given the apparent progress made by the Roma in Macedonia, especially compared to neighbouring states,[81] this

80 Tanjug, 27 March 1993, in BBC SWB EE/1650, 30 March 1993.
81 Elsewhere in the Balkans the Roma, by comparison, appear hopelessly fragmented and divided and often to suffer from overt ethnic repression. While

demand appears at first sight somewhat surprising. However the demand for 'Romanistan' is seen by Roma leaders not so much as a literal one for an actual state of, for example, Šuto Orizari, but more as an attempt to change general attitudes towards Roma. It was made by the PSER precisely because of the bad situation of Roma elsewhere in eastern Europe. The PSER feel that Roma are badly treated by neighbouring countries but that neither the UN nor the international community as a whole takes any real notice. They believe that this is because the Roma are a non-territorial people without a state of their own, and that if there was a Roma state—e.g. a 'Romanistan'—the international community would do more to protect them from attack. There were attempts in the late 1970s to have Roma recognised by the UN as 'an indigenous people' which would thus bring them under UN protection, but this was not accepted—former Yugoslavia being among the member-states that obstructed this initiative. Given this, and the Roma's continuing problems (not so much in Macedonia as elsewhere—e.g. in Romania), the PSER are attempting to raise the idea of a Romani nation by explicitly referring to the mythical state 'Romanistan'. They thus hope to enlist UN support for the protection of Roma. Their leaders stress that they want to be good neighbours with surrounding countries

---

many Roma in Greece enjoy economic advantages over those elsewhere in the Balkans, Greece continues to refuse recognition to any ethnic minorities within its territory and there have been reports of pressure on Muslim Roma to convert to Orthodoxy—see Gratton Puxton, *Roma: Europe's Gypsies*, MRG Report, 1987, p. 8. Although there is little information on the Roma in Albania it appears that their position has deteriorated in recent years—see *New York Times*, 12 March 1992, quoted in Barany, *op. cit.* Elsewhere in former Yugoslavia there have been reports of political discrimination and occasionally violent attacks against Roma—see Barany, *op. cit.* In Bulgaria the fledgling Roma parties appear seriously divided along religious, occupational and traditional settler/nomadic lines. They also suffer from the constitutional ban on ethnic and religious parties which forbids the formation of an explicitly Roma political party. There have been serious incidents, and public perception, bolstered by a rising crime rate in which Roma are seen as the culprits, has led to social tension. Sections of the Bulgarian media are openly racist against Roma—see Ivan Ilchev and Duncan Perry, 'Bulgarian Ethnic Groups: Politics and Perceptions', RFE/RL, vol. 2, no. 12, March 1993. However the worst situation in the Balkans is in Romania where there have been a number of serious incidents including full-scale pogroms and arson attacks against Roma, and there are reports that the Roma may even resort to their own para-military formations for self-defence in the face of the authorities' failure to protect them.

but at the same time they want their co-nationals living in those countries to be protected.

In contrast to other Balkan governments, the authorities in Macedonia appear genuine in viewing the Roma as an integral part of the new state and there is an evident lack of tension between Roma and the majority Slav Macedonians. It was noticeable that at the independence celebrations on the evening of 8 April 1993 in the main square in Skopje, somewhat muted, as we have seen, due to widespread dissatisfaction over the new state's compromise temporary name, there were many Roma who had apparently been specially bussed in. Their presence in the dancing was not seen as odd and caused no comment. Albanians were completely absent—reflecting the distrust and almost total lack of communication between them and Slav Macedonians.

Other minority groups

Tensions have risen lately over Islamicised Macedonians (Torbeshi) and Muslim refugees from Bosnia-Hercegovina. While the old authorities actively encouraged self-identification among smaller Muslim groups, like the Turks and Muslim Macedonians, since they feared that they were becoming Albanianised,[82] they now appear nervous of possible leverage by Turkey as the main regional power. It was announced in early 1992 that the Torbeshi would form their own political party.[83] A number of them in Debar region requested that schooling be in Turkish not Macedonian, which the authorities turned down.[84] The presidium of the Republican Community of Islamicised Macedonians issued a statement in early January 1993 that the Democratic Party of Turks in Macedonia (DPTM) was behind the 'pan-Turkish ideas' in the Moša Pijade school, the centre of the controversy, which was demolished at the end of December 1992.[85]

The DPTM for their part told the CSCE mission in January 1993 that the status of the Turkish minority was under threat.[86]

82 See Poulton, *op. cit.*

83 *Nova Makedonija*, Skopje, 13 February 1992, in JPRS- EER-92-028.

84 Tanjug, 30 September 1992, BBC SWB EE/1502 C1/9, 3 October 1992, and Tanjug, 29 Dec. 1992, BBC SWB EE/1575 C1/8, 31 Dec. 1992.

85 Tanjug, 4 January 1993, BBC SWB EE/1580 C1/11, 7 January 1993.

86 Tanjug, 22 January 1993, in BBC SWB EE/1597 C1/15, 27 January 1993.

In March it issued a statement alleging that the authorities were taking reprisals by fines and other measures against parents whose children were boycotting primary school education in Macedonian and demanding education in Turkish instead; since the beginning of the school year there had been such boycotts in many schools in Western Macedonia. A team of experts from the Education Ministry rejected the demands, stating that 'the main reason for this decision was linguistic not ethnic' but did agree to the introduction of optional Turkish classes if resources proved adequate.[87] The DPTM followed this with a press conference at which it declared a state of emergency for its members and threatened mass emigration to Turkey if the authorities continued with their 'crude harassment'. The DPTM specifically called for the removal of police from the Debar area and the reinstatement of expelled teachers.[88]

However a CSCE mission to Debar in April reportedly found no evidence of major abuses.[89] As noted above, Turkey has increasing influence in the central Balkan region and appears to want to keep the Turkish minority from possibly provoking the authorities too much. When President Özal of Turkey visited Macedonia, the Turkish consulate tried to prevent the DPTM from making inflammatory statements. It seems that the Torbeshi are identifying with the ethnic Turkish community in spite of not speaking Turkish, but their numbers remain small. A problem for ethnic Turks is finding marriage partners; they occasionally marry Muslim Albanians but rarely Orthodox Macedonians. At the time of writing, the Minister of Culture, Junar Ismail, is an ethnic Turk (but not a DPTM member): this brave appointment in the face of nationalist objections is welcome in the Balkans where culture is so often heavily politicised. Ismail incurred the wrath of the Orthodox Church when, in spite of large protests, he refused to ban a controversial theatre piece in Strumica which was seen as being anti-Jesus.

The building by the authorities of a refugee village in the Skopje suburb of Djorče Petrov with the help of finance from Germany to accommodate some of the influx of Muslims fleeing

87 Tanjug, 3 March 1993, BBC SWB EE/1629 C1/15, 5 March 1993.
88 Tanjug, 9 April 1993, BBC SWB EE/1660 C1/18, 12 April 1993.
89 Interview with General Giorgio Blais, deputy head of mission, 12 April 1993, Skopje.

Bosnia-Hercegovina was halted after protests and demonstrations by local inhabitants in February 1993.[90] The large number of Muslim refugees from Bosnia at one time threatened to cause great problems, and the settling of some 2,000 refugees in Djorče Petrov would have drastically altered its ethnic composition. Given this, the nationalist reaction, regrettable as it may have been, was understandable. The number of refugees from former Yugoslavia has since declined due to many either returning or moving on to other places. In April 1993 the Macedonian government put the current number at 30,000, the UN High Commission for Refugees at 22,000 and the Catholic Relief Service at 18,000. Whatever the true figure, the long-term impact of their presence appears to be less serious than once appeared likely. In June 1993 the UNHCR announced that it had delivered 865 tonnes of aid to refugees in Macedonia in the first five months of the year.[91] Muslim refugees have been housed in holiday camps in places like Lake Mavrovo as well as in private houses with the aid of Muslim relief organisations like 'Al Hilal'.

The economy

The economy has proved more resilient than many imagined and has even survived the rigours of three months of disruptions in oil imports from Greece during the winter of 1992/3. Many economists thought that Macedonia was incapable of surviving outside the old Yugoslav or rump Yugoslav economy. However the experience of the year following the introduction of the new Macedonian *denar* in April 1992 showed the wisdom of the move which separated it from the hyperinflation caused by the war in former Yugoslavia and allowed Macedonia to escape from financing the ruinous war. This is reflected in current average wages equivalent to about 100 Deutschmarks per month in Macedonia against 30 for Serbia and 20 for Montenegro as well as the strength of the *denar* over the *dinar*.[92] However the initial success of the

90 Tanjug, 20 February 1993, in BBC SWB EE/1620 C1/12, 23 February 1992, and Tanjug, 29 February 1993, BBC SWB EE/1621 C1/9, 24 February 1993.
91 Tanjug, 25 June 1993, in BBC SWB EE/1726 C1/8.
92 How catastrophic the war has been for the FRY economy is shown by the drop in average annual income from US$3,060 to $350 in only three years, thus reaching a level similar to that in Zambia ($420), the Central African Republic

anti-inflation programme was mitigated by problems associated with the Greek blockade and continuing non-recognition.[93] By early 1993 inflation was running at between 20 and 30 per cent a month.

In the old federal Yugoslavia, Macedonia was very much on the periphery of the periphery. With Albania almost totally isolated and Bulgaria in COMECON, towns like Debar and Strumica were as if in a state of siege—for example, all contacts with Italy had to be routed through the north via Serbia, Croatia and Slovenia despite the actual closeness of Italy via Albania. There is still no direct rail link with Bulgaria, now Macedonia's main trading partner, and the power grid was connected to Serbia. The old telecommunications system went through Belgrade, Sarajevo or Zagreb before connecting with the rest of Europe and war has severed many of these links. With almost no east-west connections, most links went along the historic route of Niš-Skopje-Salonika. The blockade of Serbia and Greek intransigence have severely disrupted this main artery and shown the need for new east-west ones. The main border crossing to Bulgaria at Deve Bair is hopelessly congested.

Thus the building of the Durrës-Skopje-Sofia-Istanbul highway, the new Via Egnatia, is of great potential importance. The largely unused capacity in Macedonia's building industry can be used for this project, which could revitalise Albania and Bulgaria as well as Macedonia. It is reported that Albania will receive credit under favourable terms to build its sector of the road, which if built should help to consolidate Turkish influence throughout this central band of the Balkans. Greece appears, by its intransigence over the republic, to have thrown away the chance to help develop the whole Vardar valley and thus gain immensely from Macedonia, and instead to have helped its arch-rival Turkey. If this road is completed, it will also be of great use to Serbia when it emerges from isolation, and Greece will have lost incalculably. On 9 May 1993 at Ohrid a protocol between Albania, Macedonia and Bulgaria over the road-rail link was signed, with Turkey and Italy (which

---

($390) and Uganda ($220). Furthermore these African countries do not have the same winter heating problems as FRY—*Politika* (Belgrade), 7 July 1993, quoted by Tanjug, 7 July 1993, in BBC SWB EE/1736 C1/10, 9 July 1993.

93 See Mihail Petkovski, Goce Petreski and Traijko Slaveski, 'Stabilization Efforts in the Republic of Macedonia,' RFE/RL, vol. 2, no. 3, 15 January 1993.

is expected possibly to extend the link onwards to North Africa) to join later.[94] Additionally there are plans to build a direct rail link with Bulgaria as well as to extend telecommunication links through Albania to Rome and through Bulgaria to Istanbul (although Albania and Bulgaria have worse systems than former Yugoslavia and themselves need much renovating). Power supplies are the other vital feature and a pipeline for natural gas from Russia through Bulgaria could also have vital ramifications in the future.

There is a readily observable private sector but this is mainly concentrated in small retail businesses. Like all the other former Communist East European countries, Macedonia is in the middle of a transformation from the old centralised state-controlled system to a system run more by the market. Nowhere is this more obvious than in the shops. The old state-run supermarket chains like 'Centro' and 'Slavija' still exist, and their large premises are everywhere, but nobody uses them since their goods are more expensive than the small private rivals, which pay lower taxes. To enter any such state-run store with its half-filled shelves and hordes of idle assistants standing around in the gloom, is to step back into the old period. Like dinosaurs they face extinction and will certainly be superseded by the new stores with their plethora of goods on offer, all crammed into a small space. Already new private chains like 'Evropromet' and 'Dragstor' are springing up, which may well supersede the smaller private companies, and they may also eventually take over the old state supermarket network which retains only its property as fixed assets. Already the main 'Stokovna Kucha' store in the city centre of Skopje has leased off the ground floor to small independent traders.

The new private sector, in classic Balkan fashion, avoids paying taxes on a huge scale and there is no doubt that some have taken advantage and amassed large amounts of personal money in a short period. It is possibly to buy all food, clothes, cosmetics, etc. without paying any turnover tax. This appeals to a population whose living standards are falling but causes problems with the budget. Additionally there have been opportunities, up till the present tightening of restrictions, for sanctions-busting to Serbia, and the black market possibly accounts for up to 30 per cent of GDP. The huge 'grey sector' helps to explain the anomaly

94 BTA, 10 May 1993, in BBC SWB EE/W0282 A/9, 20 May 1993.

of the population not appearing at first sight to be in dire straits despite the high price of most goods and the low wages. The size of this grey economy is apparent in the balance between cash and deposits in the money supply (M1) which is about 50-50 —this very high percentage for cash reflects the demand for it so as to facilitate tax evasion.

However, the new private sector is unable to accommodate all the people who face redundancy in their jobs in the near future. In 1991, about 40 per cent of the workforce were in manufacturing—of the former Yugoslav republics only Slovenia was more heavily weighted towards industry—but drastic reorganisation is needed. For example, the massive steel industry faces general collapse due both to the loss of its traditional markets—75 per cent was with the old federal Yugoslavia[95]—and to overstaffing. The workforce of 9,000 needs to be halved but with unemployment already above 20 per cent such a loss cannot be absorbed by the new private economy. Thus in the short term it seems likely that overstaffing will continue and living standards will fall. Some small firms have already gone bankrupt but the political fallout caused by the bankruptcy of the giant ones is seen as too great for it to be allowed to happy. Some workers have been laid off. In Veles in early 1993, 150 women from a textile company were made redundant, and the possible reaction to such acts in a society used to the security of guaranteed employment was illustrated when the women affected physically attacked the director and those who remained. The strategy of pensioning off as many people as possible at fifty or fifty-five years of age is being pursued, as is the bribe of paying people off with two years' salary with which they may be able to open their own small business.

Privatisation is on the agenda and the draft act is likely to become law. Some 15,000 enterprises have been registered in the republic but the first phase of privatisation will only cover 880-1,400 small firms employing up to fifty people, 435 medium-sized ones with up to 250 employees, and 135 large enterprises. Monopolies, 'non-economic enterprises' and 'losing enterprises' would not be privatised.[96] It was announced by the minister in charge of the privatisation, Jane Miljovski, that small retail

95 Figures from *Euromoney Supplement*, no date but probably November 1992.
96 *Nova Makedonija*, Skopje, 7 March 1992, in JPRS-EER-92-004, 10 April 1992.

outlets, as noted above, are no problem but the medium-sized and large enterprises are different since there is a lack of private funds available to buy them out. To overcome this, the minister offered a scheme whereby buyers of medium enterprises initially pay only 20 per cent of the purchase price (10 per cent for the big companies) but are expected to pay at least 51 per cent in the first five years from profits. Critics say that this scheme will not work since experience in other East European countries has shown that even private companies need large inputs of capital for restructuring and that the initial period almost always sees losses rather than profits; hence the new owners will be obliged to resort to asset stripping in order to pay the required amount. However even some harsh critics see the proposed measures as better than no measures at all, and hope that once the privatisation gets under way the system will be modified in a more realistic direction.

One negative aspect of the change-over period is the growth of corruption. With the increase in the private sector and the decline and bankruptcy of social ownership, there is ample scope for shady dealings. It is fairly usual for directors of social firms to own private ones, or to use intermediaries like wives, children and other relations to buy them cheaply at a large profit with mutually accepted pay-offs all round. There is also scope for directors to lead companies deliberately into bankruptcy so as to purchase them more cheaply. The connections of these new entrepreneurs with government make some observers see the system as having Latin American symptoms—the so-called 'Colombian syndrome'—and refer to such practices as *de facto* 'criminal privatisation'.

Macedonia's share of former Yugoslavia's debt is US$850 million, and servicing it will cost US$140 million a year—$80 million in principal and $60 million in interest.[97] At the time of the stabilisation programme and introduction of the new currency in April 1992, the republic had virtually no foreign exchange reserves. At the time of going to press, it has US$64 million—an improvement, but there is still a long way to go. Another problem is how to repay (the government, in contrast to Slovenia and Croatia where moratoriums have been announced, has pledged to do this) the estimated US$1 billion in hard currency lost by investors in the old banking system due to the collapse of former

97 *Ibid.*

Yugoslavia. Estimates of the amount the population has in hard currency outside the system (which must partly explain how the population manages to survive) range from US$600 million to 1 billion. Currency speculation is rife throughout the republic, with the Deutschmark the preferred currency.

The lost markets in former Yugoslavia have not yet been replaced by new ones although there have been successes like the contract, worth over US$100 million, to make buses for Turkey. GDP dropped by 15 per cent in 1992, but an equally dramatic decline was experienced by most other East European economies in this transitional stage. Although there was scope for illegal sanction-busting,[98] sanctions have nonetheless cost Macedonia dear—the government estimated that losses due to this cause totalled US$1.2 billion in the year following their initiation in May 1992. The biggest losses were in the metallurgical, chemical and textile industries as well as in agriculture.[99] An indication of Macedonia's position in relation to rump Yugoslavia was the number of Serbian traders who came to Skopje to sell their wares for currency.

The economy is crucial and the attitude of the international community will be of major importance. The World Bank Economic Mission in February/March 1993 painted a gloomy picture of the loss of government control over the economy and decline due to the loss of old markets. The IMF is also due to make an investigation, and any help from it will depend on results. However, as noted above, there is scope for constructive help—for example, in helping to finance the new east-west highway which could play so great a role in both trade and stability for the whole region. Macedonia, with its population of just over 2 million, does not need the massive aid of, say, Poland or Russia. While

98 CSCE Deputy Chairman Ritt Bjerregaard from Denmark visited Macedonia and saw such widespread violations of sanctions that he said they could not all be from Macedonia and accused Greece—see Yleisradio, Helsinki, 6 July 1993, in BBC SWB EE/1735 C1/13, 8 July 1993. Tanjug claimed the sanctions were being 'strictly enforced' by Macedonia, while the main Macedonian opposition party, the nationalist VMRO-DPMNE, welcomed the sanctions and called on the government to enforce them strictly—see Tanjug, 28 April 1993, in BBC SWB EE/1676 C1/13, 30 April 1993. Prime Minister Crvenkovski on a visit to Germany pledged to do all he could to enforce the sanctions but added that it was not possible to carry out complete checks without foreign help—DPA, 14 July 1993, in BBC SWB EE/1745 A1/2, 20 July 1993.

99 Tanjug, 15 May 1993, in BBC SWB EE/W0283 A/5, 27 May 1993.

in its level and pattern of development it cannot bear comparison with Slovenia, the Communist period was not a wholly negative one for Macedonia, which had been so backward before. There is now an educated workforce. One major negative legacy of the Communist period common to many East European societies is that a whole generation has lost the work ethic. The 'right not to work too hard' and 'a job for life' in exchange for abdicating politics has had a baleful effect on a traditional, hard-working population. Bulgaria similarly had historically a '*rabota*' (work) culture rather than the '*hajduk*' (outlaw warrior) which is more prevalent in Serbia and Montenegro.[100] However, the new young generation of entrepreneurs show that given the right opportunities they are willing to work extremely hard in the new private sector.

External relations

As noted above, Turkey has been extending its influence through the central Balkan band of Bulgaria, Macedonia and Albania, and the proposed *Via Egnatia* will if completed help to cement this process. An unattributed article first published in the Skopje newspaper *Puls* and reprinted in *Nova Makedonija* in May 1992 called for a policy of looking to Turkey rather than the European Community (although Macedonia has inherited former Yugoslavia's Most Favoured Nation status with the EC[101])commenting that Turkey had 'already openly offered Macedonia its good services for economic co-operation and for both an economic and political initiative of creating a Black Sea trade community and an Eastern Mediterranean integration initiative'.[102] It was noticeable that the first foreign ambassador to take up residence in Skopje was the Turkish one in May 1993.[103]

Additionally, Bulgaria has great influence for reasons which should by now be apparent. However, the perennial polemic over the 'Macedonian Question' tempers this natural alliance,

100 See J.R. Rothschild, *East Central Europe between the Two World Wars*, University of Washington Press, Seattle, 1974.
101 For a detailed breakdown of the EC quotas etc. see Stojmirka Tasevska, 'Maintaining the Continuity' in *Nova Makedonija*, Skopje, 8 September 1989, in JPRS-EER-92-144, 8 October 1992.
102 Reprinted in JPRS-EER-92-080.
103 Tanjug, 7 May 1993, in BBC SWB EE/1684 C1/21, 10 May 1993.

and although one of the first countries to recognise the new state, it does not officially recognise the Macedonians as a people separate from Bulgarians. The Bulgarian Foreign Minister Stoyan Ganev raised the Bulgarian concern over Article 49 of the constitution, which stipulates that the republic will be concerned with the ethnic Macedonian minority outside its borders—again an illustration of the constitution's ethnic aspects.[104] Bulgarian sensibilities were outraged by the Macedonian Prime Minister Crvenkovski's use of an interpreter when he met his Bulgarian opposite number, Berov, in Skopje in June 1993.[105]

Despite the polemics, links remain strong in many fields such as banking and military training. Many Macedonian businessmen are opening companies in Bulgaria, and there is mutual trading between the two countries. For example, Astibo from Štip has opened a modern store in the centre of Blagoevgrad.[106] When Ganev came to Skopje and met his counterpart Denko Maleski in February 1992, it was announced that Bulgaria had asked for the payment of US$15 needed for Macedonian citizens to cross the border to be abolished and that there would be an intensification of cultural relations especially in mutual mass-media exchanges.[107]

These links are to some extent forced on Macedonia due to the blockade of the Federal Republic of Yogoslavia (the rump state consisting of Serbia, including Vojvodina and Kosovo, and Montenegro) and the dismal relations with Greece which blocked its admission to the CSCE despite strong urging from most other members.[108] Despite the problems over the position of the Albanian minority within Macedonia, Defence Minister Vlado Popovski during a visit to Albania in April 1993 said that Macedonia looked to Albania to help its entry into the CSCE and NATO,[109] un-

104 *Nova Makedonija*, Skopje, 7 May 1992, in JPRS-EER-92- 070.
105 BTA, 6 June 1993 (quoting *Otechestven Vestnik*, Sofia) in BBC SWB EE/1710 C1/13, 9 June 1993. Bulgarian and Macedonian are of course mutually intelligible, being essentially the same language.
106 *Nova Makedonija*, Skopje, 1 June 1992, in JPRS-EER-92-085, 7 July 1992.
107 *Nova Makedonija*, Skopje, 28 February 1992, in JPRS-EER-92-040.
108 At the CSCE parliamentary congress in Oslo in July 1993, 158 members voted in favour of entry with only four against. The final communiqué was opposed only by Greece and Croatia who opposed due to accusations over human rights and education— Yleisradio, Helsinki, 9 July 1993, in BBC SWB EE/1738 A2/1, 12 July 1993.
109 ATA, 29 April 1993, in BBC SWB EE/1677 A2/3 1 May 1993.

derlining the official view that Macedonia firmly wants to join the West European international institutions. This was further underlined by the arrival of United States troops to bolster the UN presence in Macedonia despite Serbian President Milošević apparently persuading Gligorov, at a meeting in Ohrid at the beginning of June, not to accept them.[110] Macedonia was admitted to membership of the Central European Initiative, a scheme for regional development, on 17 July 1993.[111]

Politics—democracy or 'neo-Communism'?

The largest party in the parliament of Macedonia is the nationalist VMRO-DPMNE, which went into open opposition to the government in October 1991 when its leader Ljupco Georgievski resigned as Vice-President of the republic due to what it saw as the revival of 'neo-Communism' of the authorities led by President Gligorov, who of course was a member of the old Yugoslav Communist élite.[112] A government led by Branko Crvenkovski took over after Petar Goshev resigned as Prime Minister as the result of failure to resolve the name issue. This government was a coalition of the Albanian PDP and the three parties formed out of the remains of the former Communist authorities: the biggest being the Social Democratic Union (SDU), formerly the League of Communists of Macedonia—Party for Democratic Renewal (SKM-PDP); the reform liberals which emerged from the remains of the former Yugoslav Prime Minister Ante Marković's attempted all-Yugoslav party; and the Socialist Party. On 17 May 1993 Petar Goshev, who had also left the SDS, formed a new centre party, the Democratic Party, and was joined by veteran human rights legal expert Georgi Marianovich's League of Democracy and the Green Party.[113] This new party set out to gain the middle ground between the VMRO-DPMNE and the SDU.

The presence of many former Communists (like President Gligorov himself) as well as the tendency of the President to

---

110 *Borba*, Belgrade, 1 June 1993, and Tanjug, 2 June 1993, in BBC SWB EE/1707 C1/11, 5 June 1993.
111 *MTI*, 17 July 1993, in BBC SWB EE/1744 A2/2, 19 July 1993.
112 Tanjug, 22 and 23 October 1991, BBC SWB EE/1213 B/14, 26 October 1991.
113 Tanjug, 17 May 1993, in BBC SWB EE/1693 C1/13, 20 May 1993.

overshadow parliament at times has prompted some observers to agree with Georgievski that the system shows signs of reverting to a neo-Communist system. Defenders of the current *status quo* admit that the republic is more centralised than is desirable for a developed democracy, but point to the problems faced by the authorities in a transition period and look forward to a more open democratic system developing when conditions improve. They classify the government of Crvenkovski as one dominated by young professionals most of whom have careers outside politics and are thus not identical to the old *nomenklatura*. They also point to the relative freedom for the independent press, like the weekly *Puls*, to criticise the authorities. Time will tell whether democratic structures will take firmer root. There were few dissidents in Macedonia under the old Communist system, which is perhaps an indication of the lack of any democratic culture in the Western sense.

VMRO-DPMNE and the 'defence committees'

Georgievski himself had been one of these, and when he set up VMRO-DPMNE in June 1990 its activities were closely watched by the police. The nationalists among the old establishment intelligentsia who formed the Movement for All-Macedonian Action (MAAK) always appeared by contrast to be excessively timid and to be at least one step behind VMRO-DPMNE. The electoral support for the latter appears to be waning at the time of writing, and it suffers from splits between pro-Bulgarian factions and those who espouse independent Macedonia. In 1992 there was a leadership struggle, and the deputy chairman of the Veles section, Vladimir Golubovski, who warned of the threat from pro-Bulgarian elements, was ousted and formed a splinter party called VMRO-DP (Democratic Party).[114] However, it was not clear how much of this apparent wrangle over orientation was really a struggle for internal power. By May 1993 the infighting appeared to have ended with Georgievski still very much in control.

The aggressive independent Macedonian wing of VMRO-DPMNE arouses Greek (and Bulgarian) fears of irredentism—fears which are not allayed when, for example at a celebration to mark Macedonia's entry into the UN, the renowned performer

114 *Nova Makedonija*, Skopje, 17 March 1992, in JPRS-EER-92-049.

Vaska Ilieva sang before the President and Prime Minister about 'our Macedonia' stretching from the sea (i.e. Salonika) and from Pirin (i.e. south-west Bulgaria) to the Šar mountains (similar songs are also frequently broadcast on Macedonian television).

VMRO-DPMNE plays a disruptive role in inter-ethnic relations through the above-mentioned armed 'defence committees' which appeared along the ethnic dividing line between Slavs and Albanians in western Macedonia, especially around Ohrid. The Ohrid Assembly chairman, Blagoja Siljanovski, initially described these paramilitary organisations as useful in helping to maintain public order and security in the region, but later withdrew this tacit support and excluded any possibility of official co-operation with them.[115] Just how strong these committees are is hard to assess. Also problematic is their actual relationship to VMRO-DPMNE. Their self-styled 'commander', Nikola Veljanovski from Ohrid, claimed the huge figure of '100,000 in Vardar Macedonia and as many outside of it, ready at all times to defend Macedonia'—although the reality was certainly nowhere near such figures.[116] Veljanovski—nicknamed 'Bikcheto' (the young bull)—had been prominent in the extreme nationalist wing of VMRO-DPMNE, even issuing death-threats to fellow-members he perceived as traitors. His extremism caused him to be expelled from VMRO-DPMNE, but it seems that there was at least tacit co-operation between these paramilitaries and certain elements within VMRO-DPMNE. A number of VMRO-DPMNE activists were implicated in an attempt to blow up the JNA building in Veles as well as the houses of two 'directors' (presumably JNA officials). One of them, Goce Chushkov, denied the charges, and claiming that they were an attempt to discredit VMRO-DPMNE and alleged that he had been ill-treated to get him to confess to connections with Bulgaria.[117]

However, VMRO-DPMNE is as fiercely anti-communist as it is nationalist. As such, along with its actions in the inter-ethnic arena, it has taken to hounding the government at every opportunity. Thus, for all its regrettable Balkan nationalism, it acted the role of an opposition party—an important role given the lack of a democratic culture and parliamentary experience.

115 *Nova Makedonija*, Skopje, 19 May 1992, in JPRS-EER-92-080 24 June 1992.
116 *Ibid.*
117 *24 Chasa*, Sofia, 7 July 1992.

10

CONCLUSION—WHITHER MACEDONIA?

In the preceding chapters an attempt has been made to give an overview of the history of Macedonia as well as of the competing claims to its inhabitants throughout the ages. We have naturally concentrated in greatest detail on the post-Second World War era as this period is of immediate relevance to today's events. However, as so often in the Balkans, the seeds of present controversies can be found in the past. The initial divide has historically been between the Slavs and Greeks, and that this still continues is illustrated by the hostility of Greece towards the new Macedonian state. One factor in the Greek attitude, which the Greek Macedonian expert Evangelos Kofos points out,[1] is the high degree of ignorance and misinformation among all sections of Greek society towards developments in Bulgaria and Yugoslavia over the last forty years, which have helped to fuel the nationalistic climate in Greece today over the whole issue.

Within the Slav camp the Serb claims appear to have retreated, and the issue remains one of whether the Slav inhabitants of Macedonia are Bulgarian, Macedonian or both. As we have seen, the relationship between Bulgarians and Slav Macedonians (whether they be classified as Bulgarians, Macedonian-Bulgarians or Macedonians) has been complex since before the end of the nineteenth century. The Tito regime's ethnogenesis after the Second World War appears to have had a large measure of success. However, this success remains qualified; the new state is vulnerable both to possibly fatal internal conflicts with the Albanians and to problems with the economy. Tito's Macedonian policy benefited from the

1 Kofos, *The Macedonian Question: The Politics of Mutation*, Salonika, 1987, pp. 12-13.

208

lack of communication with Bulgaria caused by the 1948 rupture. With Serbia to the north a pariah and economically broken due to the war in Bosnia-Hercegovina, and Greece unremittingly hostile to the south, the answer to the question 'Whither Macedonia?' appears to be, in the short term at least, that it will become more closely oriented towards Bulgaria—which will surely demonstrate to both peoples just how close they really are.

Despite all this Macedonia, after its acceptance into the UN, displayed a guarded optimism. The threat of civil war breaking out between Slav Macedonians and ethnic Albanians appeared to have receded despite continuing poor relations and mistrust between the two communities. If outright war can be avoided in Kosovo—and this is something about which any prediction would be foolish—the immediate future looks relatively peaceful, although the continuing lack of communication and escalating bad relations between the two communities must cause anxiety. The drastic under-representation of ethnic Albanians in all levels of the state apparatus needs to be addressed urgently in a practical way—words and good intentions will not be enough. There is also an over-reliance, in a possible echo of the Tito era, on the personality of seventy-six-year-old President Gligorov as a guarantee of stability. There also remains the possibility of a more serious breakdown between Slav Macedonians and Albanians if he should be replaced by more overtly nationalistic Macedonian leaders.

The economy is vital and Macedonia has so far shown a remarkable resilience in the face of Greek blockades and the long delay in international recognition. The separation from Yugoslavia has proved wise in the short term, and Macedonia may well have gained by the blockade of Serbia. However, despite the explosion of small entrepreneurs, the economic future remains precarious and the effects of the privatisation of medium and large companies are not yet clear. Western financial aid for the new Durres-Skopje-Sofia-Istanbul highway and for a natural gas pipeline from Russia through Bulgaria could help to revitalise the whole region. If this happens, it will surely underline how self-destructive the Greek policy of hostility has been. Greece had the opportunity to aid the new state and develop the entire Vardar/Axios valley but its attitude has instead forced Macedonia to look to Bulgaria and Greece's principal *bête noire* Turkey. In addition the extreme nationalistic climate in Greece whipped up over the issue endangers its internal politics and risks alienating the other members of the European Community.

Western policy over the break-up of former Yugoslavia has been characterised by ineffective stop-gap actions which have often exacerbated the problems. Macedonia has historically been the apple of discord in the Balkans. A stable prosperous country of 2 million acting as a bridge between Albania and Bulgaria and, in due time, between Serbia and Greece could transfrom this sorry legacy.

INDEX